Foreign Communities in Hong Kong, 1840s–1950s

Foreign Communities in Hong Kong, 1840s–1950s

Edited by

Cindy Yik-yi Chu

palgrave
macmillan

First published in 2005 by
PALGRAVE MACMILLAN™
175 Fifth Avenue, New York, N.Y. 10010 and
Houndmills, Basingstoke, Hampshire, England RG21 6XS
Companies and representatives throughout the world.

PALGRAVE MACMILLAN is the global academic imprint of the Palgrave Macmillan division of St. Martin's Press, LLC and of Palgrave Macmillan Ltd. Macmillan® is a registered trademark in the United States, United Kingdom and other countries. Palgrave is a registered trademark in the European Union and other countries.

ISBN 1–4039–7059–9

Library of Congress Cataloging-in-Publication Data

Foreign communities in Hong Kong, 1840s–1950s / edited by Cindy Yik-yi Chu.
p. cm.
Includes bibliographical references and index.
ISBN 1–4039–7059–9
1. Ethnic groups—China—Hong Kong. 2. Hong Kong (China)—History. 3. China—History—19th century. 4. China—History—20th century. I. Chu, Cindy Yik-yi.

DS796.H79E82 2005
305.8′0095125′09034—dc22 2005043433

A catalogue record for this book is available from the British Library.

Design by Newgen Imaging Systems (P) Ltd., Chennai, India.

First edition: October 2005

10 9 8 7 6 5 4 3 2 1

Printed in the United States of America.

To Sister Rose Duchesne Debrecht, M.M.

Contents

Preface

This edited volume studies ethnic minority groups in Hong Kong from the 1840s through the 1950s. It aims to portray Hong Kong history through the perspectives of foreign communities—the British, Germans, Europeans, Americans, Indians, and Japanese—and to understand how they perceived the political administration, economic situation, and culture of the colony. In the chapters, Hong Kong history is seen from the viewpoints of foreign adventurers, businessmen, traders, missionaries, teachers, diplomats, servicemen, officials, artists, ramblers, and opportunity-seekers. The arrangement of chapters follows a chronological order, beginning with the arrival of the British who were a small and unstable community in the nineteenth century. The chapters also examine German businessmen and missionaries up to the eve of the First World War, the Japanese community before 1941, minority Catholics before the Second World War, diverse Indian groups up to the mid-twentieth century, and American diplomatic personnel in the 1950s. This book assesses the changing circumstances of Hong Kong over a period of more than one hundred years, and traces the rise and fall of various groups, and the continued development of some of them.

This edited volume, *for the first time*, brings together the histories of different foreign communities in Hong Kong. Foreign presence exerted its influence through big companies, churches, prominent individuals, and families. Instead of focusing on each of them separately, as the existing literature has done, this book argues that foreign sectors and people were well-connected both within and outside their own communities, and that *together* they contributed to Hong Kong society. This book represents the first attempt to study the various foreign communities, to see from the perspective of each, and to stress diversity within unity. Previous works deal with a single community, or a sector within a community. What has not been so far produced is a book that draws attention to these various groups, and this edited volume will certainly contribute to scholarship.

This is a cross-cultural study, examining the adaptation of foreigners to Chinese culture, the colonial rule, and the response of local people.

Also, it is a book in the field of ethnic studies. It should interest students, professors, and researchers of Asian studies, ethnic studies, Hong Kong history, and cultural relations.

Chapter 4 is a revised version of an article, "The German Community in 19th Century Hong Kong," previously published in the *Asia Europe Journal* (vol. 2, 2004, pp. 237–55). The editor would like to thank Springer-Verlag for permission to include a version of the article in this book. She is also grateful to the contributors for their tremendous effort and cooperation in making this book possible.

CINDY YIK-YI CHU
May 2005
Hong Kong

A Note on Romanization

For people, companies, streets, places, and so on in Hong Kong, this book spells the names in the same way that they have been spelled officially in Hong Kong (close to Cantonese pronunciation).

As for names of people, places, and so on in China, *pinyin* is used instead. The only exception to this is the Romanization—Sun Yat-sen—which is familiar to both Chinese and non-Chinese readers.

About the Contributors

Gillian Bickley recently retired from the rank of Associate Professor at the Hong Kong Baptist University, where she was a member of the Department of English Language and Literature for twenty-two years. She previously taught at Departments of English in the University of Auckland, New Zealand; the University of Hong Kong; and the University of Lagos, Nigeria. She is the author of *The Stewarts of Bourtreebush* (Aberdeen, Scotland: Centre for Scottish Studies, University of Aberdeen, 2003); *Hong Kong Invaded! A '97 Nightmare* (Hong Kong: Hong Kong University Press, 2001); and *The Golden Needle: The Biography of Frederick Stewart (1836–1889)* (Hong Kong: David C. Lam Institute for East-West Studies, Hong Kong Baptist University, 1997). She is also the editor of *The Development of Education in Hong Kong 1841–1897* (Hong Kong: Proverse Hong Kong, 2002).

Cindy Yik-yi Chu is Associate Professor of History at Hong Kong Baptist University. She received her Ph.D. from the University of Hawaii at Manoa, and was a degree fellow at the East-West Center (1992–1996). She is the author of *The Maryknoll Sisters in Hong Kong, 1921–1969: In Love with the Chinese* (New York: Palgrave Macmillan, 2004), and the coeditor of *Yapian zhanzheng de zai renshi* (A reappraisal of the Opium War) (Hong Kong: Chinese University Press, 2003), and *China Reconstructs* (Lanham: University Press of America, 2003). She has published almost thirty articles in journals such as the *Historian, American Journal of Chinese Studies, Asian Perspective*, and *Hong Kong Journal of Social Sciences.* She specializes in contemporary China, Chinese foreign relations, Sino-American relations, and Hong Kong politics.

Ricardo K. S. Mak is Professor of History at the Hong Kong Baptist University. He received his Ph.D. from the University of Regensburg. Specializing in modern Western intellectual thought and Sino-German relations, he has published a dozen of articles and reviews on related topics in academic journals in China, Taiwan, Hong Kong, and the United States. He is the author of *The Future of the Non-Western*

World in the Social Sciences of 19th Century England (Frankfurt am Main: Peter Lang, 1999). He is also the coeditor of *China Reconstructs* (Lanham: University Press of America, 2003) and *Sino-German Relations Since 1800: Multidisciplinary Explorations* (Frankfurt am Main: Peter Lang, 2000).

Chi-kwan Mark is Lecturer in International History at Royal Holloway, University of London. He studied at the University of Hong Kong and received his doctorate from the University of Oxford. In 2003–2004, he was a postdoctoral fellow at the University of Western Ontario, Canada. A specialist in Anglo-American relations and East Asian international history, he is the author of *Hong Kong and the Cold War: Anglo-American Relations 1949–1957* (Oxford: Clarendon; New York: Oxford University Press, 2004). His article appears in *The International History Review.*

Benjamin Wai-ming Ng is Associate Professor of Japanese Studies at the Chinese University of Hong Kong. He is an intellectual and cultural historian specializing in the history of Sino-Japanese and Japan–Hong Kong relations. His main publications are mainly on Tokugawa intellectual history, Japanese popular culture in East Asia, and Sino-Japanese cultural interchange. His book, *The I Ching in Tokugawa Thought and Culture* (Honolulu: University of Hawai'i Press, 2000) won the Choice Outstanding Academic Book of 2000.

Caroline Plüss is Adjunct Assistant Professor of History at the Chinese University of Hong Kong. She received her doctorate in Sociology from the University of Oxford, and was a postdoctoral fellow at the University of Hong Kong. She has published on the Indian, Jewish, and Muslim diasporas in Hong Kong, and her articles appear in *International Scope Review, China Perspectives, Jewish Culture and History, International Sociology*, and so on. She is now preparing a book manuscript on the history of the Jewish community in Hong Kong.

Chapter 1

Introduction

Cindy Yik-yi Chu

We present what we feel is a timely book on foreign *communities* in Hong Kong. What do Hong Kong people want the rest of the world to think about Hong Kong? Hong Kong is a cosmopolitan city with traders, businessmen, and merchants coming from almost everywhere in the world. It has a culture, which while fundamentally Chinese, has long been under foreign influence. Its people speak the English language, receive Western education, and adopt Western lifestyles. It is a place where foreigners have settled down, formed their families, and made their home. Hong Kong is a "world city," a city that belongs to the international community, and which recognizes the contribution of local people and foreigners alike in making the place what we find today.

The Hong Kong Chinese have a long history of living with other cultures and other peoples. Companies, clubs, and religions—all introduced from overseas—have long made their presence felt. These foreign presences have been the subject of numerous academic works, leisure-reading material, and even official publications dealing with particular individuals, or detailing the histories of particular corporations, Christian Churches, foreign communities, and clubs. Some foreign expatriates have written memoirs of their long years of service in government. Others have recorded their experiences in wartime and other unusual circumstances. All of these works deal with a single community, or a sector within a community. What has not so far been produced is a book that brings together *the histories of the different foreign communities* in Hong Kong.

Many foreigners came to trade and to set up their own businesses, but it was through the large overseas corporations that the influence of the foreigners was most clearly felt, as they maintained cooperative relations with the British colonial government, employed local people, and had a strong say in economic decision making. Not surprisingly, there have been a number of works on corporate and merchant history, and on trading firms within the foreign communities. Such titles include Colin N. Crisswell's *The Taipans*, and Frank H. H. King's four-volume series on the "History of the Hongkong and Shanghai Banking Corporation."[1] Besides studies on individual firms, there have been publications on clubs and associations within foreign communities. Examples are Andrew Coe's history of the American Club—*Eagles & Dragons*—and the description of the Goethe-Institut in the book, *Germany in Hong Kong*.[2]

Other foreigners came to Hong Kong to establish the Christian Church and to proselytize. These missionaries, along with traders and merchants, were the pioneers in the earliest colonial days. Through their work of evangelization and their inclusion of local converts that greatly exceeded their own numbers, foreign Churches have had a prominent presence in Hong Kong, a long and enduring impact on Hong Kong society, Hong Kong culture, and even on its education. Foreign missionaries had much closer contacts than most foreign residents did with the Chinese, and in many cases actually lived among the local people. Some Church histories have been written. For example, Father Thomas F. Ryan, himself a Jesuit, recorded the history of other Milan missionaries, who had jurisdiction over the Hong Kong Catholic Diocese, in *The Story of a Hundred Years: The Pontifical Institute of Foreign Missions, (P.I.M.E.), in Hong Kong, 1858–1958*.[3]

Some foreign expatriates have been willing to have published their own personal accounts of their time in Hong Kong. See, for example, *Foreign Devils: Expatriates in Hong Kong* by May Holdsworth; and *Hong Kong Remembers*, edited by Sally Blyth and Ian Wotherspoon. Both volumes contain fascinating recollections of foreign individuals of various occupations.[4] Susanna Hoe explored the life of Western women in the first hundred years of the colony in *The Private Life of Old Hong Kong*.[5] Others wrote their own memoirs at the conclusion of their long service, including, in some cases, records of unforgettable ordeals in Hong Kong. After surviving the Japanese occupation, George Wright-Nooth wrote *Prisoner of the Turnip Heads: Horror, Hunger and Humour in Hong Kong, 1941–1945*.[6] More recently, the last British governor had his story published in Jonathan Dimbleby's *The Last Governor: Chris Patten and the Handover of Hong Kong*, and in his own work, *East and West: The Last Governor of Hong Kong on Power, Freedom and the Future.*[7]

The existing literature shows the foreign presence making its impact most noticeably through big companies and Churches, as well as through prominent individuals and families. The present book will not focus on one company, one Church, one person, or one family alone, as previous works have done. Instead, this book shows that foreign sectors and foreign people were well connected both within and outside their own community, and that together they exerted an impact on Hong Kong society. While acknowledging diversity within foreign communities, it is well to remember that these sectors and individuals did not exist in a vacuum, and that they shared similarities of culture and of language, of customs and of values. There was always the collective identity, in addition to the diversity that did exist within the foreign communities.

With these points in mind, this book assesses the contribution of several foreign communities in Hong Kong, recognizing the distinct characteristics of each community on the one hand, and emphasizing the existence within each community of different occupations, opinions, and class interests on the other. This book also describes how foreign communities learned to live with one another and with the local Chinese. Foreigners made up minority groupings in Hong Kong. People belonging to different ethnic groups cultivated working relationships among themselves, and in some cases, a particular community might play a more dominant role than others. This book represents the first attempt to study the different foreign communities in Hong Kong, to see the city from the perspective of each, and to stress the diversity within each unity.

THEMES OF THIS BOOK

1. History from the Perspective of each Minority

This book aims to portray Hong Kong history through the perspectives of certain ethnic minority groups—the foreign communities of the British, Germans, Europeans, Americans, Indians, and Japanese—and to understand how they perceived the colony, its economic situation, political administration, and culture. In the chapters that follow, Hong Kong history is seen from the varied viewpoints of foreigners of very different types and backgrounds: adventurers, businessmen, traders, missionaries, teachers, diplomats, servicemen, officials, artists, ramblers, and those opportunity-seekers who tried to find in the colony whatever it was that they needed, but most of whom, when they stayed, became contributors to the colony.

The arrangement of chapters follows a chronological order, from Hong Kong's precarious beginnings as a British colony with the arrival of the British, who were then no more than a small and unstable community, looking for suitable roles and responsibilities. The British community, as described in two of the chapters, was in a state of flux in the nineteenth century. Its people came and went without any obvious national policy for the future of Hong Kong. Further chapters examine the small group of German businessmen and missionaries up to the eve of the First World War (1914–1918), the Japanese community before 1941, and minority Catholics before the Second World War (1939–1945). The chapters also consider diverse Indian groups up to the mid-twentieth century and American diplomatic personnel in the 1950s.

By assembling the accounts of these various groups together, the book assesses the changing circumstances of Hong Kong over a period of more than one hundred years, and traces the rise and fall of various groups as well as the continued development of some of them. The book thus also amounts to a history of the minorities in Hong Kong, the groups of people whose significance to the local Chinese society has far outweighed their numerical size.

2. History on Societal, Community, and Individual Levels

The chapters look at foreign communities on a societal level, focusing on the process of adaptation and adjustment after their arrival in Hong Kong, and the changes in their composition over the course of time. Much use is made of the recollections of individuals, especially in the most difficult periods of the colony's history. Whether or not individuals or groups came on their own initiative or were sent to the colony by their governments, they somehow managed to form a different perception of the local situation from that of their people at home. Having formed a better picture of circumstances in Hong Kong, foreigners who opted to settle down here became more sympathetic toward the needs of the society. They learned to live with the local people. In the latter half of the nineteenth century, British missionaries and teachers were more eager for conversion and education among the Chinese than the administration and general public at home in the United Kingdom. Before the 1870s, the Germans became more interested in integrating in British circles, and working with the Chinese, than in maintaining their ties with their own governments at home. In order to expand and consolidate the Catholic community in Hong Kong, the Catholic Church underwent an evolution in its objectives and work, devoting more attention to secular activities and to gaining acceptance from Chinese people. Indian businessmen became more ready to adjust their traditional practices, where they feared that a too inflexible approach might affect their business in Hong Kong. In the 1950s, American consulate officers had to find a balance between patriotism and pragmatism in the face of the precarious existence of the colony at the time.

3. Diversity within Foreign Communities

Foreign communities were far from being monolithic entities. There were different ethnic groups; within each group, members pursued different occupations, had different class backgrounds, and worked toward different objectives. Initially, the British community was composed of people from all walks of life. The Japanese came at first from the lowest classes of their society, but these people were gradually replaced by businessmen working for large corporations. To deal with the pressing needs, the Catholic Church recruited personnel from congregations in Europe and America, and trained local people for service in the community. The Indians came from a number of migrant groups, and took up positions as soldiers, policemen, and businessmen. As for the American consulate establishment, its officers stood out from the other American communities, having come with set agendas and purposes, principally the upholding of their government's line. How far was the behavior of a foreign individual influenced by his or her community, cultural and religious background, class identity, or simply by the need to survive? The Germans and Japanese set up their own clubs to promote unity within their communities and to maintain their cultural values and identities. Foreigners might be eager to preserve their own customs and traditions in Hong Kong (as Chinese communities have done in Chinatowns in overseas cities), or they might not. They might or might not seek to keep abreast of developments in their home countries. In either case, they were always changed by their experience of living in the colony. There was always a degree of divergence between the foreigners who had spent years adjusting to life in the community here and the foreigners who had spent the same years living through the changes in their home countries.

4. History of Multi-Archival Research

The history of foreign communities in Hong Kong is a history of cultural exchange, involving people of different languages, traditions, and customs. It is therefore important that the stories be drawn from a number of different sources. Almost all contributors to this book are Hong Kong-based, either local Chinese or foreign expatriates; and they have without exception produced many works on topics related to this project. Not only have they made very good use of material available locally; their contributions also benefit from their long experience with foreign-language (i.e., non-Chinese language) material, and with using overseas (i.e., non-Hong Kong) libraries and archives. Locally, contributors have explored government publications and special collections in university libraries, Colonial Office records in the Main Library of the University of Hong Kong, material stored in the Public Records Office (of the Government Records Service), and the archives of local Churches (such as the Hong Kong Catholic Diocesan Archives). To see from the perspective of foreign minorities one needs to be able to read their languages and to take advantage of their records and recollections. Contributors have conducted intensive research into published and unpublished material in a number of languages—Chinese, Japanese, English, German, and Italian. In addition, they have consulted sources from the Lauinger Library (of Georgetown University, Washington, D.C.), Princeton University Library (Princeton, New Jersey), the National Archives (College Park, Maryland), the Harry S. Truman Library (Independence, Missouri), the Dwight D. Eisenhower Library (Abilene, Kansas), the Maryknoll Mission Archives (Maryknoll, New York), Britain's National Archives (formerly known as Public Record Office, Kew, United Kingdom), the Church Missionary Society Archives (at Birmingham University Library, Birmingham, U.K.), the Bodleian Library of Commonwealth and African Studies at Rhodes House (formerly known as Rhodes House Library, Oxford, U.K.), the Archives of Commerzbibliothek Hamburg (Hamburg, Germany), and so on. It is believed that the collaboration in multi-archival research that this work has occasioned, particularly in the preparation of the contributions from members of minority groups, will bring considerable benefits to the study of the history of Hong Kong and to the recognition of the complexity of its society.

Beginnings of the British Community

The British acquired Hong Kong in 1841 and their hold on the island was consolidated by the Treaty of Nanjing in 1842. They proceeded to rule over Hong Kong as their colony on the southern edge of the Chinese mainland. Since that time, the British had played the role of colonial rulers, bringing with them their administration, legal practice, educational system, and many other things. The British community always had pride of place among the various foreign communities in Hong Kong. In her two chapters, Gillian Bickley traces the emergence and the making of the British community from the 1840s to the end of the nineteenth century. In chapter 2, "Early Beginnings of British Community (1841–1898)," she argues that the British in both the United Kingdom and Hong Kong could not agree among themselves on the purpose of the acquisition of the colony and the functions it would serve in their country's overseas empire. There was therefore no grand scheme as to how to make use of the colony and as to how the British community in Hong Kong should develop. The only things of which the British were certain were that their administration would be permanent, and that they had the responsibility for governing and defending Hong Kong, then their possession, so as to safeguard their own people and interests in the faraway land. As Bickley points out, at the core of the British community were the members of the armed services and those who arrived to take up posts in the British Hong Kong government. Even these people were always on the move, as officials and servicemen came on short assignments and then left. Outside this core, the community was composed of people from all walks of life—teachers, missionaries, performers, ramblers, and others. Bickley emphasizes that the British community was small and its members were mostly temporary residents. Chapter 2 shows how a foreign community—the British—appeared on the scene, and how it gradually grew and took on an identity of its own through responding to local needs and circumstances. The process was one of adaptation and adjustment. A foreign community was in the making in Hong Kong. Through its own initiatives, the British community began to acquire the personnel and the experience to venture into different areas in education, religion, business, and trade. More importantly, members of the British community came from diverse backgrounds, and they had to learn to live with each other as well as with others in Hong Kong.

These ideas—that a foreign community acquired its identity through the process of adaptation and adjustment, and that it adopted certain attitudes toward various issues and toward other cultural groups over the course of time—are further elaborated in chapter 3, "British Attitudes toward Hong Kong in the Nineteenth Century." Here, Bickley continues her argument that the British (in both the

United Kingdom and Hong Kong) did not have any set policy or plan on how the colony should develop. The British disagreed among themselves on how much effort should be invested in the work of evangelization and education in Hong Kong. At the same time, the British in Hong Kong tended to be more conservative than their fellow countrymen in the United Kingdom in handling social issues and in enforcing the rule of law. They had to strike a balance between morality and pragmatism in the face of local circumstances, problems, and culture. In working with the Chinese, some individual British were more successful and more willing to learn the Chinese language, while others relied on middlemen in their communications with the local people. Naturally, the British had mixed feelings about the Chinese. Some developed a sense of emotional attachment while others had negative attitudes toward Hong Kong and the local people.

Subordination to the British and Subsequent Tensions: The German Community

Faced with the predominant position of the British, how did other foreign communities react? The Germans, having searched for opportunities in cities on the Chinese mainland in the 1840s, became interested in Hong Kong in the 1850s. Those of them who settled in Hong Kong belonged to two groups, businessmen who came for monetary gain, and missionaries who came to spread the Christian faith. As Ricardo K. S. Mak explains in chapter 4, "Nineteenth-Century German Community," the Germans, a minority group in the British colony, tangoed between "integration and segregation, cultural assimilation and dissimilation, national identity and marginalization." Being very small in number, and being cautious and pragmatic, the Germans cooperated closely with the British and downplayed their own national identity in public life. Since the British Hong Kong government was rather receptive toward Germans, the latter had no difficulty in integrating into the British community. German merchants chose not to challenge the position of their British partners, and because of their success in working with the British authorities, they made no effort at cultivating political ties with their governments at home. The major German companies in Hong Kong at that time were Melchers & Co., Siemssen & Co., and Carlowitz & Co. The community also produced prominent missionaries such as Karl Gützlaff and Ernst Johann Eitel. Despite their stature, these

Germans were very willing to assimilate into British circles. In their private and cultural lives, however, the Germans were quite a closed community, with attitudes greatly at variance with the openness they exhibited toward the British in public. Before 1870, the Germans could be described as maintaining a strong sense of solidarity while trying not to display nationalistic sentiments or behavior, following the lead of the British administration. As Mak points out, German unification in 1871 began to change things in Hong Kong. Beginning in the 1870s, the Germans promoted trade between the region where Hong Kong lies and their home country, developed better connections with their new government at home, and embraced rejuvenated nationalistic feelings. Tensions began to enter into their relations with the British in Hong Kong in the 1890s, and the situation deteriorated on the eve of the First World War.

SUBORDINATION TO THE DEMANDS OF LOCAL PEOPLE: THE CATHOLIC COMMUNITY

Foreign communities needed not only to adjust to British rule in Hong Kong, but they also had to live with other ethnic groups and make themselves useful to the Chinese people. This process of adaptation and adjustment was of particular importance to the Catholic Church, which was under the jurisdiction of Milan missionaries, and which comprised congregations from Italy, France, Ireland, Spain, the United States, and Canada. The Catholic community grew rapidly with the expanding population of the colony and the inclusion of a Portuguese population. The number of baptisms increased, as did the number of Chinese converts. Over the course of time, there was an *evolution* in the objectives, work, and outlook of the Catholic Church, resulting from a better understanding of local circumstances and a recognition of the need to integrate into Hong Kong society. As Cindy Yik-yi Chu elaborates in chapter 5, "Catholic Church between Two World Wars," the Church was able to adapt, to adjust its activities, and to successfully fit in with local demands through a growing emphasis on secular activities. In other words, the Church recognized that it had more than a religious role to play. It had to fulfill certain social duties as well.

When the Church established itself in Hong Kong in 1841, it had only temporary personnel and no mission policy. However, with the growth in the local population came increased opportunities for evangelization, and the Church moved to consolidate and expand the Catholic community. This entailed the promotion of the Christian faith, the erection of church buildings, and the assignment of a responsible institute to Hong Kong to shoulder the greater responsibilities that the future would bring. The Church was also preoccupied with recruiting personnel from abroad, as well as with training local clergy. In order to be accepted by Hong Kong society, the Church underwent a transformation in the way it approached its work. It became more involved in secular tasks, as a means to attract people, who were curious about its activities, and to strengthen its position in Hong Kong. These activities, especially its work for the less fortunate—such as running old folks' homes, orphanages, hospitals, and schools for poor children—grew from the necessity to reach out to society and to remove suspicion among the Chinese. As Chu points out, from being primarily concerned with the pursuit of converts, the Catholic Church went on to assume increasing responsibility for the provision of relief, welfare, and education to the local people.

A Neglected Community: The Japanese before the Outbreak of the Pacific War in 1941

The Japanese played an influential role in Hong Kong before the Pacific War (1941–1945). However, as Benjamin Wai-ming Ng points out, this has not received sufficient scholarly attention owing to the greater emphasis placed on Japanese aggression and the Japanese occupation of Hong Kong. In chapter 6, "Making of a Japanese Community in Prewar Period (1841–1941)," Ng says that there has been almost nothing written in the English language on Japanese people and their activities in Hong Kong before the Pacific War. Such negligence should not obscure the fact that in 1941 there were significant numbers of Japanese in Hong Kong. They formed a united group, steadily gaining in both size and influence. With the establishment of the Japanese consulate in Hong Kong in 1874 (this became one of the largest foreign consulates in the colony in the early twentieth century), the Japanese population began to grow and the Japanese community came more into notice. The Japanese in Hong Kong played an important part in the ever vibrant Sino-Japanese and Anglo-Japanese political, economic, and cultural relations. Ng shows how a foreign community could undergo all these changes while being itself under the larger influence of both internal developments at home as well as its own country's foreign policy agenda. From the 1870s onward, the Japanese community in Hong Kong grew considerably; and unlike in the late nineteenth century when most members of the community came from the lowest sectors of Japanese society, the Japanese in the early twentieth century were mainly businessmen, many of them working for big companies such as Mitsui and Mitsubishi. Not only did the size, composition, and outlook of the Japanese community change, its members became more united and prominent in Hong Kong. In the early twentieth century, the Japanese took advantage of the geographical location of the colony, which to them was the "Casablanca of the Far East," to gather information about the Chinese mainland, the United Kingdom, and the outside world. In other words, they used Hong Kong as a base for intelligence activities. Hong Kong was also the ideal place for the Japanese to promote relations with the United Kingdom, and to facilitate diplomatic, military, and economic exchanges. The dominant status of the Japanese community was well evident, as maritime trade constituted its major economic activity in Hong Kong. As Ng remarks, had it not been for the Pacific War, the Japanese would have become a significant ethnic group in Hong Kong, like those of the Indians, the Jews, and the Eurasians.

ANTIFOREIGNISM FROM AN UNEXPECTED SOURCE: THE JAPANESE OCCUPATION (1941–1945) AND STANLEY CIVILIAN INTERNMENT CAMP (1942–1945)

The Pacific War finally broke out in 1941. The Japanese invaded Hong Kong on December 8, and the colony came under Japanese occupation after the British surrendered on Christmas Day. The Japanese occupation lasted from December 1941 to August 1945, a unique period in Hong Kong's history, when it was subject to control by a foreign power other than the British. As Chu argues in chapter 7, "Stanley Civilian Internment Camp during Japanese Occupation," this period deserves close attention because antiforeignism had never before been so systematically expressed in Hong Kong. Before this time there had been outbreaks of antiforeignism in the colony, for example, the 1922 seamen's strike, in which Chinese seamen demonstrated against differential treatment between themselves and their European counterparts. From 1941 onward, however, antiforeignism came from an unexpected source—not from local Chinese, but from Japanese who acted against enemy nationals, including the British, Europeans, Americans, and Canadians. In order to secure their control of the colony, not only did the Japanese intern combatants, they also interned nationals of the Allied Powers in the Stanley Civilian

Internment Camp from January 1942 to August 1945, though during this time some internees were repatriated.

The Stanley Civilian Internment Camp was the greatest manifestation of antiforeignism in local history up to that time. It was surely the most peculiar episode in the story of foreign communities in Hong Kong. When the British surrendered, an estimated 3,000 non-Chinese civilians from the Allied Powers remained in Hong Kong. In the first two months of internment, there were around 2,400 British, more than 300 Americans, and about 60 Dutch in the camp. In time, the internees settled into a routine and found their place by taking up responsibilities in work teams and squads. Throughout the internment, food remained *the* problem, as there was never enough to eat, not to mention that rations were basically filthy rice and a few vegetables. Not surprisingly, malnutrition was "the disease" among internees, leading to associated problems such as dysentery, beriberi, and diarrhea. Because of Japanese neglect, infectious and insect-borne diseases were common, including typhoid, tuberculosis, typhus, malaria, and others. Extreme poverty also meant insufficient clothing, bedding, and basic necessities. Besides deteriorating physical conditions, overcrowding in the camp imposed severe psychological pressure on internees, resulting in constant conflicts and nervous breakdowns. During internment, foreign nationals not only lost their freedom, but they also lacked adequate care, and were beyond the reach of the outside world. The memoirs of these internees remain vivid many decades after internment, containing all manner of details, a testament to an extraordinary period.

Diversity within Foreign Communities: Indians; A Distinct Sector within a Community: The United States Consular Establishment within the American Community

No foreign community has demonstrated as much internal diversity as the Indian community. In chapter 8, "Migrants from India and Their Relations with British and Chinese Residents," Caroline Plüss examines four migrant groups—Parsees, Muslims, Sikhs, and Hindus—and their different relations with Hong Kong society from the mid-nineteenth to the mid-twentieth century.

The Parsees came to trade in the earliest colonial times, taking advantage of the geographical location of Hong Kong and the stable British administration, to promote their economic undertakings, which they had already set afoot in Guangdong. The Parsees had been receptive to the English language, and to English social manners and business style, and they already had experience in serving as middlemen between the British and other peoples. As middlemen, they adopted a Westernized and cosmopolitan outlook, were willing to speak English and to adopt Western manners and even English names, and to show much loyalty to the British. As Plüss says, they continued this tendency toward Anglicization well into the twentieth century.

Another group of traders consisted of the Muslims—Bohras and Sunnis—whose economic connections with India helped them develop their business in Hong Kong. In the early twentieth century, Bohra and Sunni Muslims broadened and strengthened their networks in both Hong Kong and China. In the process, they identified more with local societies and cultures, and took a more relaxed attitude toward those of their own traditional practices, which might stand in the way of trading opportunities. Because of their business concerns, Bohras and Sunnis were flexible in following traditional customs and rules. The third group was the Sikhs, who worked in the police and the military in the nineteenth century. Although they were loyal to their British employers, the Sikhs found it difficult to move up the ranks in the police force. As a result, they took advantage of other opportunities in Hong Kong, and were often found taking up openings with European employers on the Chinese mainland, or moving to other parts of the world. From the mid-twentieth century onward, Hindus rose to become prominent Indian traders in Hong Kong, having discarded traditional prejudices against a number of occupations. In short, Indians in Hong Kong adopted pragmatic attitudes toward working with the British and the local Chinese. They were willing to take up whatever opportunities became available to them at different times.

Different times brought different challenges. The Cold War in the 1950s and the emergence of a Communist regime on the Chinese mainland saw the rise of a sector within the American community, namely the U.S. consulate establishment. In chapter 9, "American 'China Hands' in the 1950s," Chi-kwan Mark looks at this sector, its relations with the British Hong Kong government, and the distinct functions it served in a new stage of international relations. The expansion of the American consulate in the 1950s was sudden and unprecedented, and aroused considerable attention. The consulate establishment can be called "distinct," given its outlook, functions, and prominence. As Mark explains, with the Communist victory in 1949, American consular officers transferred their operations from the

Chinese mainland to Hong Kong, a colony of their Cold War ally, leading to the establishment of the huge U.S. consulate there. By the latter half of the 1950s, the U.S. consulate in Hong Kong was among the largest American consulates in the world, with consuls, vice-consuls, economic officers, and information officers in charge of intelligence gathering, export controls, and overt propaganda. As Mark points out, these American "China hands" gradually found themselves caught up in a struggle between their American background (and anti-Communist stance) and the local perspectives (which they came to learn about and understand). They were able to develop a more practical understanding of Hong Kong's situation, and of the colony's precarious existence on the edge of the Chinese mainland. The "China hands" had to strike a good balance between patriotism and pragmatism. To facilitate their work, they cultivated a cordial working relationship with the British Hong Kong government. As in the case of other foreign communities, U.S. consulate officers in Hong Kong tended, after their arrival, to form new and different judgments, being more sympathetic toward the local situation than was their government at home.

REMARKS

This book does not claim to deal with all foreign communities in Hong Kong. It includes discussion of the colonial ruler (the British), European businessmen and missionaries (Germans, and the Catholic community), Asian neighbors (Japanese and Indians), and the new world power (the Americans). Nor is it *only* about foreign communities since—while foreigners were making their impact—they in turn were being impacted by Hong Kong's culture and people. The contributors are at pains to emphasize Sino-foreign exchanges, cooperation among ethnic groups, adaptation, and change. When foreigners first appeared on the scene, they saw Hong Kong from foreign perspectives, but they gradually became less "foreign," and as they learned to be pragmatic, they discarded some of their prior cultural baggage, and began to find a balance between their "foreignness" and the local realities. Together with the Chinese people, foreigners found Hong Kong a place of diversity, a place of mixed identity, and a place of tolerance.

NOTES

1. Read e.g. Colin N. Crisswell, *The Taipans: Hong Kong's Merchant Princes* (New York: Oxford University Press, 1981); and the four-volume series

of Frank H. H. King—*The Hongkong Bank in Late Imperial China, 1864–1902* (Cambridge: Cambridge University Press, 1987), *The Hongkong Bank in the Period of Imperialism and War, 1895–1918* (Cambridge: Cambridge University Press, 1988), *The Hongkong Bank between the Wars and the Bank Interned, 1919–1945* (Cambridge: Cambridge University Press, 1988), *The Hong Kong Bank in the Period of Development and Nationalism, 1941–1984* (Cambridge: Cambridge University Press, 1991).

2. Andrew Coe, *Eagles & Dragons: A History of Americans in China & the Origins of the American Club Hong Kong* (Hong Kong: American Club, 1997); *Germany in Hong Kong: 50 Years Consulate General of the Federal Republic of Germany, 40 Years Goethe-Institut Hong Kong, 20 Years German Chamber of Commerce* (Hong Kong: German Chamber of Commerce, Goethe-Institut, Consulate General of the Federal Republic of Germany, 2003).
3. Thomas F. Ryan, *The Story of a Hundred Years: The Pontifical Institute of Foreign Missions, (P.I.M.E.), in Hong Kong, 1858–1958* (Hong Kong: Catholic Truth Society, 1959).
4. May Holdsworth, *Foreign Devils: Expatriates in Hong Kong*, with additional text by Caroline Courtauld (Hong Kong: Oxford University Press, 2002); Sally Blyth and Ian Wotherspoon, eds., *Hong Kong Remembers* (Hong Kong: Oxford University Press, 1996).
5. Susanna Hoe, *The Private Life of Old Hong Kong: Western Women in the British Colony, 1841–1941* (Hong Kong: Oxford University Press, 1991).
6. George Wright-Nooth (with Mark Adkin), *Prisoner of the Turnip Heads: Horror, Hunger and Humour in Hong Kong, 1941–1945* (London: Leo Cooper, 1994). A paperback edition was published a few years later: *Prisoner of the Turnip Heads: The Fall of Hong Kong and Imprisonment by the Japanese* (London: Cassell, 1999).
7. Jonathan Dimbleby, *The Last Governor: Chris Patten & the Handover of Hong Kong* (London: Little, Brown & Co., 1997); Chris Patten, *East and West: The Last Governor of Hong Kong on Power, Freedom and the Future* (London and Basingstoke: Macmillan, 1998).

Chapter 2

Early Beginnings of British Community (1841–1898)

Gillian Bickley

Introduction

According to British chroniclers and historians, it was news of the preliminaries of a Sino-British treaty that led to the originally unofficial British settlement of Hong Kong Island, which took place in 1841; and subsequently, in 1843, the island was declared a British colony. Seventeen years later, by the Beijing Convention (1860), the territory administered by Britain was expanded, when Kowloon Peninsula (with Stonecutters Island) was also ceded to Britain on the same terms. But a further and final expansion, in 1898, when the New Territories and numerous islands were added, was for a limited period only. This final addition of territory was for a period of ninety-nine years: the New Territories were leased by Britain from China, beginning on July 1, 1898. Paradoxically, it was this lease—designed, by providing a buffer of territory, to preserve the British administration in the face of threat from expansionist European Powers in the region—which ultimately led to the close of British administration at midnight, June 30, 1997, when Britain ceremonially handed Hong Kong back to the government in mainland China.

From 1843 to June 1898, at least, therefore, Britain had reason to believe that its administration in Hong Kong would be permanent, while those British living in Hong Kong had strong reason to believe that Hong Kong was theirs. Nor were the British alone in these assumptions. Citizens of other countries also, seeking to trade or otherwise to have relationships with the Chinese mainland, based themselves in Hong Kong, precisely because they believed that the existence of a permanent British administration offered greater security, protection, and legality than elsewhere in the region. In time, informed and educated Chinese also accepted these points, and planned business and personal relationships within these contexts. When considering the British community in Hong Kong during the period 1843 to 1898, therefore, in contrast with the period 1898 to June 30, 1997 and the period from July 1, 1997 onward, these are basic points to bear in mind.

BRITISH PERSPECTIVES ON THE PURPOSE OF HONG KONG

Accepting, therefore, that from 1843 to 1898, Hong Kong was a British possession, what purposes did the British government in the United Kingdom and the British Hong Kong administration, British citizens and the British community in Hong Kong consider that Hong Kong could or should fulfill, from a national or British perspective?

"Tot homines, quot sententiae."—"There are as many opinions as people."—It should not be surprising that there was no single opinion on this question, nor should it surprise us, perhaps, that this topic was a matter of opinion rather than a matter of fact.

It is well known that the British Foreign Secretary, Lord Palmerston, was mortified that British Captain Charles Elliott had chosen, "a barren island with hardly a house upon it"[1] as their prize of war at the conclusion of hostilities with the Chinese Empire, and that the British monarch, who ruled throughout the period under discussion, Queen Victoria (1819–1901, queen 1837–1901), reported her husband as amused over her new possession.[2] And the first Colonial Treasurer of the British Hong Kong administration, Robert Montgomery Martin, took a very gloomy view of the future economic value to Britain of this new acquisition.[3]

But was the purpose of Hong Kong, in fact, to add to or enhance the economic power of Britain? Was it not, rather, to provide a military and naval base, close to the Chinese mainland, ready and able to enforce British views and British interests on the mainland itself? And how could these two purposes—economic and military—be separated? Were not British interests largely mercantile? Would not the military and naval protection of British trade lead to increases in British economic power? As a refueling and refitting station for ships and as part of the communication network for mail and goods, did Hong Kong not serve both purposes? Additionally, to what extent, if any, did the authorities in Britain perceive Hong Kong as a base for the protection of British citizens in the area, merely in their capacity as British citizens; a duty of protection that was simply an extension of their duty, within the British Isles itself, of protecting British citizens from foreign powers?

It was in an 1850 House of Commons speech that the classically educated Lord Palmerston, then Foreign Secretary, reminded members of the British House of Commons that, wherever they were in the world, citizens of the Roman Empire had believed themselves immune from harm, simply because they were citizens of that Empire. Citizens of Britain, Palmerston asserted, should be similarly protected. "As the Roman in days of old held himself free from indignity when he could say 'Civis Romanus Sum' [I am a Roman citizen], so also a British subject, in whatever land he may be, shall feel confident that the watchful eye and the strong arm of England will protect him against injustice and wrong." This was not, the speech shows, a formulation of a new policy, for in it, speaking of Britain as, a "political, a commercial, a constitutional country," Palmerston refers to, "the principles which can be traced through all our foreign transactions . . . the guiding rule and directing spirit of our proceedings . . . the principles on which the foreign policy of Her Majesty's Government has been conducted . . . the sense of duty which has led us to think ourselves bound to afford protection to our fellow subjects abroad."[4]

Palmerston's views were not however accepted by all. For the purpose of this particular speech, unusually made in the House of Commons, was to defend his decision to blockade Greece after an Athenian mob had burned down the home of a British citizen (Gibraltar-born Jew, Don Pacifico). It is not surprising, however, that the attitude of British citizens beyond the British Isles tended to favor opinions like Palmerston's, which would lead to greater security for themselves. Indeed, Hong Kong complaints were occasionally expressed, during this period, that a British gun-boat had been slow to appear on the scene of some temporary disturbance or hot spot in the region. And, as in other colonies at the time, it was a recurrent bone of contention between Hong Kong and Britain as to what proportion of Hong Kong's defense should be paid for by the central government in Britain, and how much from Hong Kong taxes.[5] Concern for an effective defense was constant throughout the period under discussion. The New Territories lease, signed in 1898, was itself a product of this concern. Before it was signed, in 1897, a pamphlet,

The Back Door, gathering together and republishing a story first serialized, the same year, in the *China Mail*,[6] called for the defense of the south side (the back door) of Hong Kong Island. And it made its point by describing the fictional successful invasion of Hong Kong from the south by the combined forces of France and Russia.

As for the purposes that Hong Kong served for the individuals who were resident here, from time to time; in general, for those (men and women) whose occupations were beyond the home, Hong Kong was a base from which they directed their activities in China or in the region, or among the Chinese generally. These included trade and varieties of evangelization—including the spreading of the Christian Gospel and the proselytization of the Chinese. But they also disseminated the content and views of a liberal Western education, the benefits and knowledge of Western medicine (culminating, for this period, in the establishment of the College of Medicine for Chinese in 1887),[7] the benefits and knowledge of Western science and technology. And—from a broader perspective and among the idealists that there were among the residents—they also promoted friendship and understanding among the peoples and races of the world in ever improving human society.

Government servants were a special case. Their job was to administer Hong Kong well, so that its purposes (from the point of view of the home government) might be facilitated and not hindered, and in such a way as to serve and not hinder the well-being and goals of the multifarious individuals living here. As for the families (if any) of those whose work or interest had brought him or her to Hong Kong, their view of Hong Kong must have been similar to that of family members anywhere in the world to their location, and varying according to personality and economic circumstances. They must have sought to make of the place what they could, liking or disliking it, to the extent that they were or were not able to give acceptable moral support to the economic head of the family and to build an acceptable personal, family, social, and in some cases, spiritual life.[8]

Size, Degree of Permanence, and Composition of the British Community

1. Size of the British Community

The British community in Hong Kong during this period was comparatively small. Census statistics, although acknowledged even by contemporaries, for some part of this period, as not absolutely reliable, nevertheless give a workable indication of the size of the community and there are other sources of population statistics also.[9] The indications are that, early in the period under study, in 1845, probably excluding the troops of the garrison, there were no more than 595 Europeans—men, women, and children (*including* British)—and in 1898 there were 8,732 non-Chinese civilians and 6,458 non-Chinese in the armed services (both figures *including* the British figures). In about 2000, the total population was 6.9 million and the number of British residents was given as 0.5 percent of the whole.[10] (The total population figure given in about 2002 is the same.)[11]

2. Degree of Permanence of the British Community

As broadly indicated by some of these figures, a substantial part of these totals was composed of *temporary* residents only. Military and naval personnel, both officers and men, were stationed in the territory for a period of years or sometimes only of months. Senior administrators also were not necessarily permanent residents. Governors, notably, had terms of office usually of a maximum of five years. Other senior officials might be appointed to or from Hong Kong as part of their career progress, seen in terms of the British Empire as a whole, and not as related to one territory alone. For example, C. C. Smith, when a generally well-thought-of cadet, with good performance as Registrar General and in other Hong Kong positions, fell foul of the uncertain temper of Governor John Pope Hennessy and, on application, was appointed to the British administration in the Straits Settlements.[12] When Frederick Stewart, then Colonial Secretary, died in 1889, his position was seen as a career opportunity for colonial servants not only in Hong Kong, and the position went to Francis Fleming, who was transferred from another colony.[13] Missionaries and those teachers who had a vocation to work among the Chinese might be more permanent members of the community, but even these could have long periods of absence, whether on the Chinese mainland, in Europe, or elsewhere in the world, either for home visits or to perform business—including fund-raising—supportive of their work. Members of the merchant class may possibly have been among those residents who remained for the longest number of years, although these also tended to retire to Europe at the end of their career, or when ill-health made this advisable. Although a visit to the Protestant and Roman Catholic cemeteries in Hong Kong shows many from this period memorialized there (the Jewish cemetery was established in the

1850s), to be buried in either place was not an expected conclusion to the lives of most of the British civilians who spent time in Hong Kong.

As early as the governorship of John Pope Hennessy, local private naturalization ordinances were passed, by which local residents were individually made British subjects in Hong Kong.[14] The first of these, in August 1880, was on behalf of the German missionary, Ernst Johann Eitel, who, in 1866 had married the English woman, Winifred Eaton, sent out to Hong Kong under the auspices of the Society for the Promotion of Female Education in the East, as the first lady superintendent of the Diocesan Native Female Training School.[15] All residents, including therefore Indians, Portuguese, and the Chinese (to name some of the main groups), could apply for British citizenship if they wished;[16] and to serve on the Legislative Council, it was necessary to be a British citizen or to become a Hong Kong British citizen. The numbers who applied were not great. From 1880 to 1900, fifty-three such ordinances were passed, and of these only three related to persons not bearing Chinese names.[17] Most Chinese had no need to do this. Chinese nationals could come in and out of Hong Kong freely throughout the whole of this period. As for the Portuguese, in 1897, only as many as fifty-one—perhaps on the basis of place of birth—claimed to be British.[18] It is beyond the scope of this discussion to bring these groups of Hong Kong British citizens—including several individuals among the most substantial citizens in Hong Kong—into consideration, although this would obviously be a most interesting study.

3. Composition of the British Community

The British community, then, included members of the armed services, government servants, merchants, and professional people such as missionaries, teachers, clerics, engineers and architects, bankers, and journalists. One of these—the banker, Sir Thomas Jackson—was so popular that his statue was among those erected and still remains prominent in central Hong Kong.[19] There were businessmen (in both a large and small way of business), and people in service occupations such as publicans and shopkeepers. Some were here because of an independent intellectual interest in the place and some others were remittance men. As well as the respectable working class, there were beachcombers, out-of-work merchant seamen (some, without a ship through no fault of their own), and drifters. Considering these residents also from the perspective of their leisure pursuits, there were amateur sportsmen, amateur actors, musicians, botanists, graphic artists, diary and letter writers, readers of new books in English and students of Chinese, members of the various clubs and associations, gamblers, ramblers, whore-mongers, and family men.

Taken as a whole, members of each of the various groups within the British community were very different from each other. They had very different objectives, work ethics, and points of view, and were subject to different, as well as to different degrees of discipline, whether internalized through association and training, or in response to any or all of local, national, or professional authorities. These divisions were further transected by extent and group of religious adherence, as well as by attitudes toward the issues of the day, by regional provenance, education, training, and class background, as well as by marital and family status, and of course also by personality. Each group, as well as each transected group, had its own hierarchies. Additionally, the wives and families of the economic members, while taking on at least some of the color of the providers, had concerns, activities, and attitudes deriving from their own personalities; also, their own education and roles and perhaps from their own as well as the families' social and friendship groups.

As the years passed, some of those who had been in Hong Kong or mainland China as children, but had left to study "at home" would have come back to spend their working lives here in Hong Kong. (James Dyer Ball is an American example. And Victoria Smith, daughter of the first Anglican Bishop of Victoria, certainly sought to do so.) Siblings came out to join siblings. (One example is William du Flon Hutchison, who came out to join his brother, John du Flon Hutchison, founder of the company now known as Hutchison Whampoa, owned by the Chinese multimillionaire, Li Ka Shing.) Wives came out to join their husbands, and fiancées to join those to whom they were betrothed. But the proportion of European women to men was low. In 1856, Matilda Lincolne Sharp commented that, of fourteen guests at Bishop George Smith's house for tea, only three were ladies.[20] Like some other non-Chinese men, some British men established liaisons with Chinese women (some in the absence and some in the presence of their British wives) and, in time, the children of these common-law marriages—Eurasians—became a significant Hong Kong group.

The number and variety of British residents was regularly temporarily increased by travelers, going out to, or returning home from postings, business, or visits of a personal nature on the mainland of China, Singapore, and elsewhere in the region. Although the aim was that some visitors, such as Queen Victoria's two young sons, when naval cadets, should be kept out of the public eye and out of Hong Kong society, professional British travelers such as Isabella Lucy Bird (1831–1904) and entertainers such as Albert Smith (1816–1859), who visited Hong Kong in 1858,[21] added to the diversity of residents, bringing quite different perspectives to bear on the social scene.

4. Members of the British Armed Services

Since, to some extent, Hong Kong was a prize of war, and also because of its importance as a military and naval base, members of the British armed services must have had a particular view of the place, different from that of all other groups. As for the army, in particular, their difference must have been further accentuated by the fact that they were a uniformed, disciplined group, living separate from the rest of the residents, and because, when in Hong Kong, they both lived and went about their duties on prime sites located in the center of the island.[22] Although segregated and set apart in these ways, their presence was certainly prominent. They could be seen on their parade ground daily, and those who were Protestants attended Sunday church parade at St. John's Anglican Cathedral.

Officers and men came from quite different classes, had different education, training, and background as well as different responsibilities. They had different visibility and different varieties of integration with civil society. Both officers and men participated with Hong Kong civilians in sporting events (notably cricket and sailing regattas) at the various clubs and other sporting locations. And officers and men contributed their different skills to the organizing of colony-wide events such as the celebrations for Queen Victoria's two jubilees.[23] Military and naval men also participated in theatricals and pantomimes. But only officers would have had an entrée into the Hong Kong Club, established as early as 1846.[24] And it seems unlikely that any but an officer would have been interested in forming a Madrigal group, as did Lord Saltoun, Military Commander of Hong Kong from 1842 to early 1844—in effect, the first General Officer Commanding British Forces in Hong Kong.[25]

The Commander of British Forces in Hong Kong was always a member of the Hong Kong Executive Council and, on occasion, acted as Governor in the absence of the Queen's representative of the time.[26] Sometimes there could be friction between the two leading men. On one occasion, Governor John Pope Hennessy quarreled with the General for refusing to lend him the one military band for his planned splendid dinner to celebrate the Queen's birthday in

May 1880. The Band was already booked to do duty at the General's own celebratory ceremonial dinner. Hennessy appealed to London and the General was ordered to cancel his event,[27] hardly making for happier future relations.

In the early years of the colony, the mortality among the troops, stationed in then malarial Happy Valley, was terrible. But Reverend George Smith, during his first visits to Hong Kong, reported that the gun salutes, which were normal at military funerals, were suppressed, so as not to alert the civil population of the situation and give them alarm.[28] And, as already implied, the majority of British deaths in this period, recorded on the monuments in the Hong Kong cemeteries, are of officers and men belonging to the armed services. Much can be gleaned from these memorials, including the sense of group loyalty that these deaths evoked.

5. British Government Servants

The Hong Kong civil service consisted of recruits from Great Britain and other British colonies as well as of people locally hired. In the early years, appointments to clerical work as well as to decision-making posts went to British men; but later, Portuguese, Indians, Malays, Chinese and others were given clerical and other posts in the Service, including work in the police force and prisons. At times during this period, the opinion in London was, that there was little to be done in Hong Kong, and that government officials had a generally relaxing time. But those who were at the interface between government and the majority of the population undoubtedly had major problems to address.

The problem of language was a part of all other problems. The learning of the Chinese language was regarded as essential but also virtually impossible for the majority. Luckily, there were always one or two, or a small group of individuals, willing to grapple with the task, and they served as a conduit for basic communications with the Chinese majority. The Cadet Scheme, introduced by Governor Sir Hercules Robinson in 1862, used competitive examinations to select a number of young men from Britain—the number over the whole period was fewer than twenty—to be trained in the Chinese language. Once judged adequately competent, they were appointed to high positions within the Hong Kong administration, being particularly recommended to positions where their skill in the Chinese language would be particularly useful.[29]

For much of this period, the position of Registrar General contained within itself the role of Protector of Chinese. His office dealt with a wide range of practical and cultural matters, where the needs and demands of the administration came into touch with the daily lives of the Chinese majority and with the needs and demands of this part of the population (as of others).

6. British Merchants

The surnames of the major British merchants of this period are well known—Jardine, Matheson, Swire, Keswick. Their early and continuing success indicates a great ability to deal with other cultures, to operate in a strange geography, and to secure the services of able assistants—including locals—in addition to the possession of the business skills and attitudes needed anywhere at that time. The personal integration of some of these leading merchants with Chinese social life has led to what is supposed to be romantic exaggeration, in blockbuster novels like James Clavell's *Tai-Pan*.

In *The Taipans: Hong Kong's Merchant Princes*, Colin N. Crisswell, drawing to some extent on the research of the Reverend Carl Smith, comments on the fortunes of British merchants as a group, and on the great change in the degree of success achieved at the end of the period, compared with the beginning. Crisswell quotes the Hon. G. N. Curzon, 1894, as follows: "The merchant princes and magnificent houses of an earlier day have disappeared . . . . Men do not now expect fortunes; they are content with competencies . . . ."[30] In effect, the huge successes of the early years of Hong Kong were now achieved, instead, by Chinese merchants and businessmen.

But whatever the excitements of life at the top, the experience of British assistants was apparently much less eventful. Writing of his experience of Hong Kong during his brief visit in August to September 1858, British entertainer Albert Smith commented on the boring, idle, and vacuous life that young men in this sphere of work in Hong Kong, experienced. "The young men in the different large houses have a sad mind-moldering time of it. Tea-tasting, considered as an occupation, does not call for any great employment of the intellect: and I never saw one of the young clerks with a book in his hand. They loaf about the balconies of their houses, or lie in long bamboo chairs; smoke a great deal; play billiards at the club, where the click of the ball never ceases, from earliest morning: and glance vacantly over their local papers."[31] And, as late as 1875, the visiting photographer, John Thomson, as Crisswell quotes him, commented: "nothing surprised me more in Hong Kong than the expensive way in which English assistants were housed and the luxury with which they were indulged."[32]

7. British Missionaries

An important group within Hong Kong society was composed of Protestant missionaries of many nationalities—some independent, some agents of missionary societies—and missionary families. These included British scholars and priests such as James Legge (1815–1897), of the London Missionary Society (LMS), pastor of Union Church (1849–1867, 1870–1873), his two successive wives, and the Legge daughters while still living at home.[33] They also included George Smith (1815–1871), originally of the Church Missionary Society (CMS), who later returned to Hong Kong as the first Anglican Missionary Bishop of Hong Kong, and Mrs. Smith, formerly Lydia Brandram, only daughter of a famous preacher, one of the Secretaries, in its London headquarters, of the British and Foreign Bible Society. The position that missionaries and their families occupied was complex. On the one hand, they were often well respected members of the British community, helping to set the moral tone of a society, which in the first few decades from 1841 onward was in effect a frontier, port, and garrison town, and they performed those acts of social usefulness and kindness that were an accepted part of life for members of their class and persuasion. Lydia Smith for example, extended welcome general hospitality to new and old residents in her home. In company with family friend and independent missionary, Miss Harriet Baxter, she would visit the ordinary British soldiers' wives in their lodgings (away from barracks), to offer whatever acceptable assistance might be needed.

On the other hand, the missionaries' main or original purpose in being in Hong Kong had nothing at all to do with the British community as such. They were in Hong Kong because they sought to contribute toward the Protestant mission to China and the Chinese mainland was their primary focus and objective. Nevertheless, when their observed actions were consistent with this focus, they could experience misunderstanding, jealousy, criticism and resentment from the broader British community, as further discussed below.

As a young man, George Smith was one of the first missionaries sent to China by the CMS and he first arrived in Hong Kong on his way to the Chinese mainland in September 1844. He spent periods of time traveling on the mainland, interspersed with periods in Hong Kong. He read what missionaries and others earlier in the field had written, and studied the Chinese language. Unfortunately, he ruined his health, and, in May 1846, left Hong Kong to return to England, knowing that a life's work as a missionary to China, based on the

Chinese mainland, was no longer possible for him. China was still his focus, however, and he was used by the CMS to advocate the China mission in meetings throughout Britain and also in private conversations with important government figures, including Lord Grey and Lord Palmerston. Largely through his efforts, working on the generous financial support of a small number of committed Christians, the Anglican See of Victoria, Hong Kong, China, was established, as a missionary See (with no direct funding from the public purse), to work for the conversion of the Chinese and China.[34]

8. Teachers

For at least part of this period, the British missionaries in Hong Kong, together with their wives and families, were associated with education, some as teachers and some as administrators or fund-raisers. Bishop Smith founded St. Paul's Missionary College; and his wife founded two schools for girls. One of these—the Diocesan Girls' School, which also gave rise to the Diocesan Boys' School—is still prominent today, as is St. Paul's Boys' School (descended from the St. Paul's Missionary College). Similarly, the first Colonial Chaplain, Reverend Vincent John Stanton (not a missionary but much interested in missionary work), was active on behalf of education, and his wife did at least part of the teaching in his Colonial Chaplain's School. At least one British woman, Emily Bowring, daughter of Governor Bowring, after being admitted as a Roman Catholic nun, worked for her order (the Canossian Sisters) as a teacher. Others, not missionaries or religious themselves (e.g., Winifred Eaton and John Fryer), came out, funded by or under the auspices of missionary organizations, and thus worked in Hong Kong within a broadly Christian context. Some existing Hong Kong British residents undertook to teach while in Hong Kong, in response to new needs or demands, surfacing within the community, usually either in denominational schools or in small, often short-lived, private schools.

But there was another important group. These were the British teachers in the Hong Kong Government Central School for Boys, founded in 1862. Toward the end of the period, in 1890,[35] the Government Central School for Girls (soon after known, as it still is, as Belilios Public School for Girls) was founded. And women teachers were hired for this school on a similar pattern. The first of the men, Frederick Stewart, was a Scot of exceptional character and ability.[36] Coming out to Hong Kong as a young man, he built up the new school beyond expectations, at the same time managing the whole of the government education system, and, in time, became known as the founder of Hong Kong government education. He studied Chinese conscientiously, using it as a medium of instruction in his classes, and he insisted that equal time in the curriculum be given to the English language and the Western curriculum and the Chinese language and the traditional Chinese curriculum. Over time, he came to possess considerable patronage. Governor Sir George Bowen, when recommending that the decoration of Companion of the Order of St. Michael and St. George (CMG) be bestowed on Stewart, wrote that the younger generation of Chinese had been trained by him. After a disagreement with Governor Hennessy, Stewart resigned from the Education Department, but was gradually advanced through the service to occupy the position of Colonial Secretary, head of the permanent Hong Kong civil service.

Although several other masters at the school also had high ideals, ability, and conscientiousness, such as the Scot Alexander Falconer and the English A. J. May, others—notably two men appointed in a hurry, one after a forced resignation and another while Frederick Stewart was absent on leave—caused a scandal. The first was a gambler and debtor, and the other impersonated other men while visiting brothels, in order to avoid paying the bills he incurred in them.[37] As the numbers of the staff increased, so the likelihood of their possessing the outstanding degree of commitment to their mainly Chinese pupils, that Frederick Stewart had possessed, decreased. And, as Stewart put it, teaching at the school became more of a job of work rather than a life's vocation.[38] As for the women, there were additional problems. The first appointee fell in love with a man she met on the ship, while coming out to take up her position in Hong Kong, and resigned after only a few months in post. Officials in the Colonial Office in London wondered where they could find a "celibate" for the position.

Religion

One major Hong Kong issue or cluster of issues during this period—religion, or related to or deriving from religion—took its origins from the United Kingdom and not in response to the Chinese or China at all. The nineteenth century was a turbulent time for religion in Britain itself. On the one hand, modern science seemed to some to challenge the whole basis for religious belief. On the other hand, social divisions based on religion were still strong, well understood and very visible. The repeal of British laws (in place since the last decades of the seventeenth century), discriminating against those who were not prepared to take the sacrament according to the rites of the Church of England, by excluding them from membership of town corporations and any civil or military office, had taken place as recently as 1828 and 1829. Jewish emancipation took even longer and was not fully achieved until 1890.[39] Nevertheless, the 1858–1859 Parliament made the admission of Jews to Parliament legal, and the first and only British Jewish Prime Minister, Benjamin Disraeli, first took office as Prime Minister in 1868.

The British Protestant missionary movement, begun at the end of the eighteenth century, accepted the duty of preaching the Christian Gospel beyond Britain itself, and became more and more active and prominent as the nineteenth century progressed. Evangelistic groups continued to assert that their simpler forms of worship and organization were closer to the original ideals of Christianity, while the established Anglican Church continued to have the benefits and power of its close association with the British government. The difficult relations between the Roman Catholic Church and the established Anglican Church entered a new stage with the arrival of the Oxford Movement (1833–1845). Notable conversions from the Anglican to the Roman Catholic Church (such as that of the Oxford scholar, John Henry Newman in 1845, created Cardinal in 1879) were only the tip of the iceberg, and many families were split and traumatized by disputes and conversions of family members. These were the days of violent newspaper debate, with strong views, unsparing of personalities. Even those who had no leadership involvement in the issues would be aware of the ongoing debates and open to strong influence by the violence of their expression.

Individuals within the small Hong Kong British community brought with them the religious beliefs and practices, opinions or prejudices, which they had developed at home, often uncomfortably reflecting in their much smaller locality the variety of issues and emotions of the larger. Sir John Bowring, Governor of Hong Kong from April 1854 to May 1859, and his family encapsulated some of these issues. Himself a Quaker, he could not have become Governor had the Test Acts not been repealed by the British Parliament. And, in his family life, he suffered severe disappointment when both a son and a daughter converted to Catholicism, his son becoming a priest and his daughter a nun. His daughter's case must have been particularly painful. While accompanying her father during his tour of duty in Hong Kong, Emily Bowring (one of the "very pleasant and charming social girls" commented on by Matilda Lincolne Sharp)[40] converted secretly; and on the day when her father set sail to return to Britain, at the end of his term of office, she was nowhere to be found. She had "run away from home" to join the Canossian Sisters in Caine Road, not far from Government House. Later, as Sister Aloysia, she became headmistress of the "English School," which the "Italian Sisters" ran for the benefit of European and probably also for Eurasian girls.

Another Governor, John (later Sir John) Pope Hennessy, a Roman Catholic, would similarly have been unable to achieve public office had the Test Acts not been repealed. There seems little doubt that Hennessy's mismatch with the British Hong Kong community, which became almost complete as his years in office accumulated, was at least partly caused by his religion, and, specifically, from his perceived—and real—advocacy of a generally unpopular educational policy under the influence of Catholic opinion and, probably, in the present writer's view, from a desire to ingratiate himself with the international Catholic hierarchy.

Whereas, in Britain, the Anglican Church was in the majority and the Roman Catholic Church in the minority, in Hong Kong, at least for most of this period (if not all) this position was reversed. "Why is it," a new Secretary of State for the Colonial Office asked, "that there are so many Catholics in Hong Kong?" And the answer was, because of the large numbers of Roman Catholic Portuguese who had moved to Hong Kong from Macau, particularly following the murder of the Governor of Macau, João Maria Ferreira do Amaral,[41] in 1849[42] and the terrible typhoon of 1874.[43] In fact, the Catholic population far exceeded the Protestant population (a position, which in 2001, was no longer true).[44] But since Hong Kong was a colony of a Protestant country, it was assumed, from the beginning, that, if any, the religion of the government would be Protestant. And since the established Church in England was the Anglican Church, it was assumed that this situation would be echoed in Hong Kong. The church-based movement to provide for and establish a "colonial church" and the "Colonial Chaplain" for Hong Kong, coming within a period when the British-based Colonial Bishops' Fund was seeking to provide new bishoprics in Britain's various colonial possessions, was embarked on from this position.

It is not surprising that the Colonial Office in London, with its concern for appropriate use of public funds and fairness to all members of the community, demurred. And when plans for the "Colonial," that is the Anglican Protestant Christian Church, in the 1840s, sought provision for a congregation as large as 800–1,000 people,[45] this was initially accepted only because the presence of army and navy personnel and their required attendance at church parade swelled the numbers,[46] which otherwise, relying on the civil population of Anglicans only, might have been fewer even than one hundred. Nevertheless, on the basis that the Hong Kong Anglican community could and should be responsible for raising a good proportion of the funds for the building of the church, the construction of the building was finally agreed by London, but to contain the smaller number of 640 people only.[47] As a further indication of the identification between church and state that Hong Kong British Anglicans insisted on then, the colonial church—later consecrated as the cathedral—was named "St. John's" with reference not only to a Christian saint, but also to the Governor of the day, Sir John F. Davis. In keeping with this point of view, subsequently, the Colonial Chaplain's salary was paid from public funds. But the situation could not resist a determined challenge. Later in the century, the Roman Catholic Bishop, Timoleon Raimondi, when arguing that Catholics should be treated in the same way as Protestants, and similarly subsidized, caused a decision to be made, which in due course, led to the disestablishment of the Anglican Church in Hong Kong.[48] The cost of applying the undoubtedly just policy, which he urged, would have been impossible to meet. The only way to avoid a continuing unfairness was to subsidize no group of Christians, rather than to subsidize all. The strong emotions and language, which these issues evoked, are recorded in the public press as well as in private archives from the time.

Conclusion: British Community in the Making

In 1898, the lease of the New Territories for ninety-nine years added 355 square miles to the previous land held by Britain. (Hong Kong Island and Kowloon have thirty-two square miles and three and a half square miles, respectively—not including recently reclaimed land.)[49] With the territory came additional population, including people who had lived in the New Territories for generations. In contrast to the Chinese people then resident in Hong Kong and Kowloon, most of whom had migrated from the Chinese mainland to Hong Kong through personal choice, the indigenous population in the New Territories had not sought British administration, and many resented it. Thus, while the desired buffer against European expansionism in the area had been gained, with it came a population at least partially disaffected. British responsibilities increased and changed.

Nevertheless, consistent with the changed international situation, Hong Kong's role as a military and naval base continued to be as strengthened. British merchants, missionaries and traders continued to use Hong Kong as a base for their dealings with the Chinese mainland. As increasing numbers of British people of all types and callings spent at least a few years in the colony, Hong Kong came to be an accepted part of the British world.

As this chapter shows, the British community in the second half of the nineteenth century was relatively small, and its members were mostly temporary residents, coming on short assignments (as in the case of British Governors, military and naval officers, and other members of the armed services), or planning to travel on to the interior of the Chinese mainland or to other places in the region. Not surprisingly, the British community of the time was a mixed bag of people from many walks of life, including—in addition to government servants and members of the armed services—professionals such as solicitors, architects, surveyors, engineers, doctors, teachers, clergymen, cartographers, and others, who, in their leisure time, took up occupations as various as rambling and gambling, studying and writing, sport and amateur dramatics, scientific experiments, and the graphic arts. The various groups within the community were very different from each other, with different education, training, purposes, and work ethics. There continued to be no single British community, but several communities.

During this early period, these various British communities underwent a process of adaptation and adjustment, trying to work with each other as well as with the local people, seeking and finding lifestyles that were agreeable as well as useful under local circumstances. The presence of the British armed services was prominent, with their concrete responsibilities and well-defined objectives. Occasionally, the Commander of the British Forces came into conflict with the Governor, both of them being leading men in the Hong Kong British community. As for British government officials, they relied on a small group of mediators who served as a conduit for basic communication with the local Chinese population. The period of greatest relative success for British merchants was already over. As for British missionaries and teachers, well before the end of the nineteenth century, they had an adequate structure within which to develop their own work, although the acquisition of the New Territories changed the context of their work and to some extent created a new beginning. By the end of the nineteenth century, even though the individuals who made up the British community were still by no means permanent residents, very few being born and raised in Hong Kong or expecting to die there, the group of British communities had become fairly stable, with well defined roles, work occupations, and leisure activities.

NOTES

Both this chapter and the following one have been assisted, as all of the author's work in this area, by her husband, Verner Bickley, whose ready memory and useful suggestions have helped to make the best use of their joint resources of energy, information, and time.

1. G. B. Endacott, *A History of Hong Kong*, first published 1958, reissued in Oxford in Asia paperbacks (Hong Kong: Oxford University Press, 1964, second edn., 1973), p. 18.
2. Frank Welsh, *A History of Hong Kong* (London: HarperCollins Publishers, 1993), p. 108.
3. See e.g., Endacott, *A History of Hong Kong*, p. 61.
4. Speech (delivered June 25, 1850, HANSARD CXII [third ser.], pp. 380–444) added to <www.victorianweb.org/history/polspeech/foreign.html> by Marjie Bloy Ph.D., Senior Research Fellow, National University of Singapore from, Joseph Hendershot Park, *British Prime Ministers of the Nineteenth Century: Policies and Speeches* (New York: New York University Press, 1916).
5. See e.g., Welsh, *A History of Hong Kong*, pp. 309–11.
6. See Gillian Bickley, ed., *Hong Kong Invaded! A '97 Nightmare* (Hong Kong: Hong Kong University Press, 2001).
7. See e.g., Gillian Bickley, *The Golden Needle: The Biography of Frederick Stewart (1836–1889)* (Hong Kong: David C. Lam Institute for East-West Studies, Hong Kong Baptist University, 1997), p. 239.
8. See e.g., Joyce Stevens Smith, *Matilda: Her Life and Legacy* (Hong Kong: Matilda and War Memorial Hospital, 1988), passim.
9. Endacott's *A History of Hong Kong* is a useful source for population figures from censuses and other sources. In 1845, of a total population of 23,817, the total number of Europeans was estimated as 595, including 455 men, 90 women, and 50 children (p. 65). By 1847, the total population was given as 23,872, exclusive of the troops of the garrison, of which 618 were Europeans (p. 65). Between 1848 and 1853, it was estimated that the number of Europeans had increased from 642 to 776, excluding troops, and the Chinese from 20,338 to 38,000 (p. 85). By 1865, the total was 125,504, of which Europeans numbered 2,034, "colored" people 1,645, and the remainder were Chinese (p. 116). (But later, Endacott gives the number of non-Chinese as 4,007 and the number of Chinese as 121,497; slightly different figures. [p. 183]). A census held in 1876 showed that compared to the previous estimate of 1872, the population had increased from 121,985 to 138,144 and

the number of British adult males fell by 86 (pp. 174–75). The census of 1881 showed that the population had risen to 160,402, the European increase being 273 (p. 175). In 1886, the population estimates were: total 181,432, of which 10,142 were British and foreign and 171,290 Chinese. By 1898 the total was 254,400, of which 15,190 were British and foreign and 239,210 Chinese. The 50 percent increase in British and foreign between 1895 and 1898 was due in part to the increase in the garrison, owing to the growing international tension (p. 252). It is also possible, however, that some of those reported as British were Chinese and certainly, in 1897, 2,263 of the British and foreign population were Portuguese, 51 claiming to be British (p. 252). In 1898, 8,732 were non-Chinese civilians and 6,458 in the armed services (p. 276).

We can supplement these figures from at least two other secondary sources: E. J. Eitel, *Europe in China* (Kelly & Walsh, and Luzac & Co., 1895; reprint, Hong Kong: Oxford University Press, 1983) and Welsh, *A History of Hong Kong*.

Eitel (*Europe in China*, pp. 183, 186) states that, in October 1841, there were 15,000 troops and residents of all nationalities. As of March 1842, there were *over* 15,000 including 12,361 Chinese (i.e., 2,639 were non-Chinese).

Frank Welsh says that the most recent census as of 1889 showed 1,450 only as British, of which 800 only were adult males. The present writer assumes that these figures exclude the armed services.

10. *The Economist Pocket Asia*, sixth edn. (London: Profile Books, 2001), p. 67.
11. *The Economist Pocket World in Figures, 2003* (London: Profile Books, 2002), p. 146.
12. Bickley, *The Golden Needle*, p. 198.
13. *China Mail*, October 11, 1889, p. 3, col. 2.
14. Endacott, *A History of Hong Kong*, p. 181.
15. Bickley, "Reverend Ernst Johann Eitel," in Gillian Bickley, ed., *The Development of Education in Hong Kong 1841–1897: As Revealed by the Early Education Reports of the Hong Kong Government 1848–1896* (Hong Kong: Proverse Hong Kong, 2002), pp. 199–204 (with notes, pp. 509–14), p. 200 & n. 38.
16. See e.g., Welsh, *A History of Hong Kong*, p. 297.
17. Endacott, *A History of Hong Kong*, p. 245.
18. Ibid., p. 252.
19. Endacott, *A History of Hong Kong* (p. 169) refers also to the vote for a statue of Sir Arthur Kennedy to be erected in the Botanical Gardens.
20. Smith, *Matilda*, p. 23.
21. Henry James Lethbridge, "Introduction," in Albert Smith, ed., *To China and Back: Being a Diary Kept Out and Home* (1859; reprint, Hong Kong: Hong Kong University Press, 1974), pp. vii–xiv.
22. For one comment on this, see Welsh, *A History of Hong Kong*, p. 136.

23. Gillian Bickley and Verner Bickley, "Living and Working in Early Hong Kong," talk given at the Jewish Community Centre, Hong Kong, November 12, 1998.
24. Endacott, *A History of Hong Kong*, p. 70.
25. Verner Bickley, *Searching for Frederick and Adventures along the Way* (Hong Kong: Asia 2000, 2001), pp. 144–48.
26. See e.g., Endacott, *A History of Hong Kong*, pp. 165–67.
27. Ibid., p. 179.
28. George Smith [First Report], Manuscript, dated, Victoria, Hong Kong, January 7, 1845, C CH/O 79/[4B], Church Missionary Society Archives, Birmingham University Library, Birmingham, U.K. Transcribed by Gillian Bickley, see Gillian Bickley Collection, Hong Kong Baptist University, Hong Kong.
29. For a detailed discussion of this scheme and its predecessor, see Gillian Bickley, "The Student-interpreters' Scheme and the Chinese Teacher's Allowance: Translator Education in Nineteenth-Century Hong Kong," in Chan Sin-wai, ed., *Translation in Hong Kong: Past Present and Future* (Hong Kong: Chinese University Press, 2001), pp. 9–19.
30. Colin N. Crisswell, *The Taipans: Hong Kong's Merchant Princes* (Hong Kong: Oxford University Press, 1981), p. 6.
31. Quoted by Bickley, *The Golden Needle*, p. 70.
32. Crisswell, *The Taipans*, p. 5.
33. See e.g., Gillian Bickley, "Reverend Professor James Legge," in Bickley, ed., *The Development of Education in Hong Kong 1841–1897*, pp. 57–64. See also Lauren F. Pfister, *Striving for "The Whole Duty of Man": James Legge and the Scottish Protestant Encounter with China: Assessing Confluences in Scottish Nonconformism, Chinese Missionary Scholarship, Victorian Sinology, and Chinese Protestantism* (Frankfurt am Main: Peter Lang, 2004), vol. 2, p. 86.
34. Gillian Bickley, "The Right Reverend George Smith," in Bickley, ed., *The Development of Education in Hong Kong 1841–1897*, pp. 25–31.
35. Education Department, Hong Kong, "Report on Education for the Year 1890" (May 30, 1891), in Bickley, ed., *The Development of Education in Hong Kong 1841–1897*, p. 341, para. 7.
36. See e.g., Bickley, *The Golden Needle*; *The Development of Education in Hong Kong 1841–1897*, and many other articles, chapters, and mimeographs, listed particularly in the bibliography of the latter. The same author's *The Stewarts of Bourtreebush* (Aberdeen, Scotland: Centre for Scottish Studies, University of Aberdeen, 2003) includes documentation of the Scottish upbringing and education of Stewart.
37. Bickley, *The Golden Needle*, pp. 132–35.
38. Gillian Bickley, "Nineteenth Century NETs," talk to NESTA (Native English Speaking Teachers' Association), Gillian Bickley Collection, Hong Kong Baptist University, Hong Kong.

39. "The Corporation Act of 1661 excluded from membership of town corporations all those who were not prepared to take the sacrament according to the rites of the Church of England. The Test Act passed in 1673 imposed the same test upon holders of civil or military office. Roman Catholics, Protestant Dissenters and followers of the Jewish faith were therefore excluded from public office. Religious groups including Unitarians, Wesleyan Methodists, Primitive Methodists, and the Society of Friends campaigned for a change in the law. In 1828 both the Corporation and Test Acts were repealed by Parliament. Roman Catholics were prevented from holding public office until the passing of the Catholic Emancipation Act of 1829. Jewish emancipation took longer and was not fully achieved until 1890" <www.spartacus.schoolnet.co.uk/Ltest.htm>.
40. Smith, *Matilda*, pp. 22–23.
41. The Macau Governor's name was confirmed by Eric Sautede, Chief Editor, *Chinese Cross Currents*, Macau Ricci Institute, Macau. (The name given by Endacott, *A History of Hong Kong*, in both main text and index, is "Coelho Do Amaral.")
42. Endacott, *A History of Hong Kong*, p. 85.
43. Ibid., p. 175.
44. The on-line Government Information Centre of the Hong Kong Government Information Service, updated as of September 3, 2003, states that there are about 300,000 Protestants in Hong Kong, and about 230,000 Roman Catholics <www.info.gov.hk/yearbook/2002/ehtml/e18-04.htm>.
45. The "Schedule of Despatches Transmitted by the Governor of Hong Kong to the Secretary of State for the Colonies during the Year Ending 1844," Colonial Office Records, Series CO 129/7/370r.–379v., The National Archives (formerly known as Public Record Office), Kew, U.K. Copies available in Public Records Office, Hong Kong, and in the Main Library of the University of Hong Kong, Hong Kong. See Governor of Hong Kong, "Despatch No. 13 to the Colonial Office, dated June 7, 1844," which cited "Necessity for Church to contain 800 to 1,000 persons. . . ."
46. Frederick W. A. Bruce, Colonial Secretary, Letter No. 147 to Revd. Vincent Stanton and A. Anderson, Esq., dated, Colonial Office, Victoria, Hong Kong, July 8, 1844. Referred to and quoted in, E. J. R. Moncrieff, Acting Colonial Chaplain and Chairman of Trustees (with six other signatories), Printed Letter to Governor Bonham, Esq., dated, Victoria, Hong Kong, August 13, 1850. HKMS 94, D & S no. 1/1, p. 16 (4 pages), Diocesan Archives, Public Records Office, Hong Kong.

> I am directed by His Excellency the Governor in Council to state . . . that in consideration of the great want of a proper place of Worship arising from the defective condition of the mat-shed

in which Divine Service is at present conducted, His Excellency will undertake on the part of Her Majesty's Government to contribute a sum not exceeding two-thirds of the expense of building a Church. . . . Space must be reserved for the accommodation of 250 Soldiers, for their Officers, and for those employed by the Government in the Civil Department.

47. See "Ecclesiastical Return," Hong Kong Government Blue Book relating to 1847. Public Records Office, Hong Kong. (Also available as Colonial Office Records, Series CO 133, The National Archives, formerly known as Public Record Office, Kew, U.K.)
48. Writer's own reading of the archives, and see also Endacott, *A History of Hong Kong*, p. 182.
49. Endacott, *A History of Hong Kong*, p. 1.

Chapter 3

British Attitudes toward Hong Kong in the Nineteenth Century

Gillian Bickley

Introduction

By the end of the nineteenth century, the various groups that made up the British community had established patterns for their lives in Hong Kong. Benefiting from the systems put in place by previous residents, they were able to follow their different avocations somewhat more smoothly. Needing to expend less effort to create the context within which their particular activities could take place, they could carry them out more efficiently and beneficially. Additionally, benefiting from what had been learnt by their predecessors, they had access to a better understanding of the local situation. Administrative officials, naval and military officers and members of other ranks, teachers, businessmen, missionaries, and others found their place in this recently acquired colony of the British Empire. As the British community formed and grew, its members were also in search of the best ways to administer, serve, teach, profit, evangelize, or simply live with each other and people of other nationalities in Hong Kong.

This chapter considers the attitudes of the British (in Hong Kong) on a variety of topics in various areas—religion, education, social customs, and legislation—as well as the different opinions held within the diverse British community, and how these ideas developed and changed. As the chapter shows, a small group among the British residents in the colony (usually in association with a similarly small group of their fellow countrymen in the United Kingdom) was eager to promote religious and educational work for the Chinese people. But both in Hong Kong and Britain, the view was also expressed that such positive discrimination was unfair, as well as likely to be misdirected. At the same time, the British in Hong Kong often felt that they had to compromise their own cultural values and moral standards in order to deal with local circumstances and demands. It is not difficult to find examples where they tried to strike a balance between morality and pragmatism. The close and frequent contact with Chinese and other cultural groups that they experienced obviously had a significant impact as they went through the processes of adaptation and adjustment. And just as the various members of the disparate British community had different opinions on various issues, so they came to create and embrace quite diverse images of the Chinese and other foreign communities.

British Attitudes toward the Role of the Anglican Church in Hong Kong

1. Attitudes, in the United Kingdom and Hong Kong, toward Work for the Conversion of China and the Chinese

The results of a direct appeal to the British public, made by a Special Committee of the Episcopal Council, and published in its Fourth Report, dated August 21, 1848, for donations in support of missionary work among the Chinese, centered on Hong Kong, brought in much less money than was expected.[1] This confirms the view that Bishop George Smith was frequently to express, that members of the Church of England—like his countrymen in general—had little enthusiasm for the work of missionaries overseas, and he compared this unfavorably with the situation in other countries, particularly Catholic countries. Indeed, around this time, expressions of jealousy, hostility, and ridicule at the attempt to convert the people of China appeared in both the British and the Hong Kong press.

George Smith was consecrated Bishop of Victoria on May 29, 1849. To make the available funds stretch as far as possible, he was also, *ex officio*, to be warden of St Paul's missionary college. On September 17, 1849, a public meeting, "held on behalf of the fund for establishing a missionary college at Hong Kong," was held in Manchester, in the United Kingdom. It had, "the special object of listening to an appeal on the subject from the Right Reverend the Lord Bishop of Victoria (Hong Kong)" and the Lord Bishop of Manchester occupied the chair. The meeting was for a time disrupted by an individual, supported by a small group, who sought to propose two amendments to the motion before the meeting. After he had been ejected, the second amendment was read for the information of those attending. It was: "That this meeting are [*sic*] of opinion that missionary labours should be carried on in foreign climes after the spiritual wants of the people at home are duly supplied."[2]

The clergyman who proposed the main resolution, "That, considering the peculiar character of the Chinese, and especially their high standard of general education, we feel the paramount importance of a missionary college, for the purpose of training a well-educated native ministry,"[3] apologized for the disruption, as follows.

> The little handful of men who have disgraced themselves this morning do not represent the working classes of Manchester. I do not hesitate to say that the working classes of Manchester, as a body, have their sympathies and their hearts with such movements as this, and that the little knot who are trying to revive exploded socialism and infidelity in Manchester, will only find that their attempt will recoil upon their own shoulders, and that there is in Manchester that feeling of order, principle, and Christian liberty, that will spew them out of the city in due time.—This individual who has been so painfully prominent this morning, has come from London on an errand of agitation and infidelity. We will send him back to London, for we do not want him in Manchester.[4]

Nevertheless, however indignant this apology, it seems that the views of the heckler and his group were by no means idiosyncratic.

It may be that this was the event, which influenced an editorial in the Hong Kong publication, *The Friend of China*, at about this time. Certainly, it voices similar views, expressing them even more sharply. The following is a transcription of Reverend Carl Smith's unpublished transcription, kindly made available to the present writer (and which seems to include Reverend Smith's direct quotation from his source, combined with his summary and paraphrase of the source):

> During the past two years there have been current reports of an intention to appoint a Bishop to Hong Kong. We were inclined to treat the matter as a joke; but the fancied joke proves to be a substantial fact. . . . Questions giving money to missionary purpose—could it not better be used on poor; clothing naked, educating ignorant in our native land, or in supporting a missionary Bishop in Hong Kong?

> Cites needs in England—true benevolence does not require to wander for suitable field to the sterile shores of China.
>
> We did intend to have shown at some length the misapplication of £1,000 in supporting a missionary Bishop in China: but the subject is getting more serious than we anticipated when we set down in light humour to deal with it in a light way. We therefore drop it for the present by wishing Mr Smith "every success," and if in ten years hence he can with sincerity say he believes that he has really converted one Chinaman, he will be able to say a very great deal—that's all.[5]

Albert Smith, the entertainer, gives evidence of continuing feelings of this nature, among at least a portion of the British public, as reported in his private letter to Bishop Smith, dated, Egyptian Hall, Piccadilly, London, January 24, 1859. Based on his visit to China, Albert Smith included a comment in his new public lecture, that he had been led, "to one decided conviction," as follows: "I could not help thinking it was a melancholy putting of the cart before the horse to expend so much in missions, thousands and thousands of miles away, even with a doubtful result, when there is so much to educate and reclaim under our eyes, amongst the dark and wretched outcasts, crowding in the holes and corners of our own mighty London." As Albert Smith states in his letter to Bishop Smith, "These, my dear Lord, are my words, and they are always received with strong evidence of approbation. . . ."[6] Not surprisingly, as Albert Smith also states in his letter, "I have been terribly pulled to pieces by the Missionaries in print and by letter" on account of this statement.[7]

2. Attitudes toward Perceived Discriminatory Pastoral Care for the Chinese as Compared with that Provided to Non-Chinese

Some British observers, whether in Britain or Hong Kong, ignored the origins and expressed purpose of the See and criticized the work of successive Bishops precisely because they did what the terms of their appointment stipulated, but did not—in the inaccurate view of their critics—do enough of what Bishops in Britain did, or were expected to do. In short, Anglicans in Hong Kong expected their Bishops to give their time to the pastoral care of members of their Church and of the broader British community, and not to direct their efforts to the benefit of the Chinese.

This criticism was particularly marked in relation to the first Bishop, George Smith, but it also applied to some extent to his second successor, Bishop John Shaw Burdon. Indeed, when responding to a call to accept the bishopric, Bishop Burdon took care to make enquiries of the Church authorities in London about the role and function of the See. Consistent with the answer he was given, in his first sermon preached in St John's Cathedral on his arrival as Bishop, he pointed out that the role of the bishopric was not primarily to serve the foreign community, but to extend the gospel to China and the Chinese.[8] In voicing their views, critics and commentators frequently overlooked the considerable pastoral care that the Bishops did in fact give, or which was given by his direction. A leader does not undertake all tasks himself, but, if possible, achieves more by acting also through deputies. On one occasion, Bishop Smith was criticized for not attending prisoners in the goal as much as the Catholic priests did; yet his chaplains and associates did perform this duty.

BRITISH ATTITUDES TOWARD DISCRIMINATORY EDUCATIONAL PROVISION FOR THE CHINESE, NEGLECTING NON-CHINESE

Just as there was a jealous feeling arising from the perception that Anglican clerical pastoral care was being offered to the Chinese more than to the British community, so there was a period when similar jealousy was felt in relation to educational provision in Hong Kong. Up to 1862, Western provided education in Hong Kong was in the hands of missionaries and their work was mainly among the Chinese.[9] The missionaries justified this involvement in a lay occupation on the grounds that education was a necessary preparation before direct missionary work could take effect. Non-Chinese children were catered for by a Colonial Chaplain's school, but whereas the parents of *these* children paid fees for their schooling, missionaries frequently bribed Chinese parents by offering food and even money if they would send their children to school, and certainly charged no fees.[10] From 1848, the government gave a small annual grant to a handful of Chinese-run traditional Confucian schools attended by Chinese pupils only, as one means of winning the confidence and goodwill of the Chinese community and also in fulfillment of what was coming to be seen as a modern government's responsibility to provide for the education of its population. No equivalent grant was offered for schools where the pupils were not Chinese. And indeed, a grant requested for the Colonial Chaplain's school was denied. (The justification, given by London, was, that the parents of the non-Chinese pupils should be able to afford to pay for their children's education, and there was also concern that a grant given to the Colonial Chaplain's school might be resented as given to one only among several Christian denominations.)

This discrimination in favor of the Chinese was further exacerbated in 1862, when a new and important government initiative—the establishment of the Government Central School for Boys—was initiated for Chinese pupils alone. And some years later, the Head of the Government Central School for Boys, who was also head of the entire government system of education, appealed to Sir Richard Graves MacDonnell (Governor 1866–1872) for a separate school for non-Chinese boys. Following this intervention, in 1867, the school was opened to all nationalities in Hong Kong.[11] By and large, the British children who attended the school were those whose parents could not afford to send them home to Britain for their education. Of those who completed their education in Hong Kong, some—like their Chinese and Indian fellow-pupils—became notably useful members of the Hong Kong community. The Chinese language they had studied at school helped them to positions in the local government or in commerce, where bilingual skills were required. For example, former Government Central School pupil, F. A. Hazeland, became Police Magistrate. And the family names of other former Central School pupils remained well-known until quite recently, as attached to continuing businesses. They may not have acquired the success and status of some of their Eurasian fellow pupils, such as Sir Robert Ho Tung and his two brothers, but they became solid citizens known to all.

British Attitudes toward Social Conduct, Legislation, and Other Issues of the Day

Sabbath observance was an important issue in Britain, which, only in the last decades of the twentieth century, was determinedly—but still not completely unopposed—emerging from the gloom and discipline of the British Victorian Sunday. Earnest young Christians, arriving in Hong Kong in its very early years, commented with pain on the noise of construction on Hong Kong Sundays. Gambling and prostitution were other topics on which religious and moral people in Britain took a stand. In Hong Kong, this was also true. And in 1867, a group of clergymen and missionaries, based in Hong Kong, including Reverend James Legge of the London Missionary Society and pastor of Union Church, protested against the legalization of gambling.[12] It was recriminalized in 1871.[13] The Contagious Diseases Ordinance

(Ordinance 10 of 1867)—in effect the legalization of prostitution, in the interests of public health, and notably the health of the armed services—caused similar outcry. Frederick Stewart, who died in office as Colonial Secretary (head of the Hong Kong permanent civil service) and one time Registrar General, had in the early 1880s refused appointment as Registrar General, the first time the position was offered to him, because—so his colleagues believed—the position involved the administration of this Act.

Purely Hong Kong issues included Hong Kong's slave-girls (the *mui-tsai*), the associated problem of the kidnapping of women and children, Chinese emigration, and the death houses at one time administered by the Tung Wah Hospital.[14] There was also infanticide, piracy, foot-binding, opium smoking, child marriage, and concubinage.[15]

In 1858, with reference to Hong Kong, the Colonial Office made a declaration of principle that future legislation was to be uniformly applicable regardless of race, for the British Empire was "not to be preserved by forcibly creating and maintaining a dominant race or class."[16] Consistent with this, when Sir Richard Graves MacDonnell came to Hong Kong as Governor in 1866, he was handed emended Governor's instructions, which forbade him, "to agree to any ordinance 'whereby persons of African or Asiatic birth may be subjected to any disabilities or restrictions to which persons of European birth or descent are not also subjected.' "[17] Originally, however, such differential treatment was in fact provided for in Hong Kong, as a mode of coexistence and as an exercise in cross-cultural understanding. The initial agreement with China was that the Chinese community would be dealt with according to Chinese custom, and that the non-Chinese community would be dealt with under British law.[18] And indeed, writing of the period up to 1877, extending therefore beyond the enunciation of this new policy, Crisswell and Watson refer to the realistic view taken, in relation to Hong Kong, "that it was inevitable, indeed desirable, that certain ordinances, especially those relating to law and order, should be discriminatory in practice even if, in theory, all were equal before the law."[19]

In effect, however, in the early days at least, as several have commented, Chinese brought before the courts were given heavy-handed justice.[20] By today's standards the flogging sentences seem excessive; but others point out, first, that such sentences were equally applied within the United Kingdom at this time, and particularly in the British army, and, second, that the punishments meted out by the Chinese legal system were very much harsher.[21] Contemporaries felt that Chinese criminals laughed at the soft sentences of British Hong Kong.

This was a time of reforms in the British legal system in the United Kingdom, but this was one major point where the Hong Kong British public seemed to have remained very conservative in their views. There had been times when even ladies carried pistols when venturing out. Burglaries were common. As already noted, the foreign community as a whole was very much outnumbered by the Chinese majority, whose language they could not even understand. And on one famous occasion, when it was rumored that Governor John Pope Hennessy was proposing to abolish flogging as a punishment, there was a public protest meeting held in central Hong Kong.

The British Hong Kong government had the difficult task of administering, formulating, and advising on law and order, and social policy, in relation to a society, quite different from that of Britain, and, at the same time, seeking to do so from a perception of right and wrong that had evolved within, and which continued to respond to, the realities of the home country overseas. Not surprisingly, it was a position, which laid its conduct wide open to criticism, from its own British residents as much as from the residents and government of Britain, both when the Hong Kong administration inclined toward a pragmatic response and also when it favored a moral stand.

But however much the British Hong Kong government struggled for moral stature, there was of course a basic obstacle, seen as such by some contemporaries, but which has subsequently acquired such greater opprobrium, that it is now often presented as casting a shadow over all the benevolent aspects and initiatives of this administration. And this obstacle is summed up in the one word, "opium." Missionaries, such as James Legge and George Smith recorded their own and Chinese views that the missionary claim—basically that their culture brought the Chinese a superior religion and a superior morality—was contradicted by the existence of the opium trade. In fact, opium was grown on the Chinese mainland itself, although the proportion was small when compared with the amounts imported from India in British or American vessels: nevertheless, many Chinese—then, but particularly now—seem to have seen the damage to the national health and psyche, brought by the use of opium, as a purely foreign injury.

British Attitudes toward Other Cultural Groups

The observation has been made that colonial societies tended to be conservative. Separate from their culture of origin, they were uninfluenced, or influenced only slowly, by the changes—often in the direction of greater liberation and enlightenment—which occurred at home. This was most likely true of individuals within Hong Kong British society, particularly in the case of those who had been out of Britain (but not necessarily in Hong Kong only) for a very long time. And this is an argument that has been made in discussing Captain William Caine, Hong Kong's first Chief Magistrate,[22] appointed on April 30, 1841, whose methods of policing and punishment several commentators have considered excessively brutal even in the circumstances.[23] Nevertheless, the constant and frequent movement of individuals and groups also had the effect that Hong Kong British society was also stirred by the continuing issues of contemporary British society in the United Kingdom. It is true that mail (including newspapers and journals) took six weeks to arrive by sea from the United Kingdom. But, while this created an important hesitation in the formation of government policy, six weeks was not in itself a significant factor in isolating the Hong Kong British community from its home culture. More important, probably, were the conditions of life in Hong Kong, specifically the proximity of the Chinese majority, mixed with other minority groups such as Indians, Portuguese, Americans, Italians, Germans, Spanish, and others. With this variety of people came of course cultural variety also, including differences of dress, behavior, food, politics, and religious and political belief, as well as different views of civil society, law, and aspirations for life.

The armed forces were a special case. The British soldiers who acted disrespectfully and threateningly toward a small group of leading members of the civilian Parsee community, out for an evening walk in December 1881,[24] probably felt and behaved no differently than they would have done anywhere in the world. These were troops, trained for combat, and possibly battle-hardened from engagements elsewhere in Asia or the Indian subcontinent, where they had fought to the death against soldiers who (like the Parsee civilians they threatened) also looked quite different from themselves. But, in general, British public sentiment, among some groups in Hong Kong, toward other cultural groups, may also have been no more enlightened than among similar groups in Britain during this period. In Hong Kong, Sikh and Chinese members of the police force, being at the edges, as it were, of the lives of the foreign Hong Kong community, at times attracted frequent criticism.

On the other hand, proximity creates friendship as well as hostility. And one would expect that this varied from individual to individual according to their particular personality, class, upbringing, education, and religious beliefs. Nevertheless, because of their different domestic exposure to members of different cultural groups and because of their greater relative closeness to theaters of war and other forms of aggression with such groups, many British people in Hong Kong during this period may have reacted more intensely than their counterparts at home. By and large, however, like people everywhere, it seems that the British in Hong Kong responded to others in accordance with how they perceived others to behave toward them.

BRITISH ATTITUDES TOWARD THE CHINESE

While considering what the attitude of British people in Hong Kong was toward the Chinese community in Hong Kong, during the period 1841–1898, it is appropriate consider what the Chinese community itself was like. Not surprisingly, partly influenced by events on the Chinese mainland, the Chinese community in Hong Kong changed and developed as the years passed and as Hong Kong itself evolved. The number of original inhabitants of Hong Kong Island was few, estimated as about 2,000[25] and the estimated number, soon after British occupation, in 1841, was 5,650, mainly farmers and fishermen, and including 2,000 living on boats in the harbor.[26] Subsequent changes were dramatic. Many fled to Hong Kong to escape disturbances or disasters on the Chinese mainland.[27] G. B. Endacott comments on the Taiping Rebellion (1851–1864) as a cause of a large increase in the Chinese population in the 1850s.[28] Making the same point, the first English-language historian or chronicler of British Hong Kong, Ernst Johann Eitel, commented on "the [population] harvest[,] which invariably falls to its [Hong Kong's] lot whenever the adjoining districts of the Canton [Guangdong] province are in a disturbed state."[29] Many of these newcomers were in transit from the Chinese mainland to other places, which, in the 1850s included the Straits Settlements, California, and the West Indies.[30] For thousands of Chinese, however, Hong Kong was their destination, and they came to work. Some, involved in revolutionary or criminal activities, found Hong Kong a refuge. Initially, the Chinese who came to Hong Kong were mainly males, but in the 1840s and 1850s, Eitel claimed, "the proportion of males and females commenced . . . to improve, as the disturbances in the neighboring districts drove whole families to seek refuge in Hong Kong."[31]

Compared with the number of non-Chinese among the population, it is clear that the Chinese were always in the majority and the extent to which they outnumbered all other groups combined increased throughout this period. The proportions varied, from 97.54 to 2.45 in 1862 and 93.68 to 6.73 in 1867 or 1869; to 95.64 to 4.35 in 1895.[32] As Frank Welsh says, "It was this great disproportion between the races that gave rise to the most awkward problems. Chinese customs and culture were too strongly marked and deeply ingrained to adapt easily to those of the British."[33]

From the British point of view, there were times when the problem was not one of lifestyle but a question of life itself. In 1857, for example, on the orders of Chinese mandarins, an attempt was made to poison the foreigners in Hong Kong by placing arsenic in the bread.[34] In 1859, the astonished and indignant mood in Hong Kong on receiving news of the Baihe (Pei-ho) incident (the British accounts include incidents of treachery to British envoys and cruelty toward British prisoners, who died painfully of gangrenous wounds) is vividly captured in an illustration published in *The Illustrated London News*.[35] There were incidents of deceitful piracy at sea and of sudden murders of missionaries and nuns on the Chinese mainland.

The British had various and different images of the Chinese. The image presented by the English language press was that the Chinese were rude, untruthful, and quarrelsome. Emphasizing what was perceived as Chinese arrogance, and taking a lead from the contemporary designation of China as "the Celestial Kingdom," the press often referred to the Chinese as "Celestials." Chinese logic was perceived to be alien. They did not do what was expected of them. For example, when invited to Government House, they disrespectfully did not wear their best clothes. They did not visit the headmaster of the Hong Kong Government Central School for Boys to seek their children's admission to the School, as British parents in the United Kingdom might do when seeking to do the best for their sons. The photographer John Thomson, however, considered the Chinese clever. The headmaster and head of the government's Education Department, Frederick Stewart, thought them very able. John Fryer considered them money-grubbing. Albert Smith found them fascinating.[36]

The best among the missionaries set an example of respect for Chinese culture and Chinese people, often making the study of the Chinese language and Chinese writings, with a Chinese tutor, a main duty of their daily life. From a slightly earlier period of British–Chinese intercourse, a famous portrait by the leading China coast artist George Chinnery shows Robert Morrison working with Chinese scholars on the translation into Chinese of the English Bible. A matching portrait from the period under study shows James Legge, with his Chinese pupils, laboring to translate into English the Chinese classics. And this pair of images encapsulates what some in the West considered the ideal relationship: partners from each culture, working harmoniously to achieve and communicate two-way understanding and respect.

In the early days and years of the British Hong Kong administration (before two successive government schemes[37] provided a small core of government officials with Chinese language skills), the linguistic skills, which some missionaries acquired, as a necessary part of their search to convert China and the Chinese to Christianity, made them indispensable to the British Hong Kong government, which needed to communicate with the authorities in the Chinese mainland as well as with their Chinese population. British missionaries—such as John Morrison (son of Robert) and, later, James Legge—had the necessary skills. Government officials—both in Hong Kong and at home in Britain—relying on their likely greater national loyalty, preferred to use their assistance, rather than that of foreign missionaries, such as Karl Gützlaff, Wilhelm Lobscheid, or the naturalized Ernst Johann Eitel, although they requested these services from among the latter group, when they had to.

Nevertheless, as fellow missionaries sometimes commented, and as home missionary societies sometimes objected, the purpose of sending missionaries to Hong Kong or China was neither to assist the British government (although this assistance was not grudged) nor to study the Chinese language and Chinese culture, but to proselytize China and the Chinese. Unfortunately, this was an objective even more difficult to achieve, since it relied less on the abilities and personalities of individual missionaries working with a few Chinese colleagues, and much more on the willingness of numbers of Chinese to see value in a foreign religion and to experience spiritual conviction of its truth, followed by formal conversion. And in fact conversions were, from the missionary point of view, depressingly few.

In the early years of British Hong Kong, missionaries were still supported by the idea that education was a necessary or certainly helpful preliminary activity in a new mission field. Many opened or taught in small schools, supported either by their own personal funds or by those provided by their home society and supporters. As already implied, however, even a free Western education was not necessarily valued among the Chinese. Members of good families aimed at success in a Chinese education, and a career in the civil service of Imperial China, which success in the Imperial Examinations would bring. It was not until the establishment of the Hong Kong Government Central School for Boys in 1862, and growing experience of the openings made available through the bilingual education that it offered, that members of similar families, as well as those less privileged, entrusted their sons to the Western-style education offered in Hong Kong. Even so, the interest was perceived as purely pragmatic, and not at all deriving from any value or interest seen in the subjects of a Western-style education as such. In their turn, those non-missionary educationists, who had a sense of vocation and educational ideals, now also experienced disappointment at the relatively poor and inappropriate reception of the good things, which they saw themselves as offering, at some personal sacrifice, to their Chinese fellow-citizens.[38]

Some British individuals had their own very personal attitudes toward individual Chinese. On his return to England from China and Hong Kong, Reverend George Smith had written to Earl Grey, and, among other points, had urged that the Chinese be treated with kindness and respected according to their character and station. In this letter, he was the first to bring to the notice of the British government the Hong Kong practice of requiring Chinese, when out at night, to carry a lantern and a pass. There is no doubt that missionaries and missionary families, in general, took a lead in their social relations with the Chinese. Mrs. Legge, for example, regularly invited church members, English and Chinese, to tea. Bishop Smith's wife, Lydia Smith, happily offered friendly Christian support to both her own and her husband's pupils and former pupils, as well as to staff members, of St Paul's College and the Diocesan Native Female Training School. On one occasion, perhaps inappropriately to present-day views, James Legge intervened on behalf of a group of Chinese from the mainland, already found guilty by Hong Kong law, and secured their release. British teachers also had opportunities for similar relationships. Frederick Stewart, for example, invited pupils to his quarters at the school over the weekends and welcomed former pupils to his house whenever they returned to Hong Kong from overseas.

Some Hong Kong British Governors of the Nineteenth Century and the Chinese

To some extent, British Governors as well as British missionaries and teachers took a lead, in their different spheres, in social and benevolent relationships with the Chinese. Writers have emphasized the strictness with which Sir Richard MacDonnell dealt with the Chinese, in the interests of suppressing piracy and considerably enhancing law and order. Still to become widely known is his strong interest in education, particularly in the education provided for the Chinese in the Government Central School and his insistence that the teaching of Chemistry should be introduced there. The son of a distinguished educator, he speculated that experiments and demonstrations would cut through culture and language and work wonders of cultural initiation in the young pupils of the school, reducing the inhibitions and restraints imposed by centuries of Chinese traditional education.[39]

On special occasions Sir Arthur Edward Kennedy (Governor 1872–1877) invited Chinese to Government House and increased the number of Chinese in the police force. And he did this even though, as Welsh implies, Hong Kong society considered these actions eccentric.[40] G. B. Endacott, reporting on the generally benevolent and positive attitude and actions toward the Chinese of John Pope Hennessy (Lieutenant Governor and then Governor from 1877–1882), also initially implies that this was displeasing to the foreign community. "The Governor was accused of encouraging the Chinese too much."[41] Later, however, Endacott explicitly states, "He treated the Chinese as partners, and largely because of this he was hated by the Europeans. In his enlightened policy he was in advance of his time."[42]

Like others, including Hennessy's contemporaries, the present writer has questioned the disinterest of Hennessy's motives. There were many other reasons why the foreign community grew to dislike Hennessy over the course of his term of office, an attitude shared by many at the Colonial Office in London, where Hennessy's previous colonial career had already not endeared him. As for Hennessy's involvement—could we say interference?—in the government education system, the results of this (whether intended or expected by Hennessy or not) were the disablement of some of the benefits, which the system, under Frederick Stewart, had put in place for Chinese pupils, in favor of an increased share of the educational pie for Roman Catholic Portuguese pupils.[43] Again, although Hennessy did appoint the first Chinese (Ng Choy, also known as Wu T'ing-fang) to the Legislative Council,[44] it was Sir George Bowen (Governor 1883–1885), who engaged in discussions with the Colonial Office, which led to the decision that at least one unofficial member of the Legislative Council should always be Chinese, and who consequently appointed the first Chinese sitting as of right.[45] Nevertheless, whatever the rights and wrongs of the case, it is Hennessy who is now generally praised for his generous treatment of the Chinese. It seems appropriate that there should now be some recognition of the hand of friendship and help offered by other Governors. Sir George Bowen, like MacDonnell, was also enthusiastic about the work of the Government Central School for Boys, and anxious for the education given there to reach higher and higher levels.

In response to circumstances, Sir William Robinson (Governor 1891–1898), was less indulgent. Influenced by the Chinese response to outbreaks of bubonic plague in the city, specifically their rejection of the methods of control, eradication, and prevention that modern medicine and science decreed, Robinson decided that the government would discontinue the previous practice, initiated by Frederick Stewart, of protecting Chinese studies within the government-provided and government-aided education system.[46] Referring to "those Grant-in-aid Schools which give a Chinese education in the Chinese language, and contribute . . . comparatively little aid towards a promotion of modern civilization,"[47] the government announced that, "until further notice, no school for boys opened after the date of this notification shall receive any Grant-in-aid, unless such school shall give a European education in the English language besides complying with the other requirements of the Code."[48] As the then Inspector of Schools, naturalized British German, former missionary Eitel commented, "It is to be hoped that managers of Grant-in-aid Schools will see their way to adopt, more extensively than they have hitherto done, the plan of seeking to elevate the Chinese people of this Colony by means of English rather than Chinese teaching."[49]

Cross-Cultural Marriages

So much for social relations. What about the domestic scene? Writing about one particular Hong Kong government official's marriage with a Chinese Christian, Welsh makes the following comment: "Chinese mistresses were acceptable—the irreproachable Sir Robert Hart, Inspector-General of the Imperial [Maritime] Customs had a long and respectable liaison with a Chinese lady—but a Chinese wife posed almost insuperable social problems."[50] And although the example of Sir Robert Hart, who was not a member of the Hong Kong British community but resided on the Chinese mainland, is not particularly to the point with reference to Hong Kong, it seems that, in Hong Kong also, *during this period*, it would have been difficult to incorporate Chinese wives into "Society." On the other hand, since there was no question of introducing mistresses, Chinese or otherwise, into this sphere, what was not obtruded was not objected to.

The awkwardness suggested by Welsh may have had less to do with racism, however, than it did (as in the case of the fictional Eliza

Doolittle in George Bernard Shaw's play *Pygmalion*, 1913) with behavior, conversation, class, and language. In the case of Hong Kong Chinese women (as with most Chinese men who had not attended any English language school) at this time, it would not have been pronunciation, language register, and vocabulary that were deficient, as in Eliza Doolittle's case, but the very knowledge of the entire English language itself. The means of communication (including pidgin English) open to the parties themselves in such relationships would not have been helpful in more public circumstances.

But there was the occasional cross-racial (if not British–Chinese) society marriage. And extrapolating from one such case, it seems that, when the woman concerned did have the necessary social skills (and also was not surrounded by relatives who did not have these skills), undoubtedly she could be accepted. Lady Hennessy, wife of the Governor, may be taken as a case in point. She was the illegitimate daughter of Sir Hugh Low, Colonial Secretary of Labuan, with a native of the place. Although she became involved in a scandal as a result of indiscreet behavior with a prominent Hong Kong lawyer, there was no sign that Lady Hennessy was initially unwelcome or that she came to be rejected by Hong Kong society (including the British community) of which—as the Governor's wife—she was senior lady.

Some of the Eurasian children of European–Chinese extramarital relationships of more recent times have commented that they lived with their mother and had little contact with their father. And it seems to the present writer very possible that the odd relationship with her father that Irene Cheng, daughter of Sir Robert Ho Tung (1862–1956), described (she needed to seek an appointment with him when her future life was an issue)[51] had its origins in his own similarly distant relationship with his own non-Chinese father. The pattern seemed likely to have been extended to similar British–Chinese relationships.

At a different social level, there was evidence that local women provided a welcome dwelling place and finance for British men, permanently or temporarily down on their luck. We know about those relationships that played out some scenes of their lives together in the magistrate's courts,[52] but not so much, if anything, about happier arrangements and relationships.

As for British women marrying Chinese men, there were even fewer examples of this, and none seem to be known of society marriages being contracted by such couples in Hong Kong itself. However, in 1881, Miss Alice Walkden of Blackheath (1852–1884) married Ho Kai (later Sir Kai Ho Kai; son of a significant figure in

Chinese Christian circles) when he was a student in London, and returned with him to Hong Kong early in 1882.[53] Her early death, however, prevents us from knowing how she would have lived and fared in Hong Kong society as it was then. Her husband showed his respect for her memory by founding a hospital—the Alice Memorial Hospital—in her memory.

CONCLUSION

What then, did the British achieve in nineteenth-century Hong Kong? They created a modern city, where previously there was none, a place where people of many nationalities, types, and aspirations chose to come to settle down; where most made a living and a few made a fortune. It was a place open to the outside world, which traded with the outside world and facilitated international trade for other countries. The British established a Western-style administration, responsive to changes in social ideas and legislation occurring in Britain at the time. While doing so, they grappled as appropriately as possible with a population, mainly Chinese (outnumbering them, at varying times by at least ninety-seven to two, or by at least ninety-three to six, or by at least ninety-five to four),[54] but which included many other national groups; and they made provision, as far as possible, for the difference in the lifestyles and expectations of the members of all these different groups. They suppressed piracy, introduced horse racing, and worked with others to establish important social institutions—such as the Po Leung Kuk (which provided help and protection for women and children)—which are still very active today. They improved the lives of many through such institutions and by encouraging education for, and better treatment of, women and girls, and hence laid the groundwork for such assistance to continue. Through missionary activity and education, as well as through the establishment of Societies such as the Royal Asiatic Society (Hong Kong Branch) with objectives, which included (and still includes) the object of studying Chinese culture and language, they achieved advances in cross-cultural knowledge and understanding.

The strong fragmentation of Hong Kong society, separated by class and occupation as much as, for example, by nationality, national culture, religion, and particularly by language, and which is commented on by many, remained throughout the period.[55] It must be remembered, as stated at the beginning of chapter 2 earlier, that during this period the British had every reason to believe that Hong Kong was theirs. To the extent that integration with others was in the minds of any British people at all, either when they came out to Hong Kong or while they remained living in Hong Kong, it must be said that, on the whole, their objective was to integrate or convert others to their worldview and not to be integrated or converted themselves into different cultures than those into which they had already matured. This does not mean that they closed themselves off from the differences around them. Understanding others and learning their culture were necessary means to achieve their own ideological objectives of conversion and influence. Additionally, at a theoretical level at least, mutual understanding, integration, and friendship were sought. Education was recognized as an important means by which these goals were gradually being approached. The highest educational achievement of the period was the founding and continuation of the College of Medicine for Chinese. Speeches made in connection with the College urged that this was the type of initiative, which British culture should emphasize in Hong Kong; this, rather than the confrontations of war, which, in the furtherance of trade, had initially formulated the relationship.

NOTES

1. See Gillian Bickley, "The Establishment of the Colonial Bishops Fund and its Impact on the Establishment of a Bishop's See of Victoria, Hong Kong, China, and Saint Paul's Missionary College, Hong Kong, in association with the See," paper presented at the Third International Symposium on the History of Christianity in Modern China, November 21–22, 2003, Hong Kong Baptist University, jointly organized by Hong Kong Baptist University and Alliance Bible Seminary.
2. *Manchester Guardian* [Wednesday] September 19, 1849.
3. Ibid.
4. Ibid.
5. Writer's notes from Reverend Carl Smith, unpublished manuscript transcription, editorial, *The Friend of China.*
6. Copy, Albert Smith, Letter, to the Bishop of Victoria, dated, Egyptian Hall[,] Piccadilly[, London,] January 24, 1859, CCH/O 3b/54[?], Church Missionary Society Archives, Birmingham University Library, Birmingham, U.K. See also, copy in, "Victoria (Hong Kong) 1850–1859," RHL USPG D6a, the Bodleian Library of Commonwealth and African Studies at Rhodes House (formerly known as Rhodes House Library), Oxford, U.K. The present transcript represents an amalgamation of the two versions. Both have lacunae, fortunately in different places. There may be some small differences in punctuation and capitalization, etc., which have been reconciled here.

7. Ibid.
8. See Bishop John Shaw Burdon, Sermon given at his Installation at Saint John's Cathedral, Hong Kong, Sunday, December 13, 1874, *China Mail*, December 14, 1874, as transcribed in Bishops' Scrapbooks, HKMS 94, D & S no. 1/4, p. 4, Diocesan Archives, Public Records Office, Hong Kong. Also quoted in, Gillian Bickley, "Mission China," Typescript, Gillian Bickley Collection, Hong Kong Baptist University, Hong Kong. "Mission China" also quotes and documents the correspondence Bishop Burdon engaged in to ascertain this point, putting it in context.
9. See Gillian Bickley, ed., *The Development of Education in Hong Kong 1841–1897: As Revealed by the Early Education Reports of the Hong Kong Government 1848–1896* (Hong Kong: Proverse Hong Kong, 2002), passim. See also G. B. Endacott, "The Growth of a Public Education System of Education, 1841–1865," in *A History of Hong Kong*, first published 1958, reissued in Oxford in Asia paperbacks (Hong Kong: Oxford University Press, 1964, second edn., 1973), pp. 132–43, esp. pp. 135–36.
10. See Carl Smith, "Schools and Scholars: English Language Education in the China Mission in the First Half of the Nineteenth Century and Its Results" (M.A. thesis, Union Theological Seminary, 1962), passim.
11. Bickley, ed., *The Development of Education in Hong Kong 1841–1897*, p. 489, n. 9.
12. See e.g., Endacott, *A History of Hong Kong*, pp. 150–51.
13. See e.g., Gillian Bickley, "Gamblers and Informers," in Gillian Bickley, ed., *A Magistrate's Court in Nineteenth Century Hong Kong: Court in Time* (Hong Kong: Proverse Hong Kong, 2005), p. 334.
14. Endacott, *A History of Hong Kong*, p. 156.
15. Frank Welsh, *A History of Hong Kong* (London: HarperCollins Publishers, 1993), p. 253.
16. Quoted in Endacott, *A History of Hong Kong*, p. 124.
17. Ibid., p. 125.
18. Ibid., pp. 58, 124.
19. Colin Crisswell and Mike Watson, *The Royal Hong Kong Police, 1841–1945* (Hong Kong: Macmillan Publishers (H.K.), 1982), p. 60.
20. See e.g., Endacott, *A History of Hong Kong*, pp. 58, 71; Crisswell and Watson, *The Royal Hong Kong Police, 1841–1945*, p. 30; Christopher Munn, "The Criminal Trial under Early Colonial Rule," in Tak-Wing Ngo, ed., *Hong Kong's History: State and Society under Colonial Rule* (London: Routledge, 1999), pp. 52–54.
21. See e.g., Gillian Bickley, "Magistrate Frederick Stewart," in Bickley, ed., *A Magistrate's Court in Nineteenth Century Hong Kong*, pp. 55–73.
22. For example, Christopher Munn made this point at a seminar he gave at the Centre for Asian Studies, University of Hong Kong. Elsewhere,

but without making the point equally explicitly, Munn refers to the fact that Caine . . . though born in Ireland, had . . . "scarcely ever touched European soil" and was, in his philosophy of government, an "Oriental." (" 'An Anglo-Chino Conspiracy in Crime': The Caldwell Scandal, 1857–1861," unpublished draft paper delivered at a conference held at the University of Hong Kong, p. 3.)

23. Endacott, *A History of Hong Kong*, p. 29.
24. Gillian Bickley, "Soldiers," in Bickley, ed., *A Magistrate's Court in Nineteenth Century Hong Kong*, pp. 199–214.
25. E. J. Eitel, *Europe in China* (Kelly & Walsh, and Luzac & Co., 1895; reprint, Hong Kong: Oxford University Press, 1983), p. 134.
26. Ibid., p. 171. Frank Welsh, ignoring Eitel's correction of what he perceives as an obvious mistake in transcription, gives a larger number, but the overall picture is not changed (*A History of Hong Kong*, p. 137).
27. This pattern continued into the twentieth century. See Endacott, *A History of Hong Kong*, pp. 289, 310.
28. Ibid., p. 97.
29. Eitel, *Europe in China*, p. 259.
30. Ibid.
31. Eitel, *Europe in China*, p. 271.
32. Figures calculated on the basis of figures given in Welsh, *A History of Hong Kong*, p. 253.
33. Ibid.
34 Endacott, *A History of Hong Kong*, p. 93.
35. Reproduced in, Alan Harfield, *British and Indian Armies on the China Coast, 1785–1985* (London: A. & J. Partnership, 1990), p. 100.
36. Henry James Lethbridge, "Introduction," in Albert Smith, ed., *To China and Back: Being a Diary Kept Out and Home* (1859; reprint, Hong Kong: Hong Kong University Press, 1974), p. xiii.
37. See Gillian Bickley, "The Student-interpreters' Scheme and the Chinese Teacher's Allowance: Translator Education in Nineteenth-century Hong Kong," in Chan Sin-wai, ed., *Translation in Hong Kong: Past, Present and Future* (Hong Kong: Chinese University Press, 2001), pp. 9–19.
38. See Gillian Bickley, *The Golden Needle: The Biography of Frederick Stewart (1836–1889)* (Hong Kong: David C. Lam Institute for East-West Studies, Hong Kong Baptist University, 1997), pp. 107–08.
39. See Gillian Bickley, " 'Beakers, Bell jars, and Flasks': The Introduction of Chemistry into the Hong Kong School Curriculum: Two Governors as Catalysts of Educational Change," Typescript, Gillian Bickley Collection, Hong Kong Baptist University.
40. Welsh, *A History of Hong Kong*, p. 253.
41. Endacott, *A History of Hong Kong*, p. 181.
42. Ibid., p. 182.

43. Gillian Bickley, "Social Pressures on Language in Education in Nineteenth Century Hong Kong and Applications for Understanding the Social Pressures on Language in Education in Hong Kong Today," in Hong Kong Institute of Language in Education, ed., *Issues Relating to the Planning, Managing and Implementation of Language Teaching and Training Programmes in the 90's* (Hong Kong: Hong Kong Government Education Department, December 1992), pp. 54–80.
44. Welsh, *A History of Hong Kong*, p. 297.
45. Ibid., p. 297.
46. Bickley, ed., *The Development of Education in Hong Kong 1841–1897*, p. 566, n. 2.
47. Education Department, Hong Kong, "Report on Education for the Year 1895" (May 21, 1896), in Bickley, ed., *The Development of Education in Hong Kong 1841–1897*, pp. 421–22, para. 15.
48. Ibid., p. 422.
49. Ibid.
50. Welsh, *A History of Hong Kong*, p. 212.
51. Irene Cheng, *Clara Ho Tung: A Hong Kong Lady, Her Family and Her Times* (Hong Kong: Chinese University of Hong Kong, 1976).
52. See e.g., Gillian Bickley, "The Domestic Scene," in Bickley, ed., *A Magistrate's Court in Nineteenth Century Hong Kong*, pp. 237–39, 243–53.
53. G. H. Choa, *The Life and Times of Sir Kai Ho Kai: A Prominent Figure in Nineteenth-Century Hong Kong* (Hong Kong: Chinese University Press, 1981), pp. 9, 17.
54. See this chapter, and see also chapter 2 of this book.
55. See e.g., Endacott, *A History of Hong Kong*, p. 70.

Chapter 4

Nineteenth-Century German Community

Ricardo K. S. Mak

Introduction

Anthony Smith suggests that an "ethnic group" is a group of people who have a collective proper noun, a myth of common ancestry, collective historical memories, one or more differentiating elements of common culture, an association with a "homeland," and a sense of solidarity among significant sectors of its population.[1] According to historical experience, it seems to be a rule that political entities consist of different ethnic groups. Different ethnic groups in a nation or a larger community do not always coexist peacefully, because they are inevitably caught in the struggle for social, economic, and political resources. Those who are bigger in size, more coherent, and politically or militarily better organized usually prevail over the others. War, invasion, and changes in the political boundaries continue to produce privileged as well as underprivileged ethnic groups. Peoples subdued by foreign invaders are likely to be politically, economically, and culturally marginalized. Ethnic groups possessing immense wealth and social resources such as the Chinese in twentieth-century Southeast Asian countries, though small in size, can play a key role in the domestic affairs of the host-state. While few dominant ethnic groups strive to establish mono-racial states by expelling foreign communities, they can choose whether they wish to impose their culture and way of life on other groups, or tolerate cultural and national diversity. The smaller, weaker, and less organized ethnic groups, while seeking to maintain their way of living, need to come to terms with the dominant social, cultural, and political ways of life.

As Wolfgang Bergem emphasizes, "(e)thnic communities are constantly challenged by two equally threatening perspectives—maintaining their ethnicity and insisting on their cultural distinctiveness bears the danger of marginalization in their host-state, while attempts aimed at integration imply the no less troublesome possibility of being absorbed into the majority culture and the consequential loss of their particular identity."[2] Whether an ethnic minority will be integrated into the majority group is usually determined by a number of internal and external factors, including the minority groups' social and economic needs, their size and degree of cohesiveness, the majority groups' attitude toward minorities, and so on. The competition for economic resources, social opportunities, and political power may force a minority group to conceal their cultural distinctiveness temporarily. Quite often a small and loosely organized ethnic group, faced with the struggle for survival, sweeps its ethnic attributes aside and cooperates with the dominant group. However, repression and hostility will force minorities to withdraw into their own ethno-cultural environment.

While numerous studies have been carried out on national minorities in Germany, which is often presumed to be nationalistic and antiforeign, the fate of German minorities in other countries has attracted less attention than it deserves. Situated in the heart of Europe, Germany is a meeting point for a number of different European nations. Not only do Poles, Czechs, Italians, French people, Turks, Jews, and the like live in various parts of Germany, in turn Germans exist as minorities in Denmark, Belgium, France, Poland, Russia, and so on. Stefan Wolff's *German Minorities in Europe: Ethnic Identity and Cultural Belonging* (New York: Berghahn, 2000) is a collection of essays on the history, life, and future of the German minorities in these European countries. However, a thorough study of the Germans in Asia is still lacking.[3] The Germans in Hong Kong—which has since the nineteenth century been a meeting place of East and West—remains an interesting topic to be investigated.

In fact, after the conclusion of the Treaty of Nanjing in 1842, in which Hong Kong Island was ceded to Britain and the five treaty ports in coastal China were opened to foreign trade, German merchants realized that China was a new market for them. German missionaries who had been active in coastal China also saw it as a new opportunity for them to evangelize the interior of China. Having established bases in Guangzhou (Canton), they turned to explore Hong Kong, now under British administration. The political turmoil in China in the 1860s further encouraged German merchants to move to Hong Kong, which continued to grow in prosperity. The German community in Hong Kong thus grew in size and played a more active role in Hong Kong's social and economic life. However, as a minority group in a British Crown Colony, the Germans needed to choose, or at least to strike a good balance, between integration and segregation, cultural assimilation and dissimilation, national identity and marginalization. Steering a prudent and pragmatic course, they played down their national identity and decided to cooperate closely with the British who were in charge of important political and economic affairs, and with the local Chinese on a variety of social levels. The unification of Germany in 1871 strengthened the sense of nationhood among German people in Hong Kong, and their contacts with the fatherland gradually increased. However, instead of breaking with the British and Chinese in Hong Kong, they strove to strengthen the German cultural and economic network that already existed in and around the territory, without sacrificing their business and social interests, which were interwoven with those of the British and the local Chinese. In this way, they survived in Hong Kong until the outbreak of the First World War (1914–1918).

SINO-GERMAN CONTACTS: AN UNEASY START

The Germans came to Asia much later than the Portuguese, the Dutch, and the British. Before the nineteenth century, Germany was a collection of tiny states founded on self-sufficient feudal economies lacking the political and economic strength for expansion abroad. Proto-industrialization in Central Europe, which took the form of cottage industries rather than facilitating large-scale capital accumulation, only consolidated the old agricultural production mode.[4] Without adequate financial power, even the most prosperous trading Hanseatic cities such as Hamburg, Bremen, Lübeck, and the like had to be content with short-distance trade that seldom extended beyond Eastern Europe.

The lack of a strong maritime tradition also hindered the German states from expanding overseas. The medieval guild system, for instance, discouraged large-scale shipbuilding projects. According to a regulation put forth by the shipbuilding guild of Hamburg in 1514, only those who had acquired the qualification of "master" were allowed to build ships.[5] Since journeymen *(Tagelöhner)* were practically excluded from this business, the Hamburg shipbuilding industry developed slowly as a result of the shortage of skilled workers. In 1622 the Hamburg city government's attempt to recruit shipbuilders from nearby countries such as Holland and Portugal met with fierce opposition from local shipbuilders who felt threatened by the inflow of foreign workers.[6] By the time the conflict between local and foreign shipbuilders began to ease in the eighteenth century, Hamburg's shipbuilding industry lagged far behind those of Britain and Holland. The maritime development of Emden, a major Prussian seaport, was arrested by the limited supply of shipbuilding materials such as wood.[7] Politically, Frederick the Great of Prussia's *Political Testament* (1768) emphasized Prussia's status as a land power rather than a sea power, highlighting this leading German state's exclusive interest in the European continent. For him, overseas possessions would only have served to increase Prussia's burdens and would have led to an outflow of Prussian wealth and people.[8] The building of a navy, an important component of maritime activities, was therefore not on the political agenda of Prussia before 1848.[9] For small city-states like Hamburg and Bremen, which were unable to finance a navy to protect their merchant fleets, the overseas market was beyond their reach.

In the eighteenth-century German mindset, China was still a remote place. Silk, tea, and porcelain, Chinese gardening and decoration were probably the limit of what most Germans at that time knew about China. There were few direct contacts between China and the German states. Johann Adam Schall von Bell (1592–1666), perhaps one of the most important German Jesuits, worked for nearly two decades at the Chinese court. Unfortunately, he died without leaving his compatriots much information about China. Gottfried Wilhelm Leibniz's admiration for Confucianism, for the wisdom of the Chinese emperors, and for the moral life of the Chinese people seemed to typify the fascination of German intellectuals with Chinese culture. However, the question of how widely Leibniz's work was circulated among the German population is still to be examined.[10]

In the seventeenth and eighteenth centuries, Sino-Prussian trade did not function on a regular basis.[11] The failure of the *Brandenburgisch Ostindische Handelskompanie* (Brandenburg East India Trade Company), which had been founded in 1670,[12] was followed in 1750 by the setting up of the *Königlich Preußische Asiatische Handelskompanie* (Imperial Prussian Asian Trade Company) in Emden. The contribution of German merchants to this joint venture was, however, overshadowed by that of the Dutch and the Swedes.[13] Between 1752 and

1757, the fleet of the *Königlich Preußische Asiatische Handelskompanie* reached the shores of China five times. It is said that in August 1752 the flagship of the company, the "Prussian President," reached Guangzhou after a six-month journey. During its four-and-a-half-month stay in Guangzhou, the ship's crew, although unable to sell the woolen products that they had brought from Prussia, collected Chinese products such as tea, porcelain, and Chinese medicine, which they later resold in Europe at very good prices. The shareholders of the company were happy with the business, and supported further expeditions to the East. A quarrel between the shareholders in 1755, and the outbreak of the Seven Years War (1756–1763), which tied the hands of the Prussian government, brought the short history of the *Königlich Preußische Asiatische Handelskompanie* to an end, and in 1765 the company announced its dissolution. Due to a lack of funding and of new interests, Sino-Prussian trade lost its significance before the 1820s.

The conclusion of the Congress of Vienna (1814–1815), marking the end of two decades of turbulence, gave German merchants new opportunities to rebuild their businesses in coastal China. In 1822, and again in 1828, the restored Prussian monarchy sent Johann Heinrich Carl Wilhelm Oswald (1798–1859), who had changed his name to William O'Swald, to China to promote Silesian textile products. The failure of this mission shattered Prussia's dream of establishing closer commercial ties with China. Although there are a few scattered records dated between 1792 and 1797 of visits by Hamburg merchant ships to Guangzhou, the volume of Sino-German trade before the mid-nineteenth century probably remained insignificant.[14]

THE ROAD TO HONG KONG

In the 1840s, thanks to the Treaty of Nanjing, which permitted foreigners to reside in five Chinese seaports, merchants from German Hanseatic cities began to look for business opportunities in the five ports—Guangzhou, Xiamen, Fuzhou, Ningbo, and Shanghai.[15] Guangzhou, due to its long tradition of trading with Western countries, naturally became the testing ground for German merchants and missionaries. After his second expedition to Guangzhou in 1828, William O'Swald wrote a report describing the business environment and living conditions in Guangzhou. In his eyes, Guangzhou was a busy seaport where ships from Britain, Holland, and the United States congregated.[16] Thanks to its geographical advantages, the Chinese products such as silk and tea that fascinated Europeans could easily be shipped out of China through Guangzhou. In O'Swald's eyes, Chinese compradores were efficient, and the Chinese merchants were basically quite honest.[17] What bothered him most were the antiforeign attitude of the Chinese people and the pirates that threatened coastal China.[18] Both made life difficult for the Germans living in Guangzhou.[19]

His report did not frighten adventurous German merchants away. Without government support, Bernhard Harkort, Richard von Carlowitz, Hermann Melchers, and Georg Theodor Siemssen, who launched the Sino-German trade of the nineteenth century, needed a high degree of courage and the use of extraordinary methods in order to survive in China. Indeed, this group of merchants had vision and a depth of experience that few German merchants possessed. The renowned Carlowitz family, members of Dresden's gentry, from which Richard von Carlowitz (1817–1886) stemmed, had a long tradition of involvement in business.[20] Richard von Carlowitz had learned to be a trader before moving to Leipzig where he worked for the office of Carl & Gustav Harkort. Dissatisfied with his unpromising career in Leipzig, he eventually, in 1840, accepted employment in the Napier Company in New York, where he handled the company's trade with South America, but succeeded only in leaving massive unsettled debts behind. Although his life in the New World was more comfortable than in Leipzig, Richard von Carlowitz never became there the wealthy man that he wanted to be, and by 1842 he was again on the verge of bankruptcy.[21] He was therefore happy to sail east when, in 1843, the traditional manufacturing and trading house of Carl & Gustav Harkort commissioned him to explore the Chinese market.

Similarly, C. Melchers & Co. Bremen, which was developed from the Focke & Melchers Co. founded in 1806, had an extensive business network in Europe and America.[22] Laurenz Heinrich Carl Melchers, the eldest son of Anton Friedrich Carl Melchers, the founder of C. Melchers & Co., spent his early life in Baltimore in the United States. Laurenz's two younger brothers, Heinrich and Georg, extended the family business to Central America, setting up Melchers, Hermanos & Co. in Mexico in 1846. When old Laurenz died in 1854, his company was transferred to his sons, who by then had gained considerable international exposure. Hermann Melchers (1842–1918), the son of Laurenz, announced the opening of Melchers & Co., Hongkong on August 1, 1866.[23] Later he extended the family business to Guangzhou, Shanghai, and Tianjin.

The story of Siemssen & Co. began in 1837 when twenty-year-old Georg Theodor Siemssen (1816–1875) was sent by Roß, Vidal & Co.

to India and Australia as a business surveyor. He then worked in Batavia, Java for the firm T. E. Vidal between 1841 and 1846. In 1846, on his way back to Hamburg, he stopped briefly in Macau and Guangzhou. Encouraged by Carlowitz, whom he met in Guangzhou, he set up Siemssen & Co. in Guangzhou on October 1, 1847. In 1855 and 1856 he further expanded his company by setting up branches in Hong Kong and Shanghai respectively.[24]

Like these German businessmen, the German missionaries explored China under their own steam, though with some limited collaboration with British missionaries. Two good examples are Karl Gützlaff (1803–1851) and Ernst Johann Eitel (1838–1908). Gützlaff's career as a missionary began in 1816 when he felt the call from God. He equipped himself by not only pursuing an in-depth study of theology and ancient languages, but also by engaging actively in different missionary activities. He traveled through Europe and eventually decided to go to Asia. Inspired by Walter Henry Medhurst (1796–1857) of the London Missionary Society (LMS), whom he met in Java in 1827,[25] he formed his *Einmannsmission* (one-man mission), which allowed him to continue his work without interference from the Church. In the following decades, Gützlaff maintained limited contact with the *Nederlandsch Zendelinggenootschap* (NZG, Netherlands Missionary Society) and certain small missionary groups in Württemberg, Germany. After serving the Chinese community in Malaysia, Singapore, and Siam for a few years, he turned his attention to China in 1831. Working closely with the British consular authorities in China, he carried out missionary work in Guangzhou and the adjacent area. In 1843 he moved to Hong Kong.

Gützlaff's work in China set an example for Ernst Eitel, who came to China in the 1860s. Eitel joined the *Evangelische Missionsgesellschaft zu Basel* (BMS, Basel Evangelical Missionary Society) in 1861, and was dispatched to Lilang in the Xin'an district of Guangdong province by the BMS in 1862. His engagement with Miss Mary Ann Winifred Eaton forced him to break with the BMS. Recommended by James Legge and John Chalmers, he joined the LMS. In 1870 he moved to Hong Kong and joined the LMS in Hong Kong.[26]

It seems that it was only after the 1850s that Germans such as these became interested in Hong Kong. Richard von Carlowitz's first impression of Hong Kong in 1843 partly explains why, in the 1840s, Germans preferred to settle in Guangzhou and other Chinese seaports. In his eyes, Hong Kong in 1845 was still an "unfruitful, sandy, black and disgusting island."[27] However, between the 1850s and the 1870s German merchants came to realize that Hong Kong was a much better place than Shanghai, Guangzhou, Xiamen, or Ningbo. Guangzhou was aging, and the other cities also had their own problems. Xiamen had only recently become a city where international business was done, and it enjoyed only a short business boom in the 1860s.[28] Shanghai's fast rate of growth was interrupted by the Taiping Rebellion (1851–1864); it took Shanghai over a decade to overcome the disastrous effects. In contrast, under British administration, Hong Kong not only had created an excellent business environment, but also established a social and political order that Europeans found it easy to live with. For this reason, the 1860s witnessed a mushrooming of German firms in Hong Kong. Arnhold, Karberg & Co., F. Blackhead & Co., Bourjau, Hübener & Co., Hagedorn & Co., and others, all made their appearance in Hong Kong in this period.[29] Better established German firms in China, such as Carlowitz & Co., also set up branches in Hong Kong.

Integrating into the Mainstream

Though growing in size, the German community in nineteenth-century Hong Kong was still rather tiny. According to the data provided by Reverend Carl Smith, of the 320,000 Hong Kong inhabitants in 1906, 12,400 were non-Chinese. Among these, about 359 were Germans.[30] As a minority in a British colony, the Germans in Hong Kong had little choice other than to integrate into the British community. In public life, they concealed their German identity. Many of them lived close to the British and were members of the British clubs.[31] Thanks to their pragmatic character and international experience, they had little difficulty in coping with this situation.

In fact, the relationship between the British and the Germans in the nineteenth century was not as tense as might be imagined. In the initial phase of German nation-building, Britain, with the gradualness of its political changes and its economic success, appeared to many Germans to be a model of nationhood.[32] The number of Germans living and working in Britain itself was quite significant. London was not only the city where Georg Theodor Siemssen learnt his trade, but was also the cradle of the media enterprise of Paul Julius Reuter (1816–1899). The inhabitants of the German state of Hanover, nominally ruled by the British monarch, had a special affinity with Britain. Before coming to Hong Kong, Richard von Carlowitz visited Calcutta and Singapore, both of which were under British influence. Until the conclusion of the Sino-Prussian Tianjin Treaty on September 2, 1861, the interests of Germans in China were principally looked after by the British. Between 1829 and 1843, among those who were offered the position of Hamburg consul in Guangzhou were British merchants, including John MacVicar and Alexander Matheson.

The long history of Anglo-German business cooperation together with the British Hong Kong government's receptive attitude toward the Germans in Hong Kong enabled them to integrate smoothly into the British community. In fact, German business in Asia had long relied on its British counterpart. Since the demand for German industrial products was rather low in the early nineteenth century, most German merchants engaged principally in reexport trade. Between 1824 and 1841 the British parliament relaxed its restrictions on import and export trade, not only freely allowing non-British ships to load and unload goods in British seaports, but also authorizing ships owned by Hanseatic cities to export British goods from all British seaports and to carry German goods into Britain.[33] German merchants, who had little in the way of German products to sell to China, could now export British goods to China instead.

A glance at the products sold by German merchants in Hong Kong is sufficient to show their dependence on England. Melchers & Co., Hongkong prospered by importing opium and cotton from India, and reexporting these commodities to other Chinese cities. Later, the company became a major German shipping agent in Hong Kong, handling 10,152,000 tonnes of import articles and 9,906,000 tons of export goods in 1907.[34] The goods sold by Siemssen & Co. to China included Philippine and Indonesian sarongs and textiles, German beer glasses and wine, English textiles and manufactured goods, Swedish steel and iron, and English and German strip-iron.[35] As East–West trade grew in importance and the number of ships engaged in it increased, Siemssen & Co. bought in coal from Newcastle in England to refill Western ships anchored at Chinese seaports.[36] At the same time, only 25 percent of the Chinese products bought by German merchants were shipped back to Germany in German ships. The rest were handled by British and French ships.[37] It was not unusual to find companies in Hong Kong jointly owned by the British and Germans. F. Schwarzkopf & Co. and Kirchner, Böger & Co. were two examples of this.[38]

Clearly aware of their dependence on the British, the Germans in Hong Kong refrained from challenging the leading position of their British partners, even if they sometimes had the ability to do so. For instance, Siemssen & Co. contributed to the founding of the Hongkong Bank, which was set up in 1864 to provide financial services for British merchants and their Chinese customers.[39] Later, Carlowitz & Co., Wm. Pustau & Co., and Arnold, Karberg & Co. became shareholders. Even on the eve of the First World War there were four Germans on the Bank's board of directors.[40] Working together, the German shareholders in the Hongkong Bank could have contended for position with their English partners.[41] However, they made no joint bids for power, preferring to play a minor role in the daily operation of the business.

Feeling safe and comfortable under British protection, the German merchants in Hong Kong showed little interest in building up political ties with their governments at home. Theodor Johns, a Hamburg merchant working in Macau, reported in 1845 that it was not necessary for the German states to conclude an independent business treaty with China.[42] Their apolitical attitude was clearly demonstrated in the debate over the installation of an all-German consul in China. In 1846, Richard von Carlowitz and a group of German merchants in Guangzhou, seeing that their interests were not being properly protected, planned to urge the Prussian government to help create a German consul in Guangzhou who would handle all questions related to German interests in China. The move aroused fierce opposition from the Hansa German merchants in China, who believed that such a move would amount to an indirect recognition of Prussia's position as the leader of all German states.[43] Furthermore they doubted whether an official from Prussia would be in a position to represent them. Even Carlowitz himself, though he was interested in this post, was only prepared to run the office on a nonofficial basis. Later, in 1852, Siemssen was nominated Hamburg consul in Guangzhou, and in 1855 he was nominated Bremen consul in Guangzhou. In June 1856, the German state Hanover opened the first German consulate in Hong Kong.[44] Eduard Reimers became the Hamburg consul in Hong Kong in 1853. Gustav Overbeck in 1856 became the first consular agent of Prussia in Hong Kong. In 1858 the new Hamburg representative in Hong Kong, Ludwig von Weise, reported that German merchants could go on running their businesses in China without direct support from their homeland.[45] Obviously, before the founding of the North German Confederation in 1867, consular duties were performed by a number of nonofficial consuls, each representing a different small and medium-sized German state.[46]

The lives of Gützlaff and Eitel illustrate the relationship between the colonial government and the Germans in Hong Kong.[47] Following his earlier cooperation with British missionaries in Southeast Asia, Gützlaff felt comfortable working with British nationals. In June 1831, he began his first voyage along the Chinese coast on a British ship, in an effort to explore new missionary possibilities. In February 1832, thanks to his competence both in Mandarin and in a number of other Chinese dialects, he was offered the job of interpreter and doctor on board a ship of the British East India Company. The record of his second visit to major cities in coastal China and Korea was published in British and European newspapers. Gützlaff's pragmatic character and his disregard for certain rules were manifested in his third voyage. Unable to finance his new trip, he boarded a British smuggler's ship.[48] In December 1834, he succeeded Robert Morrison as Chinese secretary and interpreter to the British consular authority in China, accepting the post because it offered him more protection, a good salary, and better opportunities to preach in coastal China. In June 1840, when the Opium War (1839–1842) was still going on, he was transferred to a post with the British fleet. In 1843, Gützlaff began to work for the new colonial government in Hong Kong. He worked for the government by day, and continued his missionary work by night.[49]

Compared with Gützlaff, Eitel's integration into the British community was even more complete and thorough. In addition to having a British wife, Eitel had other assets that made him acceptable to the British in Hong Kong. Being a sinologist as well as a missionary, he pursued in-depth research into the life and customs of the Chinese, especially the Kejia (Hakka) people in South China. His *Handbook for the Student of Chinese Buddhism* won the admiration of the leading sinologist James Legge. His public lecture on *fengshui* aroused great interest among Westerners, who were fascinated by the Chinese *Weltanschauung*. For the British administrators in Hong Kong who sought to penetrate local Chinese circles in Hong Kong, Eitel was someone they could make use of. He was appointed chairman of the Schoolbook Committee, and asked to prepare "a set of three graduated readers after the pattern of the Irish National Schoolbook Society's publication," which were to be used for the aided schools in Hong Kong.[50] Governor Arthur Edward Kennedy later invited Eitel to serve on the Board of Examiners, whose main duty was to examine and issue the "certificates of proficiency in Chinese Colloquial."[51] He held a number of positions, both official and unofficial, in the ensuing decades, including head of the office of the Superintendence of Chinese studies, Acting Inspector of Schools, Supervisor of the Staff of Interpreters and Translator. He was appointed Inspector of Schools in February 1879, and resigned from the LMS on March 29, 1879 to take up this position. Later, he also worked as Governor John Pope Hennessy's Chinese secretary.[52]

Wilhelm Lobscheid, another German missionary, who became "the first inspector of schools" in Hong Kong in 1857, was in many ways similar to Gützlaff and Eitel.[53] For these German missionaries, working with the colonial government brought then unusual convenience in everyday life and helped them to carry out their missionary duties effectively. For the colonial government, despite their German nationality, these Germans could be made use of because they possessed an extensive knowledge of Chinese language and culture, something the government very much needed.

THE GERMANS AND THE CHINESE IN HONG KONG

Politically, the Chinese in nineteenth-century Hong Kong had less influence than the British. Cultural differences and language barriers also prevented the Germans from penetrating the local Chinese community. However, in many ways the Germans needed help from the Hong Kong Chinese. For this reason, while having little desire to assimilate into local culture, they tried to maintain a smooth working relationship with the local Chinese.

It is on record that the Germans in China were quite willing to learn the Chinese language. According to the correspondence of Richard von Carlowitz, in his early days in Guangzhou he spent at least two hours every morning learning Chinese.[54] However, he admitted that it was impossible to live in China without an interpreter. Although Solomon Matthews Bard claims that "one of the distinctive features of German trade in China was the lack of a comprador(e) system,"[55] there are written records showing that German merchants in Hong Kong, like other Western traders in the territory, did hire compradores to help them correspond, liaise, and deal with Chinese officials and clients. For instance, Carlowitz & Co. employed at least two Chinese compradores, Liang Hanbin and Wen Shufan, in the 1880s, while Lin Tai worked as a compradore for Siemssen & Co. at the end of the 1880s.[56] The records of Jebsen & Co., Hong Kong, mentioned with appreciation a compradore, whose name was "Chao Yue Teng."[57] Due to a lack of sources and scholarly attention, however, little is known about the relationship between the German merchants and their Hong Kong staff.[58]

The growth of German missionary activities in China also compelled German missionaries in Hong Kong to employ Chinese assistants. In the early phase of the Opium War, Gützlaff came to realize that "the presence of war and the lack of European helpers gave rise to the idea of native assistants."[59] After settling down in Hong Kong in 1843, Gützlaff devoted part of his energy to training local Chinese missionaries. He believed that, with the help of these Chinese assistants, he could extend the influence of his one-man mission to the interior of China. Although he was not entirely happy with the conduct and the qualities of some of these Chinese helpers, he was nonetheless happy to use them. In his correspondence with Christian Gottlob Barth of Württemberg, he maintained that practices like this, which allowed him to extend his influence as far inland as Henan, were to be encouraged.[60]

One source of tension between the Germans and local Chinese in Hong Kong was the coolie trade. Whether the Germans engaged in the profitable coolie trade remains a matter of controversy. While Siemssen & Co. admitted their involvement in this trade, Wm. Pustau & Co. strongly denied it.[61] The history of Carlowitz & Co. also provided a few details about the company's involvement in this trade.[62] Some records in the Foreign Office, nevertheless, show that a number of ships chartered under German firms were responsible for shipping coolies to Cuba.[63] We can surmise that, although the Germans in Hong Kong may not have been the chief players in the kidnapping and selling of Chinese workers to South America, they were at least indirectly involved in the business. The coolies, however, were at the lowest stratum of Hong Kong society, and their grievances were seldom heard.

THE GERMAN SOCIAL AND CULTURAL NETWORK IN HONG KONG

However, it seems wrong to assume that the Germans in Hong Kong entirely surrendered their national distinctiveness. On the contrary, in their private and even cultural lives the Germans formed an effectively closed community. As far as we can see, it was a common practice for several German businessmen, who had come to Hong Kong without their families, to live together in a single house or apartment.[64] Medical care for the Germans was provided by a few German doctors, who worked in the "Medical Hall" in Hong Kong.[65] The Germans attended the German church services, and their children went to the German school.[66] It was extremely important that those Germans who ventured to start their own businesses in Hong Kong as well as in China could benefit from substantial support from their compatriots. Only with the help of Bernhard Harkort did Carlowitz decide to set up his firm in Guangzhou. Without Carlowitz's encouragement,

Georg Theodor Siemssen might never have set foot in a city a thousand miles from his homeland. When Jacob Jebsen, one of the founders of Jebsen & Co., Hong Kong, arrived in the territory on November 20, 1894, he rushed to meet his German friends in order to familiarize himself with the business environment.[67] A network providing information and a sense of solidarity among Germans already existed in Hong Kong.

In Hong Kong as well as in Shanghai, German cultural and social life revolved around particular fraternal associations.[68] In Hong Kong it was obviously represented by the so-called German Club, later renamed the "Club Germania," to which only members of large firms had access, and the so-called Captain's Club, which owners of small stores frequented. The German Club was already established in 1859, but later changed location and operated a villa in the city center. The Club had a library, a reading room, a concert hall, a billiard room, a bowling alley, a bar, and a dining hall; it also organized concerts and lectures. If prominent Germans came to Hong Kong, they were received in the Club, as happened, for example, when the Prussian Prince Henry visited. Having few alternatives, many German merchants chose to spend their free time in the German Club.[69] In this way, the Club was of the greatest importance for access to news, for communication and the formation of opinion, and not least for the shaping of the mentality and identity of the Germans in Hong Kong. However, the fact that the middle-class Germans met in the "Club Germania," while lower-middle-class Germans gathered at the "Captain's Club," shows that class distinction in many ways overshadowed national affinity.

In sum, the Germans in Hong Kong cultivated among themselves a collective consciousness, if not a national identity. The German community, however, though having a strong sense of solidarity, showed no specifically nationalistic behavior. Before 1870 there were in fact few occasions that compelled Germans in Hong Kong to resort to collective action. For Winfried Speitkamp, "the businessmen were proud to be a part of the Hanseatic elite, and they also demonstrated national positions after the unification of Germany. In the opinion of the North German middle classes, Hanseatic and German identity could relate to one another. The social and cultural life of the Germans in Hong Kong thus transmitted a sense of community and home in a foreign land and a foreign culture. Germany was less a political symbol and much more a collective myth, a collection of values and ideals."[70] Paradoxically, the nonpolitical character of their sense of national identity contributed to the survival of their feeling of nationality.

THE BREAKDOWN OF THE EQUILIBRIUM

The 1870s was a turning point, not only in European history, but also in the history of the German community in Hong Kong. The unification of Germany meant at least three things to the Germans in Hong Kong, who had long been associated with the British in the territory. First, German economic expansion in the Far East, partly facilitated by the unified Germany's *Weltpolitik*, helped rebuild the economic connection between the German people in Hong Kong and their home market. There was a great increase in the volume of German industrial products, such as machinery, armaments, and munitions, imported into China through German merchants in Hong Kong. Second, thanks to developments in communications, German nationals overseas no longer felt far away from home. The new German government, concerned with the preservation of Germandom, paid more attention to its citizens in foreign countries.[71] Third, the founding of the unified Germany generated new values for overseas Germans to embrace, recalling the German identity that they had once put aside. While this new national consciousness probably did not change the relationship between the Germans in Hong Kong and the local Chinese, it began to create tension between the British and the Germans in the closing decades of the nineteenth century.

The unification of Germany was followed by Otto von Bismarck's new foreign policy. While his policy in regard to Europe was principally a matter of isolating and weakening France, his policy in the wider arena was to increase gradually Germany's political and economic influence in various parts of the world. As a result of the Sino-Prussian cooperation, which had been growing since the 1860s, China became a factor that Bismarck could no longer overlook. Advances in communications had paved the way for Germany's expansion in the East. In 1869 the Suez Canal began to operate, shortening the trip between the East and the West. In 1872 the first Hamburg steam ship entered the harbor in Shanghai, marking the beginning of the era of German steamers. In the same year, the *Deutsche Dampfschiffs-Rhederei zu Hamburg* (German Steamers Company at Hamburg), the so-called Kingsin began to operate the first steamer line running regularly between China and Germany. In the same year, the telegraph began to function between London and Hong Kong. The rising German industrialists were ready to take this opportunity to make inroads into the Chinese market. For instance, after Chancellor Bismarck signaled in April 1870 his interest in expanding beyond Europe,[72] thirty companies in Bremen and three companies in Berlin immediately petitioned jointly for overseas colonies. China became one of their targets. In the period of recession between 1876 and 1878, the quest for overseas expansion overwhelmed the free trade doctrine advocated by the German liberals. In 1878, a number of merchants in Bremen requested a new China-policy.[73] Even Wilhelm Lobscheid emphasized that an active but not aggressive policy could help Germany to find a home, to spread its knowledge, and to fully use its capital in China.[74] It was only the opposition of the Social Democrats, the lack of a powerful German navy, and Bismarck's concern about the likely reaction of France and Britain that delayed Germany's expansion in the East.

Although the German government's plan to exert direct influence over China was slow to materialize, trade between German merchants in Hong Kong and leaders in German heavy industries, such as Alfred Krupp, increased sharply from the 1870s onward. In the early 1860s Alfred Krupp gradually built up his industrial empire by selling arms and munitions to Russia and Turkey, and steel to American railway builders. However, his early attempt to penetrate the Chinese market was less than successful. Having failed in 1866 to sell 1,000 cannons to China, Krupp employed the German merchant F. Peil in Hong Kong—he originally specialized in the import and export of wines and spirits—as an agent, to explore the Chinese market. At the end of 1870 the Chinese government eventually purchased 191 Krupps cannons, which were installed in Tianjin, Jinan, Guangzhou, and Shanghai between 1871 and 1873.[75] In the following years, F. Peil and Melchers & Co., Hongkong succeeded in finding Chinese buyers for Krupp's mining machine.[76] However, Krupp was soon faced with competition from the prestigious British company Armstrong and the *Bochumer Verein für Bergbau und Großstahlfraktion* (Bochum Mining and Steel Refining Union), which was supported by Prussian military officers. From 1878 onward, the great German industrialist sought help from Schmidt & Co., another German firm, which also had a branch in Hong Kong. In 1879 Menhausen, the former head of Schmidt & Co. in France, built up another base in Shanghai, in an effort to help establish Krupp's business in Southeast China.[77] A number of other German companies, including Carlowitz & Co., also became agents for suppliers of German military arms and munitions in the following decades. After Germany established its first naval base in Jiaozhou, German companies in Hong Kong, such as Jebsen & Co., lost no time in extending their business to Northern China.[78] As in the past, German merchants in Hong Kong continued to sell goods from various countries, but they derived a growing proportion of their income from the reexport of German industrial products.

The economic ties between the German government and the German merchants in Hong Kong became closer than ever in the 1880s when the former took active steps to extend its influence in East Asia. In 1884 the German government, seeing shipping as a lucrative trade,[79] and in response to the request of the German industrialists, who believed that a state-owned steamship line between China and Germany would be the foundation of Germany's economic expansion in the East, approached Kingsin for cooperation. Turned down by Kingsin, the government turned to *Norddeutscher Lloyd* (North German Lloyd) based in Bremen, which eventually accepted the government's offer. The line began to operate in 1885. In its early years, at least one steamer left Bremen for major cities in China and Japan every month.[80] This line soon became so profitable that in 1889 *Norddeutscher Lloyd* doubled its Far East fleet, sending one steamer to China and Japan every two weeks. In 1886 it opened an office in Hong Kong, and in 1914 the Hamburg America Line, which had incoporated the Kingsin, also ran its Hong Kong offices.[81]

In 1889 the German government entered the Chinese financial market by supporting the founding of the *Deutsch-Asiatische Bank* (German-Asian Bank). Although the early operation of the Shanghai and Yokohama branches of the *Deutsche Bank* (German Bank) in the early 1870s ended in failure,[82] Adolph von Hansemann, the head of the *Disconto-Bank* in Berlin, came to realize in 1882 that growing Sino-German trade and China's modernization program presented new opportunities to German bankers. Supported by the German representative in Shanghai, Hansemann approached bankers and entrepreneurs in Germany, inviting them to contribute to the founding of a new German bank in China, whose scale would be comparable with the English banks there.[83] In summer 1885 his plan won the support of both Max von Brandt, the German Ambassador in China between 1875 and 1893, and the German Foreign Ministry.[84] Hansemann put his plan into practice, gathering a group of bankers and industrialists in Dortmund, Bochum, and Nuremberg to form an *Eisenbahn-Consortium* (Railway Consortium), which helped finance Li Hongzhang's railway building project. It was from the *Eisenbahn-Consortium* that the *Deutsch-Asiatische Bank* was developed. In February 1889 the *Deutsch-Asiatische Bank* opened in Berlin. Its Shanghai branch aimed at providing various financial services for German merchants in China as well as loans for great Chinese projects. In Hong Kong, where the Hongkong Bank dominated the financial sector, the growth of the *Deutsch-Asiatische Bank* was rather slow, because the most prominent German merchants in Hong Kong remained directors and shareholders of Hongkong Bank, while many smaller firms were already in debt to Hongkong Bank.[85]

Growing German political and economic influence in Asia complicated the situation of Germans in Hong Kong. It is to be emphasized that they were still Germans by birth, by culture and by nationality. Their national feelings were fired by the unification of Germany and sustained by the events that had been occurring since the 1870s. For instance, their sense of nationhood was reinforced by the founding of an official German consulate in Hong Kong in 1892, by Max von Brandt's visit to Hong Kong in 1883,[86] and by Germany's acquisition of Jiaozhou as a naval base in 1897. While treasuring their partnership with the British, the Germans in Hong Kong were now less hesitant about showing their affinity with the homeland, and about initiating activities that carried national meaning, especially in the German Club. For instance, a choral society, the so-called Liedertafel, was founded in 1873. The Emperor's birthday was celebrated in the Club every year.[87] The celebration of the Emperor's birthday was not so much a demonstration of loyalty to the Hollenzollern monarchy, but a means of connection with German cultural forms and values and a symbol of German identity.[88]

Nevertheless, the Germans in Hong Kong found it more and more difficult to strike a balance between national and practical interests, especially at the beginning of the twentieth century, when ill feeling began to grow between Britain and Germany. This had appeared already at the time of the Boer War (1899–1902) in South Africa, when Germany supported the Boers against British colonial power. It intensified in the run-up to the First World War.

Conclusion

The German community in nineteenth-century Hong Kong was in fact too small to form a critical mass. While their members could *mitwirken* (play a part) in many important social and economic activities, as a group they could achieve little. For instance, the German contribution to education in Hong Kong was confined to a few minor achievements, in contrast with the Germans in Shanghai who founded the Shanghai Tongji University, and the Germans in Shandong who gradually transplanted German cultural elements into Chinese society there. As Bert Becker points out, it was the German education scheme in Jiaozhou and other parts of Shandong, not the influence of the Germans in Hong Kong, that served as a "German factor" in the founding of the University of Hong Kong.[89] More important, the

Germans depended for their economic success and comfortable social life on the goodwill and cooperation of the British. Once this goodwill and cooperation gave way to hostility in 1914, the fate of the Germans in Hong Kong took a tragic turn.

NOTES

This chapter is a revised version of an article, "The German Community in 19th Century Hong Kong," published in the *Asia Europe Journal*, vol. 2 (2004), pp. 237–55.

1. Anthony Smith, *National Identity* (Reno, Nev.: University of Nevada Press, 1991), p. 21.
2. Wolfgang Bergem, "Culture, Identity and Distinction: Ethnic Minorities between Scylla and Charybdis," in Stefan Wolff, ed., *German Minorities in Europe: Ethnic Identity and Cultural Belonging* (New York: Berghahn, 2000), p. 1.
3. There has, of course, been intensive research on the German colonists in Shandong, which was a German sphere of influence before the First World War. See for instance Mechthild Leutner and Klaus Mühlhahn, eds., *"Musterkolonie Kiautschou"—die Expansion des Deutschen Reiches in China* (Berlin: Akademie Verlag, 1997) and Klaus Mühlhahn, *Herrschaft und Widerstand in der "Musterkolonie" Kiautschou* (Munich: Oldenbourg, 2000). However there have not been enough in-depth studies of the Germans outside the German colonies, or on their lifestyles and interactions with local people and other ethnic groups.
4. For an overview of German economic conditions before the nineteenth century, please consult Hans Ulrich Wehler, *Deutsche Gesellschaftsgeschichte* (Munich: C. H. Beck, second edn., 1989), vol. 1, p. 614. Hans Medick, Peter Kriedte, and Jürgen Schlumbohm, *Industrialisierung vor der Industrialisierung: Warenprodukte auf dem Land in der Formationsperiode des Kapitalismus* (Göttingen: Vandenhoeck, 1978) also displays a clear picture of the conditions and characters of German proto-industrialization.
5. Ernst Baasch, *Beiträge zur Geschichte des Deutschen Seeschiffbaues und der* Schiffbaupolitik (Hamburg: Lucas Gräfe & Sillen, 1898), p. 10.
6. Ibid., pp. 11–13.
7. Ibid., p. 85.
8. Robert B. Asprey, *Frederick the Great: The Magnificent Enigma* (New York: Ticknor & Fields, 1986), pp. 572–73.
9. Thomas Brysch, *Marinepolitik im Preußischen Abgeordnetenhaus und Deutschen Reichstag 1850–1888* (Hamburg: Verlag E.S. Mittler, 1996), pp. 41–43.
10. According to Prof. Adrian Hsia, with whom I discussed this issue in 2002, only four copies of Leibniz's *Novissima Sinica* were printed.

11. According to Philippe Dollinger, *The German Hansa*, trans. and ed. D. S. Ault and S. H. Steinberg (Stanford: Stanford University Press, 1970), the cooperation between Belgian, Dutch, English, and German traders in the North Sea can be dated back to the twelfth century. London, Antwerp, Brugge, and Amsterdam were all founding members of the early Hanseatic organization. See especially pp. 85–92.
12. Yu Wentang, *Zhongde zaoqi maoyi guanxi* (Early Sino-German Trade Relations) (Taibei [Taipei]: Daohe Publishing Co., 1995) is one of the most comprehensive studies of this topic. Read pp. 11–12.
13. Ibid., pp. 31–32.
14. Karin Bartsch, *Hamburgs Handelsbeziehung mit China und Britisch-Ostindien* (Ph.D. diss., University of Hamburg, 1958), p. 22.
15. For statistics of German ships visiting the above cities in the mid-nineteenth century, see Bernd Eberstein, *Hamburg-China* (Hamburg: Institut für Asienkunde, 1988), p. 388.
16. Percy Ernst Schramm, ed., *Kaufleute zu Haus und Übersee: Hamburgische Zeugnisse des 17., 18. &19. Jh.* (Hamburg: Hoffmann und Campe Verlag, 1948), p. 333.
17. Ibid., pp. 339 & 342.
18. Ibid., pp. 331–34.
19. Ibid., p. 346.
20. Theodor Bohner, *Von Dresden nach China: Der Deutsche Kaufmann von Carlowitz* (Leipzig: Otto Elsner Verlagsgesellschaft, 1945), p. 10.
21. Ibid., p. 36.
22. *C. Melchers & Co., Bremen. Melchers & Co. Hongkong, Kanton, Schanghai, Hankow, Tientsin, Chinkiang, Ichang, Tsingtau* (Bremen: n.p., 1909), pp. 11, 17–18.
23. Ibid., p. 13.
24. Maria Möring, *Siemssen & Co., 1846–1971* (Hamburg: Verlag Hanseatischer Merkur, 1971), pp. 21–22.
25. Herman Schlyter, *Karl Gützlaff als Missionar in China* (Lund: Gleerup, 1946), p. 33.
26. Wong Man Kong, *Christian Missions, Chinese Culture, and Colonial Administration: A Study of the Activities of James Legge and Ernest John Eitel in Nineteenth Century Hong Kong* (Ph.D. diss., Chinese University of Hong Kong, 1996), pp. 21–22.
27. *Briefe Richards von Carlowitz aus Ostindien und China von 1844 an*, p. 32, Archives of Commerzbibliothek Hamburg, Hamburg, Germany.
28. Eberstein, *Hamburg-China*, p. 390.
29. Solomon Matthews Bard, *Traders of Hong Kong: Some Foreign Merchant Houses, 1841–1899* (Hong Kong: Urban Council, 1993), pp. 98–99.
30. Carl Smith, "The German Speaking Community in Hong Kong, 1846–1918," *Journal of the Hong Kong Branch of the Royal Asiatic Society*, vol. 34 (1994), p. 3.

31. Adolf von Hänisch, *Jebsen & Co. Hong Kong: China-Handel im Wechsel der Zeiten 1895–1945* (Apenrade: Selbstverlag, 1970), p. 33.
32. Harold James, *A German Identity: 1770 to the Present Day* (London: Phoenix, 1994), pp. 21–22.
33. Bartsch, *Hamburgs Handelsbeziehung mit China und Britisch-Ostindien*, pp. 9–12.
34. *C. Melchers & Co., Bremen*, p. 18.
35. Möring, *Siemssen & Co., 1846–1971*, pp. 59–60.
36. Ibid., pp. 60–61.
37. Eberstein, *Hamburg-China*, p. 62.
38. Bard, *Traders of Hong Kong*, pp. 98 and 101.
39. Frank H. H. King, Catherine E. King, and David J. S. King, eds., *The Hongkong Bank in Late Imperial China 1864–1902* (New York: Cambridge University Press, 1987), p. 135.
40. Ibid., p. 26.
41. Ibid., p. 135.
42. Eberstein, *Hamburg-China*, p. 113.
43. Ibid., p. 62.
44. *Germany in Hong Kong: 50 Years Consulate General of the Federal Republic of Germany, 40 Years Goethe-Institut Hong Kong, 20 Years German Chamber of Commerce* (Hong Kong: German Chamber of Commerce, Goethe-Institut, Consulate General of the Federal Republic of Germany, 2003), p. 3.
45. Eberstein, *Hamburg-China*, p. 114.
46. *Germany in Hong Kong*, p. 5.
47. For a short discussion of the German missionaries in Hong Kong, see R. G. Tiedemann, "The Early German Protestant Missions in the Hong Kong Region," paper presented at the international conference on "Church History of Hong Kong," University of Hong Kong, 1993.
48. Schlyter, *Karl Gützlaff als Missionar in China*, pp. 68–77.
49. Ibid., p. 154.
50. Timothy M. K. Wong (Wong Man Kong), "The Limits of Ambiguity in German Identity in Nineteenth Century Hong Kong: With Special Reference to Ernest Eitel (1838–1908)," in Ricardo K. S. Mak and Danny S. L. Paau, eds., *Sino-German Relations Since 1800: Multidisciplinary Explorations* (Frankfurt am Main: Peter Lang, 2000), p. 84.
51. Ibid.
52. Wong, *Christian Missions, Chinese Culture, and Colonial Administration*, pp. 217–27.
53. For a short discussion of Wilhelm Lobscheid's contribution to education in early Hong Kong, see Ng Lun Ngai-ha, *Interactions of East and West: Development of Public Education in Early Hong Kong* (Hong Kong: Chinese University Press, 1984), pp. 26–31. Wilhelm Lobscheid's observation of Hong Kong education in the nineteenth

century was summed up in his *A Few Notices on the Extent of Chinese Education and the Government Schools of Hong Kong* (Hong Kong: China Mail Office, 1859).

54. *Briefe Richards von Carlowitz aus Ostindien und China von 1844 an*, p. 58.
55. Bard, *Traders of Hong Kong*, p. 97.
56. Material from the name lists of directors given in The Board of Directors 1970–1971, ed., *One Hundred Years of the Tung Wah Group of Hospitals 1870–1970* (Hong Kong: Tung Wah Group of Hospitals, 1971), pp. 62–64.
57. Hänisch, *Jebsen & Co. Hong Kong*, p. 40.
58. For instance in Hao Yen Ping's brilliant study, *The Comprador in Nineteenth Century China: Bridge between East and West* (Cambridge, Mass.: Harvard University Press, 1970), the compradores working under Germans are briefly mentioned twice.
59. Schlyter, *Karl Gützlaff als Missionar in China*, p. 142.
60. Ibid., pp. 175–76.
61. Colonial Office Records, Series CO 129, no. 169, pp. 263–70, Public Records Office, Hong Kong.
62. *Carlowitz & Co. Hamburg, Hong Kong, New York, China and Japan* (Hamburg: n.p., 1906), p. 30.
63. Colonial Office Records, Series CO 129, no. 166, pp. 196–211, Public Records Office, Hong Kong.
64. Hänisch, *Jebsen & Co. Hong Kong*, p. 35.
65. Smith, "The German Speaking Community in Hong Kong, 1846–1918," p. 11.
66. Hänisch, *Jebsen & Co. Hong Kong*, p. 445.
67. Ibid., p. 30.
68. For a short description of the German Club in Shanghai, see ibid., p. 31.
69. Smith, "The German Speaking Community in Hong Kong, 1846–1918," pp. 9–10; Hänisch, *Jebsen & Co. Hong Kong*, pp. 33 and 444–45.
70. Winfried Speitkamp, "The Germans in Hong Kong, 1860–1914: Social Life, Political Interests, and National Identity," in Mak and Paau, eds., *Sino-German Relations Since 1800*, p. 61.
71. Rogers Brubaker, *Citizenship and Nationhood in France and Germany* (Cambridge, Mass.: Harvard University Press, 1992), pp. 116–18.
72. Helmuth Stoecker, *Deutschland und China im 19. Jahrhundert* (Berlin: Rütten & Loening, 1958), p. 73.
73. Udo Ratenhof, *Die Chinapolitik des Deutschen Reiches 1871 bis 1945: Wirtschaft-Rüstung-Militär* (Boppard am Rhein: Boldt, 1987), pp. 100–01.
74. Wilhelm Lobscheid, *China in Statistischer, Ethnographischer, Sprachlicher und Religiöser Beziehung: mit besonderer Berücksichtigung*

des Ta Tsiú, der grossen Herbst-Seelenmesse (Hong Kong: Druck von Noronha, 1871), p. 3.

75. Ratenhof, *Die Chinapolitik des Deutschen Reiches 1871 bis 1945*, p. 79.
76. Ibid., p. 80.
77. Ibid., p. 83.
78. Hänisch, *Jebsen & Co. Hong Kong*, pp. 53–55.
79. According to Eberstein, the number of steamers from Hamburg to China increased from 16 in 1871 to 100 in 1913. More significantly, in 1862 Hamburg ships unloaded 1,351 cargoes in Chinese harbors, but in 1895 the weight of cargoes from Hamburg increased to 55,000 tons. See his *Hamburg-China*, p. 160.
80. Ibid., p. 163.
81. Smith, "The German Speaking Community in Hong Kong, 1846–1918," p. 53.
82. Lothar Gall, ed., *The Deutsche Bank* (London: Trafalgar Square Publishing, 1985), p. 55.
83. Maximilian Muller-Jabusch, *Fünfzig Jahre Deutsch-Asiatische Bank, 1890–1939* (Berlin: Deutsch-Asiatischen Bank, 1940), p. 11.
84. Richard Frederick Szippl, *Max von Brandt and German Imperialism in East Asia in the Late 19th Century* (Ann Arbor, Mich.: UMI Dissertation Services, 1997), pp. 44–45.
85. Dieter Glade, *Bremen und der Ferne Osten* (Bremen: Carl Schünemann Verlag, 1966), p. 114.
86. Max von Brandt, *Dreiunddreissig Jahre in Ostasien: Erinnerungen eines deutschen* Diplomaten (Leipzig: Verlag von Georg Wigano, 1901), vol. 1, p. 287.
87. Hänisch, *Jebsen & Co. Hong Kong*, p. 445.
88. Speitkamp, "The Germans in Hong Kong, 1860–1914," p. 60.
89. Bert Becker, "The 'German Factor' in the Founding of the University of Hong Kong," in Chan Lau Kit-ching and Peter Cunich, eds., *An Impossible Dream. Hong Kong University from Foundation to Re-establishment 1910–1950* (New York: Oxford University Press, 2002), pp. 23–37.

Chapter 5

Catholic Church between Two World Wars

Cindy Yik-yi Chu

Introduction

The Catholic Church established itself in Hong Kong in 1841, in response to the religious needs of Irish troops in the recently occupied territory. At that time, the Church had not developed any plans for Hong Kong as a mission field, not to mention that personnel were deployed in Hong Kong only on a short-term basis and that the Catholics had not yet formed a stable community. However, in the ensuing few years, the population of the colony grew by leaps and bounds, and thus opportunities for evangelization increased. Evangelization was the ultimate motive of foreign missions, and Hong Kong was no exception. Very soon, the Church moved from taking care of Irish troops to working for the consolidation and expansion of a local Catholic community. The latter objective entailed the proclamation of the Christian religion, the erection of church buildings, and the appointment of a responsible institute in Hong Kong.

In setting up the Church in Hong Kong—recruiting religious personnel, training local clergy, building churches, and attracting converts—the Catholic Church reacted to changing circumstances in the new colony. As the Church adapted to the local situation, there was an evolution in its objectives and roles. It did not take long before it ventured into other fields, such as starting the Catholic press, opening schools, and offering social services. In order to increase the number of converts and to be accepted by Hong Kong society, it needed to make itself useful to the community at large, meaning that it had to become increasingly involved in *secular activities*, as a way to reach out to more people and to remove inherent suspicions. It took up the task of working to improve the general livelihood of the people, especially that of the less fortunate and the poor.

Recent scholarship stresses the evolution of missionary work, Catholic and Protestant alike, in foreign fields. In the process of adaptation and adjustment, missionaries put growing emphasis on secular activities, such as education, medical care, and social welfare, as a means to create contact and to make an impact on society. Contributors to *United States Attitudes and Policies toward China*, edited by Patricia Neils, point out that foreign missionaries moved from a Bible-centered approach to the emphasis on secular activities in their work.[1] The use of both social and religious channels to spread Christianity has been an important theme of historical research; see, for example, "Diversifying the Operation" and "From the Pursuit of Converts to the Relief of Refugees," which focus on the changing agenda of missionaries in Chinese fields.[2] Others even argue that secular activities, rather than religious teachings, were the missionaries' most useful tool in establishing themselves in local communities.[3]

Before the First World War (1914–1918), the Catholic Church, wishing to expand in Hong Kong, tried to make itself welcomed and respected by society. By inviting foreign missionary groups to the colony, it hoped that missionaries would shoulder some of the tasks in providing relief and welfare to the people, undertaking such activities as opening homes for the aged and disabled, and running orphanages and hospitals. Local circumstances demanded adjustment, and there was a gradual progression in the work of the Catholic missionaries. The interwar years between 1919 and 1941 witnessed further growth of the Church, especially through the development of Catholic schools, which were then able to create a solid foundation for future expansion. By the outbreak of the Second World War (1939–1945), the Church had already become fully integrated into Hong Kong society, shouldering a variety of responsibilities for the well-being of the people. Through their services in relief, welfare, and education in the interwar years, Catholic missionaries had won recognition from the local people, and thus paved the way for taking on still greater responsibilities in the postwar years, that is, during the 1950s and 1960s.

THE BEGINNING OF THE CATHOLIC CHURCH IN HONG KONG

The Catholic Church began to have a presence in Hong Kong in 1841, the year the British acquired the colony. While British troops were stationed in Hong Kong, the "alarming rate" of illnesses and deaths raised serious concern.[4] Many soldiers were Irish and Catholic, had no army chaplains, and only had Macau—then the administrative center for missionaries to China—to look to for religious support. Given the "frequency of the deaths" among British soldiers, the services of Catholic priests became an urgent requirement in Hong Kong. Father Theodore Joset, a young Swiss priest representing the Congregation for the Propagation of the Faith, which on behalf of the Roman Catholic Church had taken charge of missions in mainland China, wrote to Rome from Macau and urged the Church to recognize Hong Kong's situation and the need to begin a mission there. A reply arrived promptly, and on April 22, 1841 a Papal decree created a Prefecture Apostolic, independent from the Macau Diocese, including "Hong Kong with the surrounding six leagues," with Joset as Hong Kong's first Prefect Apostolic. It was recognized that, "the first need being the spiritual care of the British (Irish Catholic) Troops, stationed in the just occupied Colony," a situation of emergency existed.[5] Thus the Catholic Church began its history in Hong Kong. Its prime concern was to serve the religious needs of Irish soldiers.

In January 1842, the first Catholic priest settled in Hong Kong. He was a Spanish Franciscan. 1842 also witnessed Joset's arrival, the erection of a "matshed church," the relocation of the Propagation of the Faith office and of a seminary for Chinese priests in Hong Kong. Joset's death occurred later the same year.[6] After his death, Joset was named founder of Hong Kong's Catholic Church. From 1842 to 1855 an Italian Franciscan, Anthony Feliciani, occupied the position of Prefect Apostolic, and from 1855 to 1867 Feliciani's successor was an Italian of the Propagation of the Faith, Aloysius Ambrosi. While Hong Kong and the Church were in their preliminary stage of development, "the Colony was growing, and the Church was growing in it and they were assigned to take charge of it."[7] From "a barren rock with an uncertain population of not more than 1,500" before British rule, the colony experienced a ten-fold increase in population in its first year, and by 1858 the population had risen further to 75,000.[8] With the expansion in population, the opportunities for evangelization also multiplied. There were about 70,000 Chinese and 3,000 Europeans in the colony in 1858; and most Catholics were either Europeans or Eurasians. Among the 3,260 Catholics in Hong Kong in 1858, about 1,500 were Portuguese from Macau, 300 were Europeans (mainly Irish soldiers), 800 were Filipinos and seamen, and 660 were Chinese converts.[9] Seeing the great potential for development in this mission field, the Church made plans for a large church, a presbytery, a seminary, a school, an orphanage, a hospital, and a cemetery. Franciscans, Italian priests, priests of the Paris Foreign Missionary Society, and Chinese priests all came to Hong Kong to serve.[10]

Still, there were never enough priests, not to mention that many were destined elsewhere and were preparing to leave even from the moment of their arrival. Most of them came on a temporary basis, on their way to mainland China. Although Hong Kong had become a Prefecture Apostolic, it suffered from an inadequate and unstable supply of personnel, the root of the problem being the absence of an institute to shoulder overarching responsibility. Therefore, in 1858 when the Sacred Congregation of the Propagation of the Faith made the decision that missionaries from the newly established Seminary for Foreign Missions in Milan would leave for Hong Kong, it was understood that this Milan institute would prepare in the coming years eventually to assume full responsibility for the Prefecture.[11] In 1867 Father Timoleon Raimondi, one of the first Milan missionaries to arrive, became Pro-Prefect, and this indicates that the Prefecture came under the jurisdiction of the Milan institute. In 1926 the institute became known as the Pontifical Institute for Foreign Missions (PIME). In 1868, Raimondi was made Prefect Apostolic of Hong Kong.[12] With the Milan priests in charge and making decisions, the Church was in a position to form better defined policies and plans for future.

In 1874 the Hong Kong Prefecture was raised to a Vicariate Apostolic, and the geographic scope of its responsibilities expanded to include larger areas in mainland China. Raimondi was the first Vicar Apostolic and was consecrated bishop.[13] The Church had several goals, to serve the Catholic community, to reach out to a wider population, and to attract more converts. In order to work toward these, it created its own press and erected permanent church buildings. In 1877 the Church launched the English-language weekly, the *Hong Kong Catholic Register*; and in 1885 French missionaries opened the first printing house, Nazareth Press. By the end of the 1880s, the Cathedral of the Immaculate Conception was completed. The mission field suffered its share of illnesses and deaths, and at the turn of the century there had been a number of changes in personnel. With the death of Raimondi, Father Louis Piazzoli succeeded as second Vicar Apostolic, and in 1895 was also consecrated bishop. In 1905 Father Dominic Pozzoni became third Vicar Apostolic and bishop, the appointment being made after the death of his predecessor.

After the establishment of the Church, its efforts seemed to bear fruit, as the Catholic population continued to grow every year. The increases in the numbers of baptisms were an encouraging sign,

Table 5.1 Numbers of Catholics and Adult Baptisms in Hong Kong (1897–1913)

Year	Number of Catholics	Number of Adult Baptisms
1897	8,700	202
1898	9,000	326
1899	9,170	391
1900	9,265	297
1901	9,300	292
1902	9,900	426
1903	10,800	708
1904	11,500	702
1905	12,250	713
1906	13,275	888
1907	14,195	689
1908	14,945	529
1909	15,695	456
1910	16,201	417
1911	16,751	406
1912	17,359	474
1913	18,000	683

showing that it was on the right track in its work of expanding and consolidating the Church community. The above table 5.1[14] shows some of the statistics.

Long before the outbreak of the First World War, different European groups had appeared on the scene. The French St. Paul de Chartres Sisters arrived in 1848, and became the first congregation of Catholic nuns in Hong Kong. The second group of nuns in the colony, the Italian Canossian Sisters, came in 1860. The Paris Foreign Missionary Society started a mission in Hong Kong in 1847, long before the appointment of the Milan priests. The Spanish Dominican Fathers established their mission in 1861, and the French La Salle Christian Brothers came in 1875.

THE FIRST WORLD WAR (1914–1918) AND ITS AFTERMATH

On June 28, 1914, the assassination of the Austrian archduke in Sarajevo triggered enormous tensions, which would soon issue in the First World War. While Europe was on the brink of hostilities, the Church held the first Eucharistic Congress in Hong Kong from July 22–26, signifying the Bishop's attempt to promote devotion to the Blessed Eucharist, and frequent partaking of Communion.[15] Nevertheless, he was soon taken up by the situation in Europe. On July 28 Austria declared war on Serbia; on August 1 and 3 respectively Germany declared war on Russia and France. When German troops subsequently crossed the Belgian frontier, Britain declared war on Germany. With the British at war with Germany, Pozzoni was alert to whatever impact this might have on Hong Kong. On August 9 he appealed, in both English and Chinese, to all Church members in the colony to avoid panic and to have trust in the colonial government:[16]

> England is now at war, and the majority of you being British subjects, I wish to point out to you your duties at this important time.
>
> The Government has issued various proclamations informing the inhabitants of Hong Kong that the Colony is well protected and that there is nothing to fear. All necessary steps have been taken not only to defend the Colony, but to afford the inhabitants full protection against every danger. It is the duty of us all to place our implicit trust, faith and confidence in the Government, and to help them in every way we can. By so doing a good example will be set, while every endeavour must be made by us to impress upon the minds of the 400,000 Chinese of Hong Kong and in the New Territories that the Government will do all that is necessary for their safety. Panic must be avoided at all costs. The prices of food stuffs have been fixed. The Colony is well protected. Take every opportunity to impress this firmly on the minds of the ignorant who are so easily alarmed by an increase of a few cents in the price of food.

He called on Catholics to prepare for possible price inflation, and not to be shaken by war rumors. The Bishop was fully aware that a small incident could produce a crisis situation. In Hong Kong, life had suddenly changed, martial law was proclaimed, and foreign nationals were called back home for military duty.[17] Germans, though there were many of them, left Hong Kong and their property was confiscated; there was fear of a German attack. The colony was in a state of high alert, and many Chinese refugees, who had fled to Hong Kong because of civil war in the interior, now returned to escape from a possible German invasion.

As for Italian priests, they remained, because in Italy, missionaries were not called up for military service. Italy entered the war in 1915, having declared war on Austria and Germany. Only one of the clergy, who was Polish, had to leave Hong Kong. Therefore, the Catholic Church was able to carry on its missionary work during the First World War. This is said despite the fact that missionary work was affected by the outbreak of the war.[18] On Christmas Eve 1914 the Bishop made another announcement, setting aside a day for united prayer and saying that religious services could continue:[19]

> . . . you will undoubtedly respond with enthusiasm to the call, supported by His Majesty George V, to have a day of united prayer and intercession to attain peace. The day suggested, as you already know from the press, is the first Sunday of the year, January the 3rd. We are of the opinion that, apart from the prayers which we are already saying, there is no better way of uniting ourselves in humble supplication than to have a Procession of Penance, which will be held in the compound of the Cathedral at 6 p.m. on January 3rd. We invite all the Faithful of the Colony to attend it and to accompany in their hearts with the utmost devotion the prayers which will be recited during the Procession. . . .
>
> On the 29th, 30th and 31st instant, there will be in the Cathedral the annual beautiful devotion of the "Forty Hours." In addition to the public prayers that are usually recited during these three days, on the 1st and 2nd of January, the Litanies of the Saints will be sung at 5:30 p.m. before Benediction as a preparation for the day of a special united prayer, and we confidently call on all our Faithful to take part in these devotions.

Some projects, started before the war, were still in progress. The St. Paul de Chartres Sisters had bought the properties of the Hong Kong Cotton Mill in then remote Causeway Bay, and reshaped them to house their convent, together with a hospital, orphanage, and school.[20] Despite tremendous difficulties, the work proceeded. The largest section of the buildings was transformed into an orphanage housing a yearly average of two thousand babies. After much reconstruction, the former workers' quarters became a hospital, and the convent and school were ready for use.

In 1918 an earthquake occurred in Shantou, three hundred kilometers east-northeast of Hong Kong. The tremor was felt locally and caused damage to the chief building of the school of the La Salle Christian Brothers, St. Joseph's College, on Robinson Road. The tremor damaged "the big pile of buildings" of the College, the "veritable monument" of Catholic educational endeavor in the colony, in which the Brother Director had taken so much pride. It left cracks in the main walls of the annexes and made the chief building unusable.[21] Many buildings were left vacant during the war. With a slump in land prices, the Brothers had no trouble in securing a former German property on Kennedy Road, to which they eventually transferred the school and their residence. Like La Salle, the rest of the Church also took advantage of the situation to acquire property. For example, it used the previous rest house of the German Basel Mission in Kowloon Tong for an old folks' home. The St. Vincent de Paul Society temporarily managed this old folks' home for the Little Sisters of the Poor, whose arrival in Hong Kong, together with their other mission plans, was disrupted by the First World War.[22]

During the war, the statistics of the Catholic population were as seen in table 5.2 below.[23]

Toward the close of the war in late 1918, the Maryknoll Fathers (officially known as the Catholic Foreign Mission Society of America) arrived from the United States. Upon arrival, they found the colony "a bustling foreign settlement" with the majority of the people Chinese. The American priests described the place and activities like this: "the Island was built along the water front and as the population increased it spread out up the steep hillsides. . . . Linking the Island with the mainland [Kowloon Peninsula] was a ferry service. In the earlier days this service consisted of small steam driven wooden vessels carrying some sixty passengers."[24] There were no buses and hardly any automobiles, and people traveled in rickshaws and sedan chairs. Hong Kong seemed to have regained its spirit and energy, and things were gradually returning to normal. With the conclusion of the war, both Hong Kong and the Church moved to speed up what had been started a few years previously, and modern developments quickly took off. The government continued with reclamation projects, opened up roads and districts. For merchants, the end of the war offered many new opportunities for business. As for the Church, it focused on two areas of endeavor, missionary work and the provision of education.[25]

Since their earliest arrival in Hong Kong, Catholic missionaries had realized that the first task in the promotion of the faith was the erection of church buildings, as markers of the religion and as attractions

Table 5.2 Numbers of Catholics and Adult Baptisms in Hong Kong (1914–1918)

Year	Number of Catholics	Number of Adult Baptisms
1914	18,500	680
1915	19,100	1,737
1916	19,820	1,897
1917	20,593	1,506
1918	21,858	1,903

to draw the curious, of whom there were many. This idea was well expressed in Raimondi's report in 1889, one year after the blessing of the new Cathedral of the Immaculate Conception: "The inauguration of the new Cathedral has produced a strong impression on everybody. Even those who opposed the project were compelled to admit that it was a grand achievement.—There was some fruit also in more conversions among the Chinese; . . ."[26] To have church-goers, there must be churches built in different localities. In 1845, St. Francis Xavier's Chapel was built in Wanchai, which at that time was an area yet to be developed. By 1860, the Church of the Immaculate Conception on Wellington Street was rebuilt after a fire. In the 1870s, St. Joseph's Church on Garden Road was built, subsequently destroyed in typhoon, and rebuilt again; and Sacred Heart Church in West Point was blessed. In 1885 the Paris Foreign Missionary Society set up Our Lady of Lourdes Chapel in the celebrated Taikulao, a piece of property with a European house and offices formerly owned by a British company, but then sold to the French priests, who used it as their mission house for prayer and work.[27] The present Cathedral of the Immaculate Conception on Caine Road was blessed in 1888. On Kowloon side, Rosary Church on Chatham Road was blessed in 1905. After the outbreak of the First World War in 1914, Holy Cross Church in Shaukiwan, Hong Kong Island was blessed.

The press was also an important means of cultivating the Catholic community, as demonstrated by the publication of the *Hong Kong Catholic Register* (beginning in 1877) by the Church, and the later launching in 1914 of the Portuguese paper, *Religiao e Patria*, by lay personnel. Subsequently, in 1920, some English people started a Catholic monthly known as *The Rock*. The rationale for the endeavor was set out thus:[28]

> A want having been felt for the existence of a local Catholic magazine that would give expression to Catholic opinion in the Colony on all subjects of Catholic interest, as well as keep the community *au courant* of all matters of public concern throughout the world, the Right Reverend Bishop Pozzoni, Vicar Apostolic of Hong Kong, has given his approbation to the starting of a monthly magazine for this Vicariate. . . .

The Rock began in October, and subsequent issues appeared in the first week of every month. It was published under the auspices of the Catholic Union and the Catholic Men's Club, with a lieutenant colonel as editor. In the beginning, five hundred copies were printed

Table 5.3 Numbers of Catholics and Adult Baptisms in Hong Kong (1919–1922)

Year	Number of Catholics	Number of Adult Baptisms
1919	(lacking)	937
1920	23,477	1,034
1921	24,945	2,128
1922	26,556	2,770

for distribution not only in Hong Kong, but in Macau and Guangzhou (Canton) as well.[29] The table of contents of a 1924 issue included these items: Catholic General Council of China; Catholic University Hostel; Marco Polo; China mission fields; London letter; national pilgrimages to the Holy Land; the Society of St. Vincent de Paul; the Society for the Propagation of the Faith; Pope Pius XI; the catechist fund; and a school in Catholic England.[30] As an English-language periodical, *The Rock* attracted foreigners rather than local Chinese, though it claimed to target everybody in the Catholic community, irrespective of their class, their nationality, and the institutions to which they belonged.[31]

Immediately after the First World War, the statistics of Catholics and converts were as seen in table 5.3.[32]

THE 1920S

The other major focus of the Church was the establishment of schools for Catholics and non-Catholics, for foreigners and Chinese alike. Concern for education had begun early in 1843, when the Church opened its first school for Chinese boys. Subsequently, schools started for English and Portuguese boys. The St. Paul de Chartres Sisters and the Canossian Sisters also had their schools for girls. In 1864 Holy Savior's College opened. Later, in 1875, the La Salle Christian Brothers took over and changed its name to St. Joseph's College. In 1879 the government decided to avoid the emphasis on "secular instruction" for the grant-in-aid scheme, thus encouraging Catholic schools to apply, to benefit from government grants, and to make education available to more children. In 1919 Hong Kong Wah Yan College opened.

After the war, from 1921 to 1926 the Maryknoll Fathers took over the St. Louis Industrial School, formerly known as West Point Reformatory and Orphanage. Previously, the La Salle Christian

Brothers had managed St. Louis, equipping it with a printing press. As the St. Louis boys were competent in printing, the Paris Foreign Missionary Society employed many of them when it started the Nazareth Press in 1885.[33] By 1908 the Church no longer managed St. Louis as a reformatory, but as an industrial school and orphanage for the poor.[34] Even though St. Louis had undergone many changes, its ultimate objective was to train students with technical skills so that they could earn a living after graduation. Maryknoll continued with this mission, and Brother Albert Staubli, an architect, emphasized carpentry in its curriculum when he took over the school in 1921. The Maryknoll Fathers described the surroundings of St. Louis thus:[35]

> The site, overlooking the harbor of Hong Kong, was a striking one, albeit a rather noisy one with a row of tinsmith shops just across the street to the south, whose workers incidentally did not follow any union rules as to hours of labor, so that every night one's sleep suffered from the din. Down below on the water front there were also a number of Chinese hotels and restaurants, and every night at 10 o'clock, huge strings of firecrackers hanging from the topmost story, were set off, thus adding to the din.

These scenes were reflective of the modern economy and the growth of the working class. Therefore, St. Louis catered to the demands of the time by training young people to serve in industry. While Holy Savior's College had concentrated on commercial studies, St. Louis followed the same path of providing practical education to less fortunate children, so that they could finds ways to lift themselves from their own poverty. In this way, St. Louis pioneered industrial education in Hong Kong.[36]

Catholic schools served a number of purposes. There had been an *evolution* in the Church's understanding and priorities in its educational policies. After the war, Catholic schools moved toward emphasizing the serving of community needs, rather than functioning primarily as tools for evangelization. As Stephen H. Law observes, they were there to realize "the Church's mission of providing social services" to people regardless of race, religion, and status.[37] While initially the Church set up schools for foreign children, it was quick to recognize the need for education among the local Chinese. The less fortunate became the focus of concern as missionaries offered education to delinquent boys, to girls (who had fewer opportunities to enter public schools), and to the disabled. The successes scored by the Catholic schools confirmed the belief that the Church was heading in the right direction by focusing on meeting the demands of society—"The certificate of St. Saviour's College was by that time [1860s] said to be a passport into any office in Hong Kong; very soon too it came to be said that a diploma of the West Point Reformatory was a sure way of getting employment in any of the Colony's workshops."[38]

The emphasis on education in its mission, as well as the recognition of the social role of Catholic schools, took some time to evolve within the Church. Ever since the Church had arrived in Hong Kong, conversion was the primary goal. From the perspective of its bishops, schools were instruments for the spread of the Christian faith; this remained the objective throughout the years before the Second World War. At the same time, there was an inherent contradiction in their thinking, one that hindered the development of Catholic schools right up to the 1870s. Joset, the First Prefect Apostolic, held two conflicting views. On the one hand he believed that schools "were of the first necessity even though a great number of the pupils, perhaps the majority, might not be Catholics"; on the other hand he thought, and his successors concurred, that "it was not sound mission policy to employ men and consume resources in the maintenance of schools, since this was not the most fruitful means of making conversions."[39] When Feliciani succeeded Joset as second Prefect Apostolic, he was more inclined to the second view, and thus the Church became sluggish in its provision of educational services, compared to Protestant and government initiatives. Later, disputes arose between Raimondi and the government concerning the grant-in-aid code. These disputes centered on the Bishop's insistence that religious instruction be an item on the curriculum of Catholic schools.[40] In 1879 the government and the Church were able to reach an understanding, as the authorities revised the code and included some of Raimondi's proposals. The "offensive term 'secular' " was removed, and "secular instruction" was changed to "instruction in the subjects of the standards."[41] In other words, grant-in-aid schools provided quality education, some of which offered religious classes as well. From then on, the Church's educational endeavors began to gather momentum. In doing so, Stephen Law believes, Catholic schools became a bridge between Eastern and Western cultures, introducing foreign knowledge and values while encouraging students to appreciate Chinese traditions and history.[42]

In 1920 the Catholic Bishop became a member of the government's Board of Education, which had just been reconstituted. This step represented both the Church's determination to promote Catholic education, and its recognition of the necessity to become involved in the overall educational development of Hong Kong. With the Director of Education as President, the Board would later make decisions on matters relating to primary education, education in the vernacular, and the promotion of students from primary schools to secondary schools.[43] When Pozzoni died in 1924, the local paper commented that he had shown a keen interest in Catholic education, which experienced great advances during his leadership. His friend, Father Peter de Maria of the Milan institute, who "saw to it that in practically every district in the Colony there was a Catholic school for boys and girls," shared his support for education.[44] Missionary groups continued their earlier efforts. In the early 1920s the La Salle Christian Brothers went ahead with their new school buildings on Kennedy Road on Hong Kong Island and Chatham Road on the Kowloon Peninsula. At the same time, the Canossian Sisters expanded their school enrolment.[45]

The 1920s also witnessed the presence of new missionary congregations, which did not take long to see the openings in the educational field. In 1921, the Maryknoll Sisters (officially known as the Foreign Mission Sisters of St. Dominic) arrived. In 1922 the Precious Blood Sisters began as an independent local group. In 1923 the Little Sisters of the Poor arrived. In 1926 the Canadian Sisters of Our Lady of the Angels started their mission. In 1928 the Canadian Sisters of the Immaculate Conception began service. Men's groups included the Irish Jesuit Fathers (Society of Jesus) who arrived in 1926 and the Italian Salesian Fathers (Salesian Society) in 1927.

The Maryknoll Sisters started a kindergarten in their convent in 1925. The Portuguese community demanded English-language education, and the Sisters responded to the need.[46] The kindergarten soon developed into a school. By 1929 the Maryknoll Convent School had already moved twice in Tsimshatsui, and offered classes from kindergarten through Class 6, with an attendance of both foreign and local students. In 1927 the Maryknoll Sisters opened their second school, Holy Spirit on Robinson Road. Holy Spirit had 120 students and initially only accepted Chinese who wanted to be taught in Chinese and English. Holy Spirit was meant to be different from Maryknoll Convent School, "which was open to any nationality, where all subjects were taught in English, with Chinese, Portuguese or French as a language."[47] Nevertheless, both schools were for girls. Other congregations made similar moves in providing female education. The Sisters of Our Lady of the Angels opened St. Clare's School in 1927, and the Sisters of the Immaculate Conception opened Tak Sun School the following year.

When the Salesian Fathers arrived in 1927, they immediately took over St. Louis Industrial School from the Maryknoll Fathers, who had become interested in other projects. St. Louis remained an industrial school and orphanage, with an enrolment of about forty.[48] It continued to provide practical instruction so that boys could make themselves useful to society, and arranged workshops to train them in special skills. In 1929, the Jesuits became involved at tertiary level, and opened Ricci Hall Hostel for University of Hong Kong students. Long before their arrival in Hong Kong, the Jesuits had won recognition for their contribution to education worldwide. In early 1919, a group of Catholics of different nationalities petitioned the Bishop for provision of higher education by the Jesuits. In response, Pozzoni proposed a college for tertiary studies, with a curriculum of the standard required for undergraduate and Master's degrees in Europe. Writing to the Milan headquarters, he agreed that the matter was of great importance. Although the plan did not materialize, the local Catholic community had already built up high expectations of the Jesuits by the time they arrived.

The expansion of the Church and winning more converts were always the Church's principal concerns. The Church continued its efforts through the press and through the construction of new buildings. In 1928 the Church began publishing *Kung Kao Po* as a Chinese monthly, and the initial circulation was 8,000 copies. The editorial office was located in Rosary Church, Chatham Road. The "long-felt needed periodical in Chinese" had at last come into being.[49] While the Church had concentrated on its educational undertakings, there was also concern for "sound information and its beneficial power upon public opinion."[50] Therefore the first editorial of *Kung Kao Po* wrote:[51]

> Nowadays, all people concerned with the Church's work cannot help considering Education the most important factor for Catholic progress and ignore that the Newspaper is a long-term school for the general public and a second breathing atmosphere for human life, with an even stronger penetrating and convincing force than the school itself.

In a circular to schools, Bishop Henry Valtorta, fourth Vicar Apostolic, encouraged distribution of the paper:[52]

> I wish to call your attention to the monthly Catholic paper, which is now being published in Hong Kong under the title of Kung Kao Po, and to recommend it very strongly to you and to your College.

> The said paper has all my support, because it fulfills admirably the role of a first class Catechist for the purpose of propagating Religious Instruction and Catholic news.
>
> As your College is a Catholic School and, consequently, ought to favour Catholic doctrine, I should like to request you to see that a copy of the said paper is offered regularly and free of any charge to all those Chinese pupils of your College who are willing to receive it.

The launching of *Kung Kao Po* represented a significant step toward consolidating and expanding the Chinese Catholic community. The blessing of St. Margaret Mary's Church in Happy Valley in 1925 and the opening of Precious Blood Church in Shamshuipo in 1929 showed that the other great way of attracting converts, the erection of new churches, was also moving ahead. The idea of a new church in Kowloon (in addition to the existing Rosary Church) had long been mooted, and its possible location discussed. Finally, in 1923, the Church decided to establish a parish in Kowloon Tong, which would soon develop as a Chinese settlement.[53] Pozzoni asked the government to grant land for a church building, but he died in 1924. Father John Spada became Pro-Vicar Apostolic, and remained in the position for more than a year.[54] After much negotiation with the authorities, Bishop Valtorta, who became Vicar Apostolic in 1926, was able to secure land for the present St. Teresa's Church in 1928. Spada, "Parish Priest of Kowloon" and builder of other churches, supervised the construction of St. Teresa's.[55]

The statistics of Catholics and converts in the latter half of the 1920s up to 1930 were as seen in table 5.4.[56]

THE 1930S

The 1930s witnessed important initiatives in the training of local clergy, in particular the opening of the Regional Seminary for South

Table 5.4 Numbers of Catholics and Adult Baptisms in Hong Kong (1926–1930)

Year	Number of Catholics	Number of Adult Baptisms
1926	30,237	537
1927	30,639	506
1928	31,120	623
1929	32,350	719
1930	32,678	598

China in Aberdeen to accommodate a greater intake of seminarians and to provide a better environment for them. Joset had transferred the seminary from Macau to Hong Kong in 1842, but it had moved several times over the intervening years. Originally, it was a "matshed building" by the side of the "matshed church" at the corner of the present Wellington Street and Pottinger Street. Later, the seminary was situated in different places—in a small house in Wanchai, on the first floor of the Mission House on Wellington Street, in a new structure at the back of the Cathedral after 1888, and in another new building close by after 1900. However, the seminary quickly became overcrowded. It consisted of a junior section, which offered middle-school education for boys wanting to become priests, and a senior section, which catered for the seven years of study of philosophy and theology that seminarians were required to complete before their ordination.[57] As Father Thomas F. Ryan pointed out, "provision of a major seminary was a serious undertaking"; and at that time "very precise directions had been given by the Holy See regarding the training of clerical candidates."[58] The decision was to combine several seminaries in South China and establish a regional seminary in Hong Kong, which not only trained local clergy but students from mainland China as well. The Jesuits were to take charge of the regional seminary, which came into being in 1931.

In spreading the Christian faith, catechists also played a crucial role. Since the Church began in Hong Kong, catechists had assisted priests in their teaching and missionary tasks. In 1921 Pozzoni started a catechist fund to support the training of catechists. He referred to the then inadequate understanding of the importance of catechists—"We have often thought that Catholics are not sufficiently alive to the necessity of supporting their missions and providing for the urgent need of our poor missionaries to be supplied with Catechists to help them in their work."[59] As well as shouldering the usual responsibilities, catechists could be models to their fellows, helping to make the foreign religion more accessible to the Chinese. As Pozzoni said, "Not only are these Catechists invaluable help to the Missionary, but they are often models of what a true Christian should be, keeping their flock in order, instructing the ignorant and helping the weak, . . ."[60] In 1930 Valtorta instructed Spada to open a school for training catechists; he sent a circular to district rectors asking them to make recommendations. In 1931 Catholic Action was organized, and encouraged a catechetical apostolate among members of various associations, meaning they would visit different districts on Sundays and teach catechism.[61]

Table 5.5 Numbers of Catholics and Adult Baptisms in Hong Kong (1931–1939)

Year	Number of Catholics	Number of Adult Baptisms
1931	31,037	701
1932	30,894	930
1933	31,105	588
1934	31,597	965
1935	32,055	935
1936	32,921	807
1937	34,413	885
1938	34,982	761
1939	35,821	846

Some statistics for the Catholic population and converts is seen in table 5.5.[62] Before the Second World War, the Church provided welfare services mainly in the form of direct relief to the poor. As the majority of local people lived at bare subsistence level and government had no policy for social welfare, the provision of voluntary services of nongovernmental groups was very much welcomed by society and authorities alike.[63] The Church performed the task on two levels: that of lay associations (as those under Catholic Action) and religious groups. The St. Paul de Chartres Sisters established the *Asile de la Sainte Enfance* in the late nineteenth century. They managed an orphanage, a nursery, and homes for the blind, destitute, and aged women. The Canossian Sisters carried out similar functions, setting up homes for the poor and the blind and an orphanage. The Little Sisters of the Poor took charge of St. Joseph's Home for the Aged. In addition, women religious opened hospitals for local people, such as Saint Paul's Hospital of the St. Paul de Chartres Sisters, Canossa Hospital of the Canossian Sisters, and Precious Blood Hospital of the Precious Blood Sisters.

The other level of Catholic service was that of lay associations. Under the Bishop's initiative, Catholic Action began in 1931 and attempted to coordinate the various social and welfare activities of the lay community.[64] Catholic Action represented an agglomerate of the efforts of Catholics to be of service to needy and less fortunate groups, while at the same time to be examples of the Christian way of life to society. According to its constitutions, Catholic Action was the "apostolate of the faithful laity who under the guidance of the Hierarchy give a helping hand to the Church of God, so completing in a certain way a pastoral ministry."[65] Its objective was the "organization of the laity in associations under the guidance of the Catholic Hierarchy, so that . . . individual lives are improved, the rights of the Church defended and the growth of Catholic Religion attended to with zeal and courage excluding any . . . participation in political parties or factions."[66] Catholic Action assumed "no political character." On the committee chaired by the Bishop, representatives came from the Catholic Union Club (the members were mostly Portuguese), St. Patrick's Club (mostly Irish and English), the Chinese Catholic Youth Society (for both men and women), St. Teresa's Association (for Portuguese women), and the Society of Catholic Men.[67] With the creation of Catholic Action, the Chinese Catholic Young Men's Society became more active. Its members were increasingly involved in the catechetical apostolate, and went on mission tours to villages in the New Territories, starting doctrine classes in places where they had previously been nonexistent.

With the outbreak of the Sino-Japanese War (July 7, 1937) in Northeast China, the Church became increasingly aware of the plight of the Chinese people. Therefore, in August Bishop Valtorta sent a pastoral letter to the Catholic community in Hong Kong, asking them to be alert to developments in the interior. As he wrote:

> . . .we wish to remind you of the general strict duty which you have to love your own country with that same kind of love which you have for your parents and, consequently your strict duty to do everything in your power to help it. We must keep in mind that the Commandment of God "Honour thy father and thy mother" applies also to our country and, consequently, failure to honour and help our country is a sin just as it is a sin to refuse [to give] honour or help to our own parents. Let all Catholics remember this and resolve to be an example to all others in the fulfillment of all civic duties towards the country.[68]

As we see, there was emphasis on the loyalty of the Chinese to their motherland. In line with this, the Bishop asked for donations to the poor in China:

> Lastly, let us give alms, according to our capabilities and in proportion of our means, for the relief of those who are made homeless or destitute or are wounded in the course of war. Any help given to the Red Cross of China would serve this purpose. Of course, the vast majority of our Christians are very poor, but even the poor can give something and add a few drops to the mighty river of charity. A good idea would be, for those who freely choose to fast once a week, to offer, at least as a

> minimum, the price of their own fasting, which would thus become a very holy and meritorious way of practicing together both mortification and alms-giving, and could not fail to call down abundant blessings from Heaven. We also suggest that all these alms be given over to specifically appointed members of the Catholic Action or even to the local Missionaries, in order that they can be collected together and, through the President of the Catholic Action, be handed over to the Red Cross of China.[69]

The following is a breakdown of the missionary groups and their undertakings in Hong Kong at the end of 1938: the Milan Seminary for Foreign Missions continued to have jurisdiction over the Hong Kong Vicariate Apostolic, with Bishop Henry Valtorta as Vicar Apostolic, 37 missionaries from the seminary, and one Brother to carry on missionary work. A Milan priest served as procurator at St. Margaret Mary's Church in Happy Valley. Twenty-one Chinese priests had come from the local native seminary. The rector of St. Anthony's Church in West Point came from the Salesian Congregation. The Salesians were also responsible for their seminary in Shaukiwan, and for the St. Louis Industrial School and the Aberdeen Industrial School. The rector of the Roman Catholic Chapel in Pokfulam was a member of the Paris Foreign Missionary Society. The Paris society had its procure on Battery Path, and ran a sanatorium, as well as Nazareth House, in Pokfulam.[70] In charge of the Regional Seminary for South China in Aberdeen, the Jesuits also supervised the Ricci Hall in Pokfulam, Wah Yan College on Robinson Road, and Loyola House (their language school) in the New Territories. The Maryknoll Fathers had their mission house in Stanley, and the Franciscan missionaries had their procure on Boundary Street, Kowloon Tong. The Dominican Fathers had their procure on Seymour Road, and set up the Dominican House of Studies on Stubbs Road. The La Salle Brothers administered St. Joseph's College on Kennedy Road, La Salle College on Prince Edward Road, and St. Anthony's Catechumens' House in the New Territories. There were also military chaplains in Hong Kong.[71]

Women's congregations were mainly involved in social services and education.[72] The St. Paul de Chartres Sisters founded the *Asile de la Ste. Enfance* in Causeway Bay, which housed the St. Paul's Institution, the Anglo-French School, an orphanage, a nursery, a home for the blind, St. Paul's Laundry, and the French Convent Hostel. They also set up Saint Paul Hospital in Causeway Bay, a Home for Destitute and Aged Women in Happy Valley, St. Theresa Nursing Home on Prince Edward Road, St. Marguerite Vernacular School, and the Chinese School in Pokfulam. The Canossian Sisters' delegation house was on

Austin Road and their regional house (convent) was on Caine Road. They founded St. Mary's School on Austin Road, the English School and Pui Ching Chinese School on Caine Road, the Canossa Free School on Mosque Street, the Chinese School in Hunghom, the Sacred Heart Foundling Home in West Point, and the Chinese School in Aberdeen. They also took charge of the Home for the Poor in Wanchai, a Chinese orphanage, Canossa Hospital, and a home for blind girls.

The Chinese Sisters of the Precious Blood had their motherhouse and novitiate in Shamshuipo, and opened the Precious Blood Hospital in the same district. They set up Tak-Ching Girls School in Shamshuipo, Ching-Kao Girls School in Saiwanho, Tak-Ying Girls' School in Wanchai, Tak-Yan Girls School, and Tak-Ying School (1st Branch) in Yaumati, and Tak-Ying School (2nd Branch) in West Point. The Maryknoll Sisters set up their houses in the two girls' schools: Maryknoll Convent School on Boundary Street and Holy Spirit School on Caine Road. They also ran a Sunday School for Mexican Children in Maryknoll Convent School. The Little Sisters of the Poor took charge of the St. Joseph's Home for the Aged. The Sisters of Our Lady of the Angels established St. Clare's English School for Girls. The Sisters of the Immaculate Conception founded Tak-Sun School for Girls. In Stanley, Sisters set up the Carmelite Convent.

Conclusion

The interwar years witnessed the growth and development of the Catholic Church, which paid particular attention to social welfare, services, and education. While the Church defined its prime objective as evangelization, it had to find ways to make its presence felt and to become an active member of society. Religious activities alone were not sufficient to attract a bigger audience and to achieve the goal of drawing in more converts. The Church came to realize that the best way to be accepted was to pay heed to the actual needs of society at large, to be sensitive to local demands, and to see matters from local perspectives. Therefore, the Church saw secular activities (not just religious functions) as a means to open opportunities for evangelization. Gradually, it became very much involved in social services, and established itself as a crucial actor in community affairs.

By making itself useful to the local community, through both religious and secular activities, the Church developed very successfully in Hong Kong. Catholic schools became a guarantee of quality education, and graduates were able to master practical skills so as to find jobs and to earn a reasonable income. It was not that many of the graduates were themselves Catholics, but through education they were able to lift themselves from poverty and secure a better standard of living. For a long time, the Church was working for the welfare of the poor and the less fortunate. Besides schools, it set up orphanages, homes for the blind and the aged, hospitals, and other welfare organizations. In a society with little concern for social welfare, the Church had found an opening for itself—a role to perform—in the wide-open fields of social service and education.

With the arrival of foreign missionaries, the Church became an agglomerate of different ethnic groups, serving a Hong Kong society of equally mixed ethnicity. The earliest missionaries were the Italians and French, later came also the Irish, the Spanish, Americans, and Canadians. Local seminaries trained Chinese priests and nuns. While they shared the same Christian faith and swore obedience to the Vatican, the Catholic missionaries had to learn to work together as a mixed group comprising people of different nationalities, languages, and cultures. On the one hand, they had to adapt to local circumstances; on the other, they had to be able to work within their own Catholic community, which was of mixed ethnicity. The years before the Second World War were years of adaptation and adjustment, and in the process the Church witnessed an evolution in its work and its emphases. It changed and grew together with Hong Kong society. These years constituted a crucial period in the early history of the Catholic Church in Hong Kong, serving as a preparation for the successes it would later enjoy in the post–Second World War era.

NOTES

1. Patricia Neils, ed., *United States Attitudes and Policies toward China: The Impact of American Missionaries* (Armonk: M. E. Sharpe, 1990).
2. Li Li, "Diversifying the Operation: Southern Baptist Missions in China at the Turn of the Century 1890–1910," *Baptist History and Heritage*, vol. 34, no. 2 (1999), pp. 42–55; Cindy Yik-yi Chu, "From the Pursuit of Converts to the Relief of Refugees: The Maryknoll Sisters in Twentieth-Century Hong Kong," *The Historian*, vol. 65, no. 2 (Winter 2002), pp. 353–76.
3. Adrian A. Bennett, *Missionary Journalist in China: Young J. Allen and His Magazines, 1860–1883* (Athens: University of Georgia Press, 1983); Lawrence D. Kessler, *The Jiangyin Mission Station: An American Missionary Community in China 1895–1951* (Chapel Hill: University of North Carolina Press, 1996).

4. Thomas F. Ryan, *The Story of a Hundred Years: The Pontifical Institute of Foreign Missions, (P.I.M.E.), in Hong Kong, 1858–1958* (Hong Kong: Catholic Truth Society, 1959), pp. 1–2.
5. *Xianggang Tianzhujiaohui yibai wushi zhounian jinian tekan* (The Special Bulletin for the 150th Anniversary of the Catholic Church in Hong Kong) (Hong Kong: Catholic Church, 1991; in both Chinese and English), p. 5.
6. Ryan, *The Story of a Hundred Years*, p. 2.
7. T. F. Ryan, "Survey of a Century," in *Catholic Hong Kong: A Hundred Years of Missionary Activity* (Hong Kong: Catholic Press Bureau, 1958), p. 7.
8. Ibid.
9. *Souvenir Number of the Golden Jubilee of the Catholic Cathedral in Hong-Kong 1888-8th December-1938: Catholic Directory of the Vicariate Apostolic of Hong-kong and Calendar for 1939* (Hong Kong: Catholic Church, 1939), p. 11; Bernard Hung-kay Luk, "A Brief Outline of the History of the Catholic Church in Hong Kong," 1991, p. 3, Folder 3, Box 22: Historical Research, Manuscripts, Booklets, Pamphlets on Hong Kong Catholic Church (1835–1991), Section I: Hong Kong Roman Catholic Church as an Ecclesiastical and Civil Entity, Hong Kong Catholic Diocesan Archives, Hong Kong.
10. Ryan, *The Story of a Hundred Years*, pp. 2, 5–7; *The Special Bulletin for the 150th Anniversary of the Catholic Church in Hong Kong*, pp. 5–7.
11. Ryan, *The Story of a Hundred Years*, pp. 2–4.
12. Ibid., pp. 47 and 51.
13. *The Special Bulletin for the 150th Anniversary of the Catholic Church in Hong Kong*, pp. 8–9.
14. *Vicariatus Apostolicus Hongkong, Prospectus Generalis Operis Missionalis*, n.d., Folder 2, Box 10: Reports, Statistics and Related Correspondence (1969), Accumulative and Comparative Statistics (1842–1963), Section I, Hong Kong Catholic Diocesan Archives.
15. Ryan, *The Story of a Hundred Years*, p. 145.
16. Sergio Ticozzi, *Historical Documents of the Hong Kong Catholic Church* (Hong Kong: Hong Kong Catholic Diocesan Archives, 1997), p. 118.
17. Ryan, *The Story of a Hundred Years*, p. 146.
18. Ibid., p. 147; Ticozzi, *Historical Documents of the Hong Kong Catholic Church*, p. 119.
19. Ticozzi, *Historical Documents of the Hong Kong Catholic Church*, p. 119.
20. Ryan, *The Story of a Hundred Years*, pp. 149–51.
21. Ibid., p. 151; Ticozzi, *Historical Documents of the Hong Kong Catholic Church*, p. 121.
22. Ryan, *The Story of a Hundred Years*, pp. 151–52.
23. *Vicariatus Apostolicus Hongkong, Prospectus Generalis Operis Missionalis.*

24. Catholic Foreign Mission Society of America, *Maryknoll: Hong Kong Chronicle* (Hong Kong: Catholic Foreign Mission Society of America, 1978), p. 1.
25. Ryan, *The Story of a Hundred Years*, p. 152.
26. *Souvenir Number of the Golden Jubilee of the Catholic Cathedral in Hong-Kong 1888-8th December-1938*, p. 12.
27. Leon Triviere, "Nazareth House, Hong Kong" (Hong Kong: n.p., 1954?), p. 2.
28. Ticozzi, *Historical Documents of the Hong Kong Catholic Church*, p. 123.
29. Ibid.
30. *The Rock: Hong Kong Catholic Monthly*, vol. 4, nos. 10–11 (July–August 1924).
31. Ticozzi, *Historical Documents of the Hong Kong Catholic Church*, p. 123.
32. *Vicariatus Apostolicus Hongkong, Prospectus Generalis Operis Missionalis; Status Animarum*, Folder 2, Box 10: Reports, Statistics and Related Correspondence (1969), Accumulative and Comparative Statistics (1842–1963), Section I, Hong Kong Catholic Diocesan Archives.
33. Catholic Foreign Mission Society of America, *Maryknoll: Hong Kong Chronicle*, p. 4.
34. Stephen H. L. Law, "Social Commitments of the Catholic Church in Hong Kong: Education," paper presented at "Seminar on Catholic Archives Records" of Hong Kong Catholic Diocesan Archives and Hong Kong Catholic Social Communications Office, January 5, 1995, p. 17.
35. Catholic Foreign Mission Society of America, *Maryknoll: Hong Kong Chronicle*, p. 4.
36. Catholic Diocese of Hong Kong, *Xianggang Tianzhujiao jiaoyu jianjie* (A Brief Introduction to Catholic Education in Hong Kong) (Hong Kong: Exhibition of Catholic Church, 1900), p. 7.
37. Law, "Social Commitments of the Catholic Church in Hong Kong: Education," p. 2.
38. Ryan, *The Story of a Hundred Years*, p. 36.
39. Ibid., p. 29.
40. Law, "Social Commitments of the Catholic Church in Hong Kong: Education," p. 2.
41. Ibid., p. 14.
42. Ibid., p. 2.
43. Ibid., p. 21.
44. Newspaper clipping, entitled "Death of Bishop Pozzoni: Succumbs Suddenly at French Hospital; Nearly 40 Years in Diocese," February 21, 1924, Folder 5, Box 8: Msgr. Domenico Pozzoni, 3rd Vicar Apostolic (1905–1924), Section II: Hierarchy, Hong Kong Catholic Diocesan Archives.
45. Ryan, *The Story of a Hundred Years*, p. 154.

46. Sister Mary Imelda Sheridan, "A History of the South China Region 1921–1958," 1959, p. 6, Folder 1, Box 1, South China Region: Hong Kong/ Macau Region, 1921–, Maryknoll Mission Archives, Maryknoll, New York.
47. Ibid., p. 7.
48. Law, "Social Commitments of the Catholic Church in Hong Kong: Education," p. 18.
49. Ticozzi, *Historical Documents of the Hong Kong Catholic Church*, p. 137.
50. Ibid., p. 136.
51. Ibid., p. 137.
52. Ibid.
53. Letter from Sister Mary Paul McKenna (Superior of Maryknoll Sisters in Hong Kong) to Mother Mary Joseph Rogers (Mother General in Maryknoll, New York State), May 9, 1923, p. 1, Folder 2, Box 1, Regional Correspondence: South China, Maryknoll Mission Archives.
54. Bishop Dominic Pozzoni, Vicar Apostolic, to A. G. M. Fletcher, Colonial Secretary, May 16, 1923, 1 page, and June 30, 1923, 2 pages, Folder 1, Box 10: St. Teresa's Church, Section IV: Territorial Subdivision, Hong Kong Catholic Diocesan Archives; Letter from A. E. Wright, Pro-Director of Public Works, to Colonial Secretary, June 5, 1923, HKRS 58-1-114–46 "Application of Roman Catholic Mission for Three Areas near Kowloon Tong for Erection of Church, Training School, Girls' School and Houses for Portuguese," Public Records Office, Hong Kong.
55. Ryan, *The Story of a Hundred Years*, pp. 197–98.
56. *Vicariatus Apostolicus Hongkong, Prospectus Generalis Operis Missionalis.*
57. Ryan, *The Story of a Hundred Years*, pp. 192–95.
58. Ibid., p. 194.
59. Ticozzi, *Historical Documents of the Hong Kong Catholic Church*, p. 143.
60. Ibid.
61. Ticozzi, *Historical Documents of the Hong Kong Catholic Church*, pp. 144–45.
62. *Vicariatus Apostolicus Hongkong, Prospectus Generalis Operis Missionalis.*
63. Stephen H. L. Law, "Social Commitments of the Catholic Church in Hong Kong: Welfare Services," paper presented at "Seminar on Catholic Archives Records" of Hong Kong Catholic Diocesan Archives and Hong Kong Catholic Social Communications Office, January 5, 1995, pp. 1–2.
64. Ryan, *The Story of a Hundred Years*, p. 202.
65. *General Constitutions of Catholic Action (Extract)* (Hong Kong: Apostolic Delegation of China, n.d. [1931?]), p. 2, Box 57: Catholic

Action, Section V: Mission Personnel, Hong Kong Catholic Diocesan Archives.

66. Ibid.
67. Ryan, *The Story of a Hundred Years*, pp. 202–03.
68. Ticozzi, *Historical Documents of the Hong Kong Catholic Church*, p. 156.
69. Ibid., p. 157.
70. The word "procure" was often used among missionaries. As Jean-Paul Wiest explains: "This word, borrowed from the French, is a term commonly used by Catholic missionary societies. It refers to a house or office in some convenient location to which missioners can look for service in procuring needed supplies, exchanging checks, and so forth. A procure also serves, when large enough, as a hostel for passing missioners." Read Jean-Paul Wiest, *Maryknoll in China: A History, 1918–1955* (Armonk: M. E. Sharpe, 1988), p. 60 footnote.
71. *Souvenir Number of the Golden Jubilee of the Catholic Cathedral in Hong-Kong 1888-8th December-1938*, pp. 21–22, 47.
72. Ibid., pp. 49–57.

Chapter 6

Making of a Japanese Community in Prewar Period (1841–1941)

Benjamin Wai-ming Ng

Introduction

The Japanese in prewar Hong Kong were a medium-sized but fast-growing, united, and influential foreign community. They played an important role in promoting Sino-Japanese and Anglo-Japanese political, economic, and cultural interaction. Yet Hong Kong people had mixed feelings toward the Japanese in this period. Japanese investment in Hong Kong and Japan–Hong Kong bilateral trade strengthened Hong Kong's position as a leading trading port in Asia as well as a business and industrial base in South China. The Japanese also introduced a new cultural diversity to Hong Kong. However, due to anti-Japanese sentiments, many Hong Kong people have chosen to ignore or deny the Japanese legacy in Hong Kong, seeing the involvement of the Japanese in Hong Kong's history solely as a succession of imperialistic acts. There have been almost no studies in English on the Japanese in prewar Hong Kong.[1] Using Japanese primary sources as the main references, this chapter aims to provide a balanced historical overview of the Japanese community in prewar Hong Kong, focusing on its political and economic activities and its impact on Hong Kong's politics, its economy, and its society.

A Changing Japanese Community in Prewar Hong Kong

The Japanese do not have a very long history in Hong Kong. Although Japanese merchants and pirates had been calling at different Chinese ports since the fifteenth century, Hong Kong was not visited because it became a trading port only in the mid-nineteenth century. In 1841, the crew of a wrecked Japanese ship, *Kannon Maru*, were carried to Macau via Hong Kong. They stayed for only two or three days, and were the first group of Japanese to visit Hong Kong. Four years later, in 1845, rescued by Macau fishermen in the Philippines, four Japanese fishermen were carried to Hong Kong via Macau. Two of them, Shozo and Rikimatsu, decided to stay, and became the first Japanese residents in Hong Kong. The former married a Chinese woman and accumulated a fortune in tailoring. The latter married an American woman and ran a grocery. Before the founding of the Japanese consulate in Hong Kong in 1874, Shozo served as a kind of unofficial consul, and generously offered his assistance to his countrymen in Hong Kong. In 1855, Rikimatsu helped the British to conclude a treaty with Japan by serving as an interpreter.[2]

After Shozo and Rikimatsu, a small number of Japanese (mostly officials, merchants, and fishermen) visited Hong Kong in the 1850s and 1860s. After the Meiji Restoration in 1868 and the opening of the Japanese consulate in Hong Kong in 1874, the number of Japanese visiting Hong Kong increased considerably and, as a result, a small Japanese community began to emerge in the 1870s.

From the 1870s to the early 1940s, the Japanese community in Hong Kong underwent several dramatic changes. First, the population greatly increased, from dozens in the 1870s to more than two thousand in the 1930s.[3] Throughout the late nineteenth century, the population rose steadily. From 13 Japanese in Hong Kong in 1875, their number increased to 86 in 1880, and 243 in 1889.[4] In the first half of the twentieth century, the Japanese population increased even more sharply. From 421 Japanese in Hong Kong in 1901, their number jumped to 1,099 in 1911, 1,585 in 1921, and 2,205 in 1931.[5] In the 1930s, the Japanese community developed into one of the largest foreign communities in Hong Kong. In 1941, due to the Second World War (1939–1945), the Japanese population dropped to 393.

It is clear that the growth of the Japanese population in Hong Kong was affected by Japan's economy and foreign relations. More Japanese came to Hong Kong when Japan experienced an economic boom (such as in the late Meiji period, itself from 1868–1912 and the early Showa period, itself from 1926–1989) or won international recognition (such as in the time following the Sino-Japanese War, 1894–1895 and the Russo-Japanese War, 1904–1905). Fewer Japanese came when anti-Japanese feelings were strong in Hong Kong due to deteriorating ties between Japan and China, or between Japan and the United Kingdom (in the 1880s, for example, and the late 1930s).

Second, there was a change in the distribution of the Japanese population by gender, profession, and geographic location. In the late nineteenth century, the majority of the Japanese in Hong Kong were females (mostly prostitutes). As increasing numbers of Japanese men came, by the turn of the twentieth century, the number of Japanese males began to exceed the females. The social status of the Japanese improved over these decades.[6] In the late nineteenth century, the Japanese residents of Hong Kong were mostly from the lower end of Japanese society. The majority were prostitutes from Kyushu, the so-called *karayuki-san* (literally, people going abroad), unskilled laborers, and gangsters. They were all but social outcasts in Japan, discriminated against by the public and unprotected by the Japanese government. They worked as prostitutes, brothel-keepers, grocery shopkeepers, and hawkers in Hong Kong. The Japanese consulate in Hong Kong initially paid little attention to these groups of Japanese. In contrast, in the early twentieth century, the majority of the Japanese population in Hong Kong were businessmen, in particular expatriates working for big Japanese corporations such as Mitsui and Mitsubishi.[7] These educated, qualified, and promising members of the social elite established and ran various Japanese organizations in Hong Kong under the auspices of the Japanese consulate. The Japanese government made use of the Japanese community in Hong Kong for various purposes, such as intelligence, propaganda, fund raising, and lobbying.

Following the rise of the Japanese population in Hong Kong, their geographic distribution also changed. In the beginning, the majority of the Japanese lived in the Central District (including Mid-Levels). By the beginning of the twentieth century, Wanchai became a more popular choice for Japanese residents. In general, Japanese executives, officials, and employees of big companies preferred Central, whereas Japanese prostitutes, small businessmen, and shopkeepers lived in Wanchai. According to a survey conducted in the mid-1910s, about 50 percent of the Japanese lived in Wanchai (including Happy Valley) and 40 percent lived in the Central District (including Mid-Levels). The remaining 10 percent lived in South Kowloon (in such districts as

Tsim Sha Tsui, Yau Ma Tei, and Hung Hom).[8] In the 1920s and 1930s, the Japanese spread all over the urban districts in Hong Kong Island and Kowloon.

Third, the Japanese community became increasingly united and influential. In the late nineteenth century, the Japanese community in Hong Kong was small and loosely organized. The Japanese consulate in Hong Kong was the center of the Japanese community, but—due to a shortage of manpower and funding—it did not exercise strong leadership. Its primary concerns were to serve the interests of the Japanese government and big companies, not the well-being of Japanese residents in Hong Kong. Thus, it organized few activities for the Japanese residents in Hong Kong. Its only regular contact with Japanese residents was made through the annual census. In the early years, brothel bosses became the de facto community leaders among the Japanese in Hong Kong. For example, they managed the Japanese Cemetery in Happy Valley (founded in 1878).

In the early twentieth century, executives of large Japanese companies (such as Mitsui, Mitsubishi, the Yokohama Shokin Bank, and the Taiwan Bank) assumed leadership of the Japanese community through the Japanese Club (founded in 1905, renamed the Japanese Association in 1921). The Japanese Club, in place of the Japanese consulate, became the center of the Japanese community. The Japanese Club was a semiofficial organization, initiated by and working closely with the Japanese consulate. The Japanese consul was also an executive member of the Japanese Club.

The Japanese Club ran the Japanese Primary School, managed the Japanese Cemetery, and organized many social and cultural activities for Japanese residents in Hong Kong. In 1911, the Japanese Primary School was founded on Kennedy Road. There were not many Japanese children in Hong Kong (usually no more than a hundred), as Japanese expatriates usually came to Hong Kong alone, and few of them settled in the territory with their families. The clubhouse of the Japanese Club (established in Central in 1906) and the Japanese Primary School became the venues for many of their functions. Under the management of the Japanese Club, the Japanese Cemetery became increasingly used, 465 being buried there between 1878 and 1945 (the majority were prostitutes who died in the Meiji era).[9]

The Japanese Club was developed from Yamato-kai (founded in 1903), a group of Japanese executives who met to socialize and play tennis, and it thus had a strong sports tradition. It held baseball and tennis tournaments twice a year. The Japanese Club also organized sports days, vaccination days, picnics, study tours, classes, concerts, parties, festivals, and many other social and cultural functions for its members. Many Japanese joined the Japanese Club to meet social, educational, and psychological needs. Its clubhouse had a billiard room, a library, a common room, a Japanese restaurant, and a bar. The Club was exclusively for Japanese. It had limited contacts with local residents and other foreign communities in Hong Kong. The Japanese government did not make full use of the Club's potential as a vehicle for cultural diplomacy.

Besides the Japanese Club, the Japanese founded other organizations to bring their countrymen together. Major Japanese companies joined the Hong Kong Japanese Chamber of Commerce (Honkon Nihon Shoko Kaigisho) for networking and information, whereas small Japanese shops could acquire loans from the Japanese Society for Promoting Business (Nihonjin Shokyosha, founded in 1915). The Honganji Temple of Kyoto sent monks to Hong Kong from 1900 onward, and was very active in providing various facilities to Japanese residents in Hong Kong, including running a Japanese primary school, a Japanese cemetery, and a temple in So Kon Po (in Wanchai).

POLITICAL ACTIVITIES OF THE JAPANESE IN PREWAR HONG KONG

Hong Kong, as the gateway to political influence with the Chinese and the British, was a place with special significance to Japan. The Japanese consulate was the second Japanese consulate established in Asia. The first one was in Shanghai. It represented Japan's interests not only in Hong Kong but also in the entire Guangdong province. In the nineteenth century, there were only three or four staff (consul, secretary, and interpreter[s]) working at the consulate in Central, Hong Kong Island. In the early twentieth century, it developed into one of the largest foreign consulates in Hong Kong. Its main objective was to protect and enlarge Japanese interests in Hong Kong and China. Japan used Hong Kong as a base in South China to conduct political and diplomatic activities.

Hong Kong, the "Casablanca of the Far East," was an ideal place to gather information about China, the United Kingdom, and the world, whether by legal means or otherwise. As early as the 1850s, the Japanese government, under the shogunate in Edo, circulated Hong Kong Chinese newspapers among high-ranking officials.[10] In 1874, the Japanese consulate in Hong Kong began reporting to Tokyo on the latest international affairs. For example, when France invaded Vietnam in 1885, the Japanese consulate in Hong Kong became

Japan's major source of information about the Sino-French War (1884–1885).[11] During the Sino-Japanese War, the Japanese sent officials to Hong Kong to gather information.[12] In 1887, the Ministry of Foreign Affairs in Japan began, every so often, dispatching Japanese students to study Cantonese (*Guangdonghua*) and English in Hong Kong. Some of these students later worked for the Japanese consulate in Hong Kong or in China for intelligence purposes.[13] The Japanese community also helped the Japanese government gather information and spread political propaganda. For instance, the *Hong Kong News Press* (*Honkon Nipposha*, established in 1911), one of the largest newspaper agencies in prewar Hong Kong, was actually financed and controlled by the Japanese government. It published three dailies (one in Japanese, one in Chinese, and one in English) as part of Japan's efforts at cultural diplomacy. It employed many reporters, some of whom performed intelligence functions. In addition, the Yokohama Shokin Bank (Yokohama Shokin Ginko) and the Taiwan Bank (Taiwan Ginko) conducted surveys on different aspects of political and economic conditions in Hong Kong.[14]

Hong Kong was important in promoting Anglo-Japanese political, economic, and military ties. British and Japanese officials in Hong Kong visited each other frequently, communicating in English, sometimes through interpreters. In the Meiji period, many Japanese noblemen, senior ministers, generals, and admirals visited Hong Kong, including such prominent figures as Ito Hirobumi, Togo Heihachiro, Kuroda Kiyotaka, and Oyama Iwao. Leading Japanese intellectuals such as Fukuzawa Yukichi, Mori Ogai, Oka Senjin, and Tokutomi Soho also visited Hong Kong. In the early Meiji period, the Japanese regarded Hong Kong as one of their models for modernization and thus some of these visits were in the nature of study tours. They usually visited government houses, military facilities, schools (in particular Ying Wa College, which was famous for Western education and Western publications), hospitals, and prisons. Besides Westernized institutes and systems, the Japanese were impressed by the British colonial administration, which emphasized economic development and made good use of the local Chinese to implement British policies and laws. When Japan conquered Taiwan, it initially sought to apply the "Hong Kong model."[15]

Hong Kong also played a role in Japan's modernization in the Meiji period. Some big British and Chinese firms (such as the Hongkong Bank, Jardine, and Lane Crawford) set up branches in Yokohama, Kobe, and Nagasaki. The Hongkong Bank offered loans to the Japanese government.[16] Lane Crawford opened the first Western tailoring outlet in Japan. The Hong Kong government sold its Mint facilities and transferred its know-how to help Meiji Japan set up the National Mint Bureau in Osaka.[17] Impressed by Hong Kong's architecture, with its mix of East and West, the Japanese built a cluster of Hong Kong-style buildings in South Kyobashi in Tokyo.[18] Hong Kong small merchants also tried their luck in areas in which Japan lagged behind Hong Kong, including Western-style tailoring, Western-style hairdressing, accounting, and engineering.

There were particularly active military exchanges between Hong Kong and Japan. Beginning in 1874, Japanese naval ships called at Hong Kong every year for supplies and exchanges. In the 1880s, the Japanese navy ordered a battleship from the British, which was manufactured at the dock in Aberdeen in Hong Kong Island. Shortly after the Mino-Owari Earthquake of 1891, Hong Kong merchants and the British military in Hong Kong raised relief funds for Japan. During the Sino-Japanese War in 1894, British ships in Hong Kong provided military supplies for Japan as a gesture of goodwill. Under the Anglo-Japanese Alliance (1902–1923), the military exchanges between Hong Kong and Japan became more frequent and formal. The British invited Japanese naval officers to visit navy bases and defense facilities in fortresses and barracks, and organized parties for officials of the two countries in Hong Kong.

Japan reciprocated British hospitality by inviting Hong Kong Governors and high-ranking military men and officials to visit Japan. The Japanese treated these official visits very seriously. For instance, in 1879 Japan invited the Hong Kong Governor John Pope Hennessy to visit Japan, the first such visit by a Hong Kong Governor. Japan hosted the two-month visit, and the Japanese consul Ando Taro accompanied the Hong Kong Governor to different parts of Japan throughout the visit. The Finance Minister of Japan, Okuma Shigenobu, even accompanied the Hong Kong Governor on his visit of Hakotate in Hokkaido.[19] At the request of the Hong Kong Governor, Japan set up several plants in Hong Kong.[20] In 1884, a second Hong Kong Governor, George Bowen, also visited Japan for about two months.

In 1894, thousands of people died of bubonic plague in Hong Kong. The Japanese government sent a medical team to Hong Kong to investigate the cause of the disease. One of the team members caught the disease and almost lost his life. Later the team leader, Kitazato Shibasaburo, became the first person to discover the bacteria.[21] The Hong Kong government highly appreciated the efforts of the Japanese medical team.

Hong Kong was important for Japan in enhancing its political influence in China. The Japanese consulate in Hong Kong was placed in charge of matters relating to Japanese interests throughout Guangdong province. In the beginning, Japan established consulates in Shanghai and Hong Kong only. These two cities were used for various political purposes. Hong Kong, as a British colony, gave the Japanese more freedom to conduct political activities such as lobbying, negotiating, spreading propaganda, and spying. The Japanese consul did not spend all his time in Hong Kong, and went to China frequently to meet with high-ranking Chinese officials. For example, in 1877, the first Japanese consul, Ando Taro, visited Liu Kunyi, the Governor of Guangdong and Guangxi. In 1884, the deputy Japanese consul Machida Sanekazu visited Zhang Zhidong, the Governor of Guangdong and Guangxi and one of the most influential statesmen in late Qing China. The Japanese government saw its consul in Hong Kong as a kind of expert and consultant on Chinese affairs. When Japanese envoys and ministers went to China, the consul usually joined the group. For instance, in 1884, Japanese Consul Ando Taro accompanied the Meiji political leader Ito Hirobumi to Guangdong province. The Japanese Army and the Ministry of Foreign Affairs sent students to study Cantonese and English in Hong Kong. On graduation, many worked for the intelligence department and some later became administrative officers in China during the Second World War. The Japanese consulate in Hong Kong also got involved in China's internal politics. It tried to influence Sun Yat-sen through Miyazaki Toten (who was a life-long friend of Sun and supported the revolutionary movement in China by providing funds and weapons).[22] It also helped Sun flee to Japan after the failure of the Guangzhou (Canton) Uprising in 1895. Likewise, after the failure of the Hundred Days Reform in 1898, the Japanese consulate in Hong Kong helped Kang Youwei escape to Hong Kong and then to Japan.[23]

Economic Activities of the Japanese in Prewar Hong Kong

The Japanese community was made up of people the majority of whom had come to Hong Kong for economic reasons. Japan's investment in and trade with Hong Kong started in the 1870s. By the early twentieth century, its investment in and trade with the territory was on a larger scale than any other country's. Japanese economic activities in Hong Kong can be divided into three major sectors: retailing and servicing, prostitution, and maritime trade. The first two sectors were influential in the late nineteenth century, whereas maritime trade became dominant in the early twentieth century.

In the late nineteenth century, some Japanese individuals and families used their limited resources to set up small businesses in retailing and servicing in Hong Kong. These small businesses included groceries, Japanese-style inns, Japanese restaurants, Japanese-style barber shops, photo shops, clinics, *kimono* shops, and Japanese bookstores. With the exception of the grocery stores, most of these shops primarily served the Japanese, both Japanese residents in Hong Kong (such as prostitutes, shop owners, and expatriates), and Japanese visitors (such as soldiers, businessmen, and officials). In terms of numbers, the Japanese set up more grocery stores than any other type of shop. Japanese products were also quite popular among Hong Kong people on account of their fine quality and affordable prices. It is said that the fisherman Rikimatsu ran a Chinese grocery store, but we do not know the details. Records indicate that Japanese grocery stores were established in Hong Kong no later than the 1870s. Since there were only a few dozen Japanese in Hong Kong at that time, these early Japanese shops targeted mainly British and Hong Kong people. Suruura and Kusakabe were two of the oldest Japanese grocery stores founded in Hong Kong. Suruura was perhaps the first. It was founded in Central in 1873 by a Nagasaki merchant, selling Japanese and Western commodities. Kusakabe opened on Queen's Road, Central in 1879, introducing Japanese goods such as chinaware, tea sets, cotton, and *yukata* (Japanese-style summer casual wear) to Hong Kong. Following the influx of the Japanese in the 1880s, various kinds of retailing and servicing shops began to emerge to serve the new immigrants. Since most Japanese lived in Wanchai and Central, the Japanese shops were also located in these two districts. In the early twentieth century, more Japanese shops were founded in these two districts, which were the general business and commercial centers in Hong Kong. Here the Chinese were in the majority, competing and working with Westerners, Japanese, and Indians in various economic activities. The Japanese were never the majority. Unlike Singapore or San Francisco, Hong Kong had no Japanese town. In terms of the geographical distribution of Japanese residents, members of the business elite and officials lived in the Central District (including Mid-Levels), whereas small businessmen, low-ranking employees, and prostitutes lived in Wanchai.

Prostitution was a major economic activity of the Japanese in prewar Hong Kong, particularly in the late nineteenth century. In the Meiji period, thousands of young Japanese women (an estimated

100,000) went to China and Southeast Asia to make their livings as prostitutes. In the late nineteenth century, Japanese prostitutes constituted the largest portion of the Japanese population in Hong Kong. They formed a consumption market to support many Japanese small businessmen such as retailers, hawkers, shopkeepers, tailors, barbers, chefs, photographers, and dentists. Hong Kong was a major distributing center of Japanese prostitution. Japanese women from poor villages in Kyushu were smuggled to Hong Kong in cargo ships (mostly carrying coal). Some died by suffocation on the way. Upon arrival, they were sold at HK$150–300.[24] The Hong Kong market was too small to absorb them, and after a short stay in Hong Kong to receive basic training, including learning simple English, most of them were reexported to mainland China or Southeast Asia.[25]

Japanese prostitutes began coming to Hong Kong in 1879. In the 1880s and 1890s, the majority of Japanese residents in Hong Kong were prostitutes. In 1885, Hong Kong had eight licensed Japanese brothels employing fifty-two Japanese prostitutes. The Japanese consulate asked the Hong Kong government to restrict the number of Japanese prostitutes in Hong Kong. In response, the Hong Kong government issued an edict freezing the number of Japanese brothels and Japanese prostitutes at the level that obtained in 1885. This edict was never strictly implemented, and the number of Japanese prostitutes continued to increase rapidly. In 1901, there were 13 licensed Japanese brothels and 132 Japanese prostitutes.[26] The number of licensed Japanese prostitutes reached a peak of 172 in 1908.[27] Hong Kong and Shanghai became the two largest markets for Japanese prostitutes in China. However, compared with Singapore, the scale of Japanese prostitution in Hong Kong was relatively small. At the same time, Singapore had more than a hundred Japanese brothels and nearly a thousand Japanese prostitutes.

There were two kinds of Japanese prostitutes in Hong Kong, licensed (or public) prostitutes and unlicensed (or private) prostitutes. Licensed prostitution was monitored by the Hong Kong government through the annual census, with the assistance of the Japanese consulate. Licensed prostitutes worked at brothels that had acquired a license from the Hong Kong government. Brothels paid taxes, and prostitutes received regular medical check-ups. These licensed Japanese brothels were called *kashizashiki* (literally, renting a small place). Each had 6–9 Japanese prostitutes. Licensed Japanese brothels were first located in Central (mostly on Hollywood Road, Stanley Street, and Wellington Street). Later, many moved to the seafront in Wanchai (mostly in the area around Spring Garden Lane and Sam Pan

Street). Japanese prostitutes working at the brothels in Central were called "shopping girls," and provided more expensive services than their counterparts in Wanchai. Spring Garden Lane and Sam Pan Street were the famous pleasure quarters in prewar Hong Kong, housing a large number of Japanese brothels. On these two streets, Japanese brothel keepers usually rented two or three-story Western-style houses for business. To make them more recognizable, Japanese red lanterns were hung in front of the building, where Japanese prostitutes wearing *kimono* or *yutaka* (usually in red color) waved and gave the eye to people on the street from the balcony on the second floor. The interior was furnished in Japanese style. Customers could have a snack and a bottle of Japanese beer on the ground floor before they went upstairs to be received by a prostitute. Japanese prostitutes provided cheap sex services to local Chinese people and Indians, as well as to foreign soldiers and merchants visiting Hong Kong. Being willing to serve anyone at affordable prices, Japanese prostitutes became the main competitors of local prostitutes at the low end of the market. Licensed Chinese brothels were located in Sheung Wan (Shui Hang Hau) and Western District (Shek Tong Tsui), and thus the competition between Japanese and Chinese prostitutes was not direct.

Many Japanese prostitutes enjoyed better economic conditions in Hong Kong than were available in their hometowns in Japan. They could eat meat and rice, have a hairdo, wear a *kimono*, as well as do some shopping. They worked hard, particularly in the evening and at night. They received about HK$7 for each transaction (a meal cost only 25 cents).[28] It usually took the first 3–5 years for the prostitutes to pay back their debt (they had obtained a loan before they left Japan). After that, they could choose to return to Japan or stay on to save money. Most decided to stay. They played an important role in helping their hometowns by remitting money. Some had extra money to lend at interest to small Japanese traders and hawkers in Hong Kong and South China. However, they were forced to retire when they reached their late thirties. Some returned to Japan and found that they were discriminated against by their government and their fellow countrymen. Some stayed on in Hong Kong as concubines of locals or Westerners.

The problem of unlicensed Japanese prostitution existed from the beginning. At first, unlicensed Japanese brothels—like the licensed Japanese brothels—were also located in Central and Wanchai, and hid themselves under the guise of cafes, Japanese-style inns, and restaurants. When the Hong Kong government tightened its control over prostitution, many unlicensed Japanese prostitutes moved out of these two districts and conducted their business secretly in other parts of Hong Kong Island. Some even went to Kowloon. Since these unlicensed Japanese prostitutes were not registered, their numbers remain unknown.[29] They offered their services at lower prices than their licensed counterparts. However, many suffered from poverty and poor health. Since their business was illegal, once caught by the Hong Kong government, they were sent to the Po Leung Kuk (a protection home for women and children founded in 1878). At one time, more than forty unlicensed Japanese prostitutes were kept there. The Hong Kong government passed them to the Japanese consulate for repatriation. However, the Japanese consulate lacked the resources to send them home. As a result, they were released, and many went back to their underground business. In 1932, the Hong Kong government abolished the licensed prostitution system, and many formerly licensed Japanese prostitutes went underground.

Maritime trade was the pillar of economic activity among the Japanese in prewar Hong Kong. Hong Kong overtook Macau to become the busiest port in South China, and one of the two most important trading ports in the China–Japan–Southeast Asia triangular maritime trade (the other was Shanghai). Maritime trade in Hong Kong was largely under the control of Chinese and British merchants. Japanese merchants only played a supplementary and secondary role. In the late nineteenth century, Japanese trading firms in Hong Kong had a difficult time competing with their Chinese and British counterparts. Several big Japanese trading firms set up their offices in Hong Kong (mostly in Central) in the 1870s and 1880s. In 1878 Mitsui Trading (Mitsui Bussan) established an office in Hong Kong (on Queen's Road, Central), marking the beginning of the influx of investment from big Japanese companies. Staffed with only five Japanese, Mitsui Trading was an import and export firm. Its main business in the early years in Hong Kong was to sell Japanese coal to Swire and Jardine, two of the largest British firms in Hong Kong. It also sold Japanese matches to Hong Kong. In the same year, another Japanese trading firm, Kogyo Commercial House (Kogyo Shokai) opened an office in Hong Kong. Unlike Mitsui Trading, it focused on imports and introduced Japanese products (in particular dried seafood) to Hong Kong. Both Mitsui Trading and Kogyo Commercial House closed in 1882, due to strong competition from British and Chinese trading houses. In 1879, Mitsubishi Steamship (Mitsubishi Kisen) launched its operation in Hong Kong. It opened direct sea traffic between Hong Kong and Japan by arranging two Japanese steamships to shuttle between Hong Kong and Yokohama/Kobe twice a month.

This made Hong Kong depend less on Shanghai in Hong Kong–Japan sea transportation.[30] When the first Japanese ship entered Hong Kong in 1879, the Hong Kong Governor Hennessy attended a reception luncheon held by Mitsubishi to show his support for Japanese investment and trade. In the 1880s, many Western firms (such as Jardine [United Kingdom], Cheung Hing [Canada], and Louis [Germany]) also operated direct sea transportation between Hong Kong and Kobe.[31] Hong Kong became Kobe's largest exporter.[32] Mitsubishi Steamship discontinued its operation in Hong Kong in 1884. In 1890, Nippon Liners (Nippon Yusen, which had been in Hong Kong since 1885) reopened the direct sea traffic between Hong Kong and Japan.

Japan–Hong Kong bilateral trade in the late nineteenth century was primarily an exchange of natural resources as well as agricultural and marine products. Only a small number of industrial products, finished or semifinished, was handled. Hong Kong functioned as a trading port rather than a consumption market for Japanese products. For some years in the late nineteenth century, Japan was Hong Kong's largest trading partner.[33] Hong Kong was important to Japan in international trade in the late nineteenth century. Products were exchanged between Japan and South China/Southeast Asia through Hong Kong. Japanese products shipped to Hong Kong included dried seafood and sundry items such as abalone, *shiitake* mushrooms and shark's fin, copper, coal, sulfur, and cotton. Products shipped from Hong Kong to Japan included rice (mostly from Vietnam), textiles (mostly from Luzon), and sugar. Japanese trade enriched the material lives of Hong Kong people and introduced them to the products of a different culture. For example, Japanese rickshaws were introduced to Hong Kong in 1874. Japanese *yukata*, beer, tea, and utensils had an impact on Hong Kong's consumption market. The Japanese also played a role in jumpstarting Hong Kong's movie industry. In 1905, when China produced its first movie, the Japanese showed a documentary film about the Russo-Japanese War in the open space in Central. It was the first time for many Hong Kong people to see a movie.

At first, the size of Japan–Hong Kong bilateral trade was very small. At the turn of the century, Hong Kong remained important to Japan in its trade with China, but became less important in international trade and total exports due to the development of Taiwan and international sea transportation. In the early twentieth century, Japan's exports to Hong Kong increased in actual volume but declined as a percentage of Japan's total exports.[34] Nevertheless, maritime trade became the largest economic activity among the

Japanese in prewar Hong Kong, overtaking servicing, retailing, and prostitution. Not only did Hong Kong continue to be a trading port for Japan–China–Southeast Asia triangular trade, it also gradually became a consumption market for Japanese products. In Hong Kong and China, Japanese products competed with European and Western products in the high-end market and Chinese and Southeast Asian products in the low-end market. The market share of Japanese products in Hong Kong expanded in the early twentieth century. Increasing numbers of Japanese firms set up their regional headquarters or branches in Hong Kong, and many enjoyed good business.

Major Japanese firms and banks were located in the Central District (especially in Mid-Levels, the area between MacDonnell Road and Bowen Road). In the 1930s, Japan became the third or fourth largest investor in Hong Kong, ranking only after China, the United Kingdom, and the United States.[35] The "big three" Japanese firms in early-twentieth-century Hong Kong were Mitsui Trading, Toyo Cotton (Toyo Menka, a subsidiary of the Mitsui Group, in Hong Kong since 1920), and Mitsubishi Trading (Mitsubishi Shoji, in Hong Kong since 1905). Fifty-five percent of Japanese investment in Hong Kong came from these three companies. Mitsui and Mitsubishi continued to be the two largest Japanese firms in Hong Kong.[36] Mitsui, the largest Japanese company in prewar Hong Kong, hired about 50 Japanese in the 1910s, and employee numbers increased to 198 (138 non-Japanese and 60 Japanese) in 1939.[37] In addition to maritime trade, the Japanese were strong in banking and sea transportation. Two major Japanese banks, the Taiwan Bank (in Hong Kong since 1903) and the Yokohama Shokin Bank, set up their branches in Hong Kong, offering services to Japanese and non-Japanese in financing, remittances, and loans.[38] The Taiwan Bank became the third largest bank in Hong Kong, smaller only than the Hongkong Bank and the Standard Chartered Bank. The Yokohama Shokin Bank, with the help of the Standard Chartered Bank in Hong Kong, issued Japanese government bonds in Hong Kong.[39] Japan Liners, Toyo Streamliners (Toyo Kisen), and Osaka Cargo Liners (Osaka Shosen, in Hong Kong since 1901) operated the busy direct sea routes between Japan and Hong Kong, both in passenger ferries and cargo ships.

The Japanese exported more and more products to Hong Kong and China, and the Hong Kong market was flooded with Japanese primary products, sundries, and the products of low-skilled industry. Japanese coal (in particular Miike coal from Kyushu) was popular for its high quality. It was the largest import item from Japan in the late nineteenth century and was the second largest in the early twentieth century. Unlike other Japanese items, Japanese coal was mainly for domestic consumption in Hong Kong, occupying about 70–80 percent of the market. Jardine, a major buyer of Japanese coal, consumed 4,000 tons of Japanese coal a month in its sugar refinery.[40] Textiles, both raw materials (such as cotton) and garments, replaced coal as the most important import item from Japan from the early twentieth century until the outbreak of the Second World War.[41] Japanese cotton and other materials were shipped to South China through Hong Kong. Japanese garments were popular among Hong Kong people for their competitive prices and unique style. *Yukata* was once popular among Westerners in Hong Kong.[42] In the 1920s, Japanese garments, overtaking their British competitors, became the number one seller in the Hong Kong textiles market. These Japanese garments came from Japanese factories in both Japan and China, and some were reexported via Hong Kong to the rest of the world.

Dried seafood and sundries were the oldest import items from Japan in prewar Hong Kong, securing the first or second place in the late nineteenth century in total imports from Japan. Their supply and the demand for them in the Hong Kong market was very stable. Sheung Wan had a high concentration of dried seafood and sundries shops, and carried a large portion of Japanese imports. This tradition survived into the postwar period. The famous pro-Japanese merchant, the late Fung Ping Fan, the so-called King of *shiitake* (a Japanese mushroom), had a family business in Japanese dried seafood and sundries. His grandfather opened a dried seafood and sundries shop, Shiu Fung Hong, in Sheung Wan.[43] The introduction of dried seafood and sundries enriched Guangdong cuisine. For example, in the late nineteenth century, chefs in Hong Kong began to use dried squid in Guangdong soups and dishes.[44]

Other popular Japanese imports were ceramics and matches. Japanese ceramics such as utensils and tea sets were the items most in demand in Japanese grocery stores. They were affordable, beautiful, and practical. Japanese matches were well-received for their high quality. In the 1890s, Hong Kong became the largest overseas market for Japanese matches, offering both expensive artistic pieces for collectors and low-end products for mass consumption. In Hong Kong, it was easy to find counterfeits manufactured in South China, a testament to the popularity of Japanese matches. A Japanese person helped a Chinese businessman establish the only match factory in prewar Hong Kong, Lung Chi Company. The Chinese owner had lived in Japan for some years. He purchased machinery and hired experts from Japan for his new factory in Hong Kong. This was one of the earliest cases of "technological transfer" from Japan in Hong Kong's history.[45] Japanese matches declined in importance in the 1920s due to competition from Macau, China, and Sweden. Japanese tea, sugar, silk, tobacco, and fruits were also very competitive in the Hong Kong market.[46] In contrast, Japan bought little from Hong Kong. Hong Kong exported agricultural and animal products (such as rice, sugar, and pork) as well as metals (such as tin, lead, and iron) to Japan, but most of these items were originally from mainland China or Southeast Asia.[47]

Hong Kong also had bilateral trade with Taiwan, a colony of Japan. Taiwan also maintained a regular surplus in its trade with Hong Kong. Taiwan exported coal, tea, leather, sugar, salt, menthol, and other primary products to Hong Kong, and imported finished products (such as clothes and shoes) from Hong Kong.[48] Many Taiwanese products were shipped to Europe and the United States via Hong Kong. Hong Kong-Taiwan trade was mostly controlled by major Japanese trading firms such as Mitsui.[49]

The Japanese also invested in various industries in Hong Kong. For example, Canton Nanyang Brothers Tobacco Company, one of the largest tobacco factories in prewar Hong Kong, was owned by a naturalized Japanese person who was originally a native of Guangdong. Employing more than 500 locals under the supervision of Japanese experts, this factory was able to export its products to mainland China and Southeast Asia.[50]

According to a survey conducted by the Japanese, in 1936, when there was a large Japanese population and a high level of Japanese investment in Hong Kong, there were 76 Japanese companies (totally 125 offices) doing trading and investment business in Hong Kong. In terms of the size of foreign investment in Hong Kong, Japan ranked only after the United Kingdom and the United States. Of these 76 Japanese companies, 4 came in the 1890s, 13 in the 1900s, 21 in the 1910s, 19 in the 1920s, and 17 in the 1930s. Of these companies, 20 were trading firms, 19 were retailers, 10 were media agencies, 3 were financial and transportation firms, 2 were factories, and one was a fishery firm.[51]

Japanese investment in Hong Kong and Japan–Hong Kong bilateral trade increased in size throughout the prewar period. Japan usually had a trade surplus with Hong Kong.[52] At times, their relationships were tense due to Japan's territorial ambitions and economic penetration in the mainland. Large-scale anti-Japanese movements appeared in Hong Kong in certain years, such as 1915, 1919, and 1931. Calls for boycotts of Japanese products were heard every now and then. Some major British and Chinese trading firms in Hong Kong (such as Sincere and Nam Pei Hong) wanted to make use of these anti-Japanese feelings to restrict and undermine Japanese business. However, the effects of the boycotts were short-lived, and each time the Japanese bounced back even stronger than before. Japanese economic interests in Hong Kong experienced a dramatic and consistent downturn only after the Marco Polo Bridge Incident in 1937. From 1937 to 1941, Japanese investment in Hong Kong was under siege by Chinese and British competitors. In addition, physical and verbal abuse against the Japanese and attacks on Japanese shops and organizations became common.[53] Some non-Japanese shops were also victimized simply for carrying or using Japanese products, such as Japanese beers and *Ajinomoto*, a taste enhancer. Japanese businessmen began to pull out. When the Pacific War started in 1941, only 393 Japanese remained.

CONCLUSION

Hong Kong and Japan maintained relatively harmonious political and economic relations during most of the prewar era. It is unfair to see all Japanese activities in prewar Hong Kong as imperialistic acts and harmful to Hong Kong. For Hong Kong, Japan was a major investor and trading partner. The Japanese community developed into one of the most influential foreign communities in prewar Hong Kong. The economic activities of the Japanese in Hong Kong helped strengthen Hong Kong's status as an international trading port and an economic center in South China. It also enriched the material lives of the Hong Kong people by introducing new products and a new culture. For Japan, Hong Kong was an important port of transit and distribution and a gateway to political influence with the Chinese and the British. Hong Kong–Japanese relations were largely mutually beneficial. In general, the Hong Kong government and Hong Kong people were friendly toward the Japanese in Hong Kong until the 1930s. Japan was once an ally of the British, and thus Japan and Hong Kong maintained close military exchanges. In the 1930s, Japan–Hong Kong relations were badly damaged by the rise of militarism in Japan and the ensuing outbreak of the Pacific War. If not for the Pacific War, the Japanese would probably have become a significant ethnic group in Hong Kong along with the Indians, the Jews, and the Eurasians.

NOTES

1. Chan Cham Yi, *Riwen Xianggang yanjiu zhushu de huigu* (A Retrospection of Studies on Hong Kong in Japanese), in *Prospects for Japanese*

Studies in the 21st Century (Hong Kong: Society of Japanese Language Education, 1999), pp. 147–56.

2. Chan Cham Yi, *Ribenren yu Xianggang: shijiu shiji jianwenlu* (The Japanese and Hong Kong: Records of the Nineteenth Century) (Hong Kong: Hong Kong Educational Publishing Co., 1995), p. 10.
3. Hong Kong was one of the most popular Asian cities among the Japanese in the pre–Second World War era. Only Taibei (Taipei) (under Japan), Seoul (under Japan), Singapore, and Shanghai could compete with Hong Kong. In contrast, Macau had few Japanese. The number of Japanese in Macau reached its all-time high of only 23 in 1941. See Yonoza Nobuharu, *Makao no Nihonjin* (The Japanese in Macau), in *The Third Macau Symposium on Japanese Studies* (Macau: Publications Center, University of Macau, 1997), p. 78.
4. Okuda Otojiro, ed., *Meiji shonen ni okeru Honkon Nihonjin* (The Japanese in Hong Kong in Early Meiji Years) (Taibei [Taipei]: Taiwan sotokufu nettai sangyo chosakai, 1937), pp. 20–21, 112, 270, 309.
5. Ibid., pp. 313–14.
6. Regarding the gender, profession, and geographical distribution of the Japanese population in Hong Kong between 1909 and 1917, see *Honkon jijo* (Conditions in Hong Kong) (Tokyo: Gaimusho tsushokyoku, 1917), pp. 348–49.
7. According to the official figures about Japanese residents in Hong Kong in 1917, the five most common professions were, employees of Japanese companies and banks (307), prostitutes (188), *kimono*-related businesses (115), dining-related businesses (67), and tailors (58). See *Honkon jijo*, pp. 348–49.
8. See table 6.1 below.

Table 6.1 The actual figures of the Japanese in Hong Kong in 1917

Items/Location	Central	Wanchai	South Kowloon
Households	66	158	21
Males	371	353	52
Females	186	407	31
Total	556	760	83

Source: *Honkon jijo* (Tokyo: Gaimusho tsushokyoku, 1917), p. 348.

9. See Akaiwa Akiyoshi, "Honkon no Nihonjin bochi" (Japanese Cemetery in Hong Kong), in Yue-him Tam, ed., *Hong Kong and Japan: Growing Cultural and Economic Interactions, 1845–1987* (Hong Kong: Japan Society of Hong Kong, 1988), p. 132.
10. Lee Pui Tak, "Xianggang Riben guanxi dashi nianbiao chugao" (A Draft on the Chronicle of Major Events in Hong Kong–Japan Relations), in *The Japan Society of Hong Kong 40th Anniversary*

Commemorative Volume (Hong Kong: Japan Society of Hong Kong, 2002), p. 174.

11. Otojiro, ed., *Meiji shonen ni okeru Honkon Nihonjin*, p. 181.
12. Chan, *Ribenren yu Xianggang*, p. 258.
13. Otojiro, ed., *Meiji shonen ni okeru Honkon Nihonjin*, pp. 236–38. See also Chan, *Ribenren yu Xianggang*, pp. 210, 244–45.
14. The Yokohama Shokin Bank published its findings in the multivolume *Tsuho gogai* (Additional References). For examples of these reports, see Okumura Niro, *Honkon heisei ni tsuite* (Regarding Hong Kong Currencies) vol. 57 (Yokohama: Yokohama Shokin Ginko, 1935) and Kaneda Shinichi, *Honkon shaku ni tsuite* (About Tin Industry in Hong Kong) vol. 36 (Yokohama: Yokohama Shokin Ginko, 1931). The Taiwan Bank published many reports on the Hong Kong economy. For example, a report, listing the background of major Chinese businessmen in Hong Kong, with special mention of their attitudes toward Japan, became an important reference for the Japanese in choosing collaborators during the Second World War. See Shimojo Yoshikatsu, *Honkon kakyo gaisetsu* (An Introduction to Overseas Chinese in Hong Kong), in *Toan chosa hokokusho* (Report on Our Investigation of East Asia) (Tokyo: Sanhai toan dobun shoin daigaku, 1940), pp. 1099–121.
15. This idea was first aired by the famous journalist Tokutomi Soho. See Chan, *Ribenren yu Xianggang*, pp. 235–38. When Japan conquered Taiwan, it accepted the proposal by some British advisors to turn Taiwan into a colony of Japan, applying the Hong Kong model. See Hamashita Takeshi, *Honkon: Ajia no nettowaku toshi* (Hong Kong: Network City in Asia) (Tokyo: Chikuma shobo, 1996), pp. 32–34, 44.
16. Frank H. H. King, Catherine E. King, and David J. S. King, eds., *The Hongkong Bank in Late Imperial China, 1864–1902* (Cambridge: Cambridge University Press, 1987), pp. 482, 491.
17. Lee Pui Tak, "Xianggang zaobichan yu Daban zhaobiju" (Hong Kong Mint Factory and Osaka Mint Bureau), in *The Japan Society of Hong Kong 40th Anniversary Commemorative Volume*, pp. 573–89.
18. Kume Kunitake, *Tokumei zenken Taishi: Beio kainan jikki* (A Factual Record of the Envoy to the United States and Europe), reprinted in Tam, ed., *Hong Kong and Japan*, pp. 103, 123.
19. "Honkon taiju juran nisshi" (The Diary of the Visit of the Hong Kong Governor), in *Hakotateshi-shi* (History of the Hakotate City), *Shiryohen* (Part on Sources), vol. 2 (Hakotate: Hakotateshi-shi henshubu, 1975), pp. 765–77.
20. Otojiro, ed., *Meiji shonen ni okeru Honkon Nihonjin*, p. 83.
21. Ibid., pp. 320–29.
22. Zuda Kunihiro, *Kanko kosu dewanai honkon* (Hong Kong, Not a Course for Tour) (Tokyo: Kobunken, 1999), p. 126.
23. Chan, *Ribenren yu Xianggang*, p. 259.

24. "Fukuroku" (Appendix), in Otojiro, ed., *Meiji shonen ni okeru Honkon Nihonjin*, p. 27.
25. James F. Warren, *Ah Ku and Karayuki-san: Prostitution in Singapore, 1870–1940* (Singapore: Oxford University Press, 1993), pp. 68–70, 83, 207.
26. Otojiro, ed., *Meiji shonen ni okeru Honkon Nihonjin*, pp. 303–06.
27. *Minami Shina no kaikojo* (International Ports in South China) (Taibei [Taipei]: Taiwan sotokufu, 1930), p. 113.
28. "Fukuroku," in Otojiro, ed., *Meiji shonen ni okeru Honkon Nihonjin*, p. 6.
29. It is said that there were more than 200 unlicensed Japanese prostitutes in Hong Kong in the late nineteenth century. See Chan Cham Yi, "Xianggang zaonian de Riben changji" (Japanese Prostitutes in Early Hong Kong), in Hara Takemichi, Chan Cham Yi, and Wang Xianghua, eds., *Riben yu Yazhou Huaren shehui: lishi wenhua pian* (Japan and Chinese Communities in Asia: Essays on History and Culture) (Hong Kong: Commercial Press, 1999), p. 139.
30. The first Japan–Hong Kong sea traffic was launched in 1867 by the Pacific Mail Steamship Company (U.S.), which operated the San Francisco–Yokohama–Hong Kong route.
31. Yu Shengwu and Liu Cunkuan, eds., *Shijiu shiji de Xianggang* (Hong Kong in the Nineteenth century) (Hong Kong: Qilin shuye, 1994), pp. 242–43.
32. Lin Man Houng, "Riben zhiminshiqi Taiwan yu Xianggang jingjiguanxi de bianhua" (Changes in Taiwan–Hong Kong economic relations during the Japanese occupation period), *Zhongyang yanjiuyuan jindaishi yanjiusuo jikan* (Bulletin of the Institute of Modern History, Academia Sinica), vol. 36 (2001), p. 74.
33. Ibid., pp. 96–97.
34. In 1900, 19 percent of Japan's total exports were shipped to Hong Kong. This dropped to 4.3 percent in the 1910s, 3.5 percent in the 1920s and 1.8 percent in the 1930s. See Chan Cham Yi, "Ershishijichu zhi 1931 nianjian de Gang-Ri maoyi—Rimao shu Gang bufen," (Hong Kong-Japan Trade between the Early Twentieth Century and 1931: Japan's Exports to Hong Kong), in *Quality Japanese Studies and Japanese Language Education in Kanji-using Areas in the New Century* (Hong Kong: Society of Japanese Language Education, 2002), p. 203.
35. Lin, "Riben zhiminshiqi Taiwan yu Xianggang jingjiguanxi de bianhua," p. 70.
36. *Nihon no taishi toshi* (Japanese Investment in China) (Tokyo: Nihon Toa kenkyujo, 1942), reprinted in Tam, ed., *Hong Kong and Japan*, p. 157.
37. Ibid., p. 159.
38. The Yokohama Shokin Bank later set up an office in Macau in 1944. The scale of Japanese investment in Macau was small and the Japanese

owned some tobacco factories, wine factories, and food trading firms. See Yonoza Nobuharu, *Makao no Nihonjin*, pp. 72–77.

39. Chosen Ginko, ed., *Honkon sanhai kinko no hattatsu oyobi sono genjo* (The History of Hong Kong and Shanghai Banking Corporation and Its Current Conditions) (Tokyo: Chosen ginko, 1929), pp. 60–62.
40. Chan, *Ribenren yu Xianggang*, p. 212.
41. See Asashi Shimbunsha Toa mondai chosakai, ed., *Honkon to Kainanto* (Hong Kong and the Hainan Island) (Tokyo: Asahi shimbunsha, 1939), pp. 46–48.
42. Otojiro, ed., *Meiji shonen ni okeru Honkon Nihonjin*, pp. 249–50.
43. Fujita Ichiro, "Senzen no daitonyakai" (The Street of Distributors in the Prewar Era), in *Honkon Nihonjin kurabu soritsu 25 shunen kinen tokushuko* (Special Issue for the 25th anniversary of the Japanese Club) (Hong Kong: Japanese Club, 1981), p. 122.
44. Otojiro, ed., *Meiji shonen ni okeru Honkon Nihonjin*, pp. 183–84.
45. Taiwan sotokufu minseibu shokusan kyoku, ed., *Honkon ni okeru kogyo* (Industries in Hong Kong) (Taibei [Taipei]: Taiwan sotokufu minseibu shokusan kyoku, 1915), p. 31.
46. Japan exported apples from Aomori Prefecture to Hong Kong from 1911. Most were reexported to China and Southeast Asia. Japanese apples were popular among Westerners in Hong Kong. See Nakahada Tatsumi, *Meiji jidai ni okeru Aomori ringo kaiai hanbaishi* (History of Selling Aomori Apples Overseas in the Meiji Period) (Tokyo: Aomoriken keizaibu, 1952), pp. 30–53, 58–60.
47. For example, Hong Kong (in particular Swire) imported raw sugar from Taiwan for refinement and then sold it to Japan.
48. See *Honkon jijo*, pp. 238–39.
49. Lin, "Riben zhiminshiqi Taiwan yu Xianggang jingjiguanxi de bianhua," pp. 57–58.
50. See Taiwan sotokufu minseibu shokusan kyoku, ed., *Honkon ni okeru kogyo*, p. 18.
51. See Toa kenkyujo, ed., *Honkon ni okeru Eikoku no keizaiteki toshi* (British Investment in Hong Kong) (Tokyo: Toa kenkyujo, 1941), pp. 7–8.
52. According to the statistics provided by the International Trade Bureau of the Ministry of Foreign Affairs of Japan, Japan had a huge surplus in its trade with Hong Kong every year between 1903 and 1914. See *Honkon jijo*, p. 228. The imbalance in trade continued in the period between 1913 and 1917. See Lin, "Riben zhiminshiqi Taiwan yu Xianggang jingjiguanxi de bianhua," p. 98. In addition, the figures released by the Statistics Bureau of Hong Kong indicate that the problem of imbalance in Hong Kong–Japan trade was not fixed at all in the 1930s. It is recorded that in the years 1937–1939, Japan had a surplus in Japan–Hong Kong trade in terms of both the money value of transactions and the percentage of trade (see table 6.2). Japan ranked second among those nations exporting to Hong Kong and only sixth among those nations importing from Hong Kong.

Table 6.2 Japan–Hong Kong trade, 1937–1939

Year/ Items	Total imports from Japan in $HKD	% of total imports in Hong Kong	Total exports to Japan in $HKD	% of total exports in Hong Kong
1937	58004	9.4	19780	4.2
1938	58093	12.8	17955	5.1
1939	43132	11.8	11497	4.2

Source: Asashi Shimbunsha Toa mondai chosakai, ed., *Honkon to Kainanto* (Tokyo: Asahi shimbunsha, 1939), pp. 44–45.

53. The Japanese finished a report on anti-Japanese feelings in Hong Kong in 1940. See Nakayama Juzo, "Honkon ni okeru Shinajin no tai-Nichi kanjo" (Chinese Attitudes toward the Japanese in Hong Kong), in *Toan chosa hokokusho* (Report on our investigation of East Asia) (Tokyo: Sanhai toan dobun shoin daigaku, 1940), pp. 807–27.

Chapter 7

Stanley Civilian Internment Camp during Japanese Occupation

Cindy Yik-yi Chu

Introduction

Hong Kong experienced three years and eight months of Japanese occupation, from December 1941 to August 1945, a long ordeal that inflicted suffering on Chinese and foreign residents alike. Before the Japanese invaded the colony, there had been fear that the ongoing Sino-Japanese War (1937–1945) would spread across the border to Hong Kong. That Hong Kong was under British rule was not proof against impending hostilities. Following the attack on Pearl Harbor on December 7, 1941, the United States entered the Second World War (1939–1945). War finally broke out in the Pacific, and the Allied Powers truly faced a war on two fronts, one in Europe and one in Asia. From then on, the Japanese moved to realize their so-called Greater East Asia Co-prosperity Sphere, aiming at the control of other countries in Southeast Asia. Seeing how events were unfolding elsewhere, the British knew they could not forestall Japanese expansion, and very quickly Hong Kong fell victim to Japanese aggression.

The Japanese invaded Hong Kong on December 8, and after days of fighting, British surrendered on Christmas Day, 1941. The Japanese occupation was unique in Hong Kong's modern history, the only time the colony was on a war footing and the only time it was under the control of a foreign power other than the British. This period was also rare in the sense that "antiforeignism" was manifested most explicitly, not by local people, but by the Japanese invaders, against enemy nationals, namely the British, Europeans, and Americans. Antiforeignism took the form of the internment of people of Allied countries in the Stanley Civilian Internment Camp from January 1942 to August 1945, though Americans and Canadians were repatriated, once in June 1942, and again in September 1943, in exchange for the repatriation of Japanese being held in other countries.

In Hong Kong, there were not very many large incidents of antiforeignism. This did not mean that British rule was not authoritarian. Tensions did indeed exist between the foreign rulers and the local Chinese, and British nationals enjoyed highly privileged status and treatment in the colony. However, as a recent study points out, the British colonial government was able to manage and accommodate conflicts by playing one party of actors against another, and to maintain its rule by producing social factions and clashes of interests to its own favor.[1] Before the Sino-Japanese War, there had been outbreaks of antiforeign feelings in Hong Kong, such as the 1922 seamen's strike, in which Chinese seamen demonstrated against the many-times-higher pay of their European counterparts, and the 1925 strike, in which people of different occupations were involved.

The Stanley Civilian Internment Camp in the 1940s was *up till then* the largest manifestation of antiforeignism in Hong Kong. This episode was the only time in Hong Kong history in which foreigners were targeted, suspected, and kept under close surveillance. For foreign communities, it was the worst time in their history in Hong Kong, the time of their worst treatment, and the time that held their worst memories. The circumstances of war led to extraordinary events, and the Stanley Civilian Internment Camp was certainly an exceptional episode in the history of foreign nationals in Hong Kong. This chapter explores the lives of foreigners during internment, making use of camp records, and their own diaries and recollections. The research material can be found in published memoirs, Hong Kong's Public Records Office, and other private archives. The chapter reveals the situation in the camp, the treatment of internees, and their psychological state. In doing so, it highlights an exceptional and significant period in the history of foreign communities in Hong Kong.

JAPANESE OCCUPATION OF HONG KONG, DECEMBER 1941

On July 7, 1937, military hostilities broke out in the Northeast of China, marking the beginning of the Sino-Japanese War. Since the start of the 1930s, aggressive Japanese expansionism had continued, and Chinese nationalistic sentiments were at the peak. In December 1937, Nationalist leader Jiang Jieshi (Chiang Kai-shek) announced that China had entered a war of attrition against Japan. Having shown great perseverance, the Chinese people had nothing to expect but a prolonged period of hardship. For the British colony of Hong Kong, there were worries that war might come close to its border. Although the threat was not imminent, Hong Kong already felt the impact of the conflict, as refugees flooded in from the interior, many of them without food and shelter. Wandering on the streets, they begged for food and jobs; refugee camps became an emergency solution to the problem. At the same time, the Hong Kong government was preparing for a defense against possible Japanese invasion. The preparation work included military and air drills, the enlistment of volunteers, and occasional sirens. Nevertheless, the British believed that if the Japanese really approached the border, the likelihood that the colony would be able to resist invasion was minimal. In April 1941, Winston Churchill claimed that Hong Kong had "not the slightest chance" of success if it was engaged in war against the Japanese.[2]

Invasion finally came, on December 8, 1941, when the Japanese moved across the border in the early hours of the day. In response, by destroying infrastructure from the border to Kowloon, the Royal Engineers, Punjabis, and Chinese Volunteers aimed at delaying the advance of Japanese troops. At five o'clock in the morning, they started work to blow up the Kowloon Canton Railway bridges over the Shenzhen River; half an hour later the bridges were destroyed. Soon the British and Japanese were engaged in fighting. Two hours later, Kai Tak airport received a warning of an imminent Japanese air attack, and at eight o'clock, Shamshuipo barracks became the target of attack. Air raids continued through the following days. On the morning of December 11, Kowloon suffered from severe shelling. In the afternoon, even the police joined the military in the evacuation to Hong Kong Island. The West Battery at Stonecutters was under fire; so was Mount Davis Fort. By the end of the day, the evacuation had been completed.[3] The fighting did not last long, however, and on Christmas Day the British surrendered. At this point, the Japanese occupation of Hong Kong began, and it was not to end until August 1945.

When the British surrendered, there were about three thousand non-Chinese civilians of Allied countries in Hong Kong.[4] For some time, these people avoided going out onto the streets, fearing for their security. On January 4, 1942, the *Hongkong News*, then the only English language newspaper (managed by the Japanese), published a notice, calling all enemy nationals to report themselves at Murray Parade Ground. The notice was the only way they could communicate with the foreigners. As one of them recollected: "Had I not been with the press, I would not have had the advance information of the move." The other thing he barely remembered was being given instructions about what to take—"We were to take blankets and whatever personal effects we could carry, and nothing else. We were to report at Murray Hill parade grounds the following morning at 10 a.m. for registration and distribution to internment billets. Just that and nothing more."[5]

Eventually, about one thousand non-Chinese civilians of Allied countries showed up at Murray Parade Ground. They were registered and escorted to hotels and brothels on the harbor-front, where they were temporarily interned. The Japanese made an exhibition of these people and their forced march to the harbor-front, and used it to humiliate the foreigners in front of the local Chinese.[6] For the next fifteen or sixteen days, these enemy nationals lived in "appallingly overcrowded, filthy conditions with very poor food."[7] Their situation was quite dreadful even before they arrived at Stanley. Then, at last, they rode by boat to the Stanley Civilian Internment Camp. Half internees left their temporary housing—the hotels—for Stanley on January 20, and the remaining half left the following day. In the camp, internees were counted, and they were then grouped into their different communities:

> Finally we were loaded on to two decrepit cargo launches. These were heavily overloaded and topheavy and it required much rearranging to make them even partially seaworthy. . . .
>
> It was a grim party that made that two-hour trip around the east end of the Island to Stanley. The air soon became putrid with gas fumes from the creaking diesel engines. Just past Repulse Bay we saw the remains of the British destroyer Thracian which ran on the rocks. . . .
>
> Due to the shallowness of the water in Stanley Bay, we were taken ashore in junks which had been towed behind us for that purpose. . . . Noses were counted and we were segregated to American, British and Dutch groups.[8]

Dr. Percy Selwyn Selwyn-Clarke, who was Director of Medical Services of the Hong Kong colonial government, suggested Stanley Peninsula as the location of the civilian internment camp. Surrounded by water on three sides, internees would find it extremely difficult to escape from the camp. After discussing it with Franklin Charles Gimson, who was Colonial Secretary of the Hong Kong government, the Japanese agreed to the site.[9] Located on the south of Hong Kong Island, Stanley Peninsula had pleasing scenery, and the blocks there were modern structures. It could be said that "a healthier site could not have been chosen."[10] Despite the perfect view of the ocean, however, the war had ruined the place, and a witness said: "Stanley Peninsula had been the scene of the gallant 'last stand' in our little war in Hong Kong."[11] Fighting was still going on in Stanley hours after the British had surrendered elsewhere in the colony. In St. Stephen's Casualty Hospital, the remains of those who died in combat, as well as bloodstains on the walls, grounds, and furniture were all evidence of the violence and horror of the war.[12] The state of alert, the anxieties, and the fear continued in the Stanley camp compound. The situation in the camp was at its worst during the first few months of internment.

The Beginning of Stanley Civilian Internment Camp, January–February 1942

The Stanley Civilian Internment Camp included the grounds of Stanley Prison (but not the prison itself) and the adjacent grounds of St. Stephen's College. The Japanese headquarters was situated on the hill overlooking the prison grounds, consisting of the former residences of the prison superintendent and the prison doctor.[13] The camp was close to the Maryknoll Mission and could be said to be on "a small peninsula." Stanley Peninsula was in fact "a narrow strip of land" with "just a narrow beach on the left, then a road, and a Chinese village" and another beach on the right.[14] Behind barbed wire were the former prison warders' apartments, St. Stephen's College, and buildings. Maryknoll Father William Downs, an American internee, describes the camp's layout. As he writes, Stanley Civilian Internment Camp consisted of seven blocks of prison warders' apartments, St. Stephen's College, six blocks of flats formerly occupied by Indian prison guards and their families, a block for single warders, the prison officers' club, a building then serving as camp hospital, and another building then allocated for British doctors.[15] Internees spent hours reading and chatting in the cemetery; some went swimming in Tweed Bay but were closely watched by Japanese soldiers. This was the extent of the area in which the internees could move about, the camp itself being isolated from the rest of Hong Kong and far from the city.

Twenty-four Maryknoll priests and Brothers were told to leave Maryknoll House nearby on January 20, 1942, and were interned in the camp. They occupied the top (third) floor of Block E of the former prison warders' apartments, which had two flats, each with three rooms, a bathroom, a kitchen, and a pantry.[16] Their first night was described thus: "We are billeted four to seven in a room and have camp cots for beds. There is little other furniture save a chair here and there, or a small table and a wardrobe or bureau in some of the rooms. . . . After stowing away our belongings under camp cots and in corners, we make up our cots and prepare to retire."[17] Other internees had similar experiences. It did not take long for the Maryknoll men to realize how crowded the camp was to be. The only thing they could do was to adapt to the new environment and to get the most out of the meager resources of the place. There was no electricity. The morning after their arrival, they lit a fire in the kitchen to prepare coffee and oatmeal, which they had managed to bring with them. Very soon, however, they had to rely on what was available in the camp, and like everybody else, their share was always limited and inadequate. For daily meals, they would receive daily rations. Everyone had the same food prepared from the same kitchen:

> We have already been informed that the Japanese authorities will give us rice, meat, vegetables, tea, salt, and sugar—all of which will be strictly rationed—and that we may be allowed to purchase other foods, such as fish and vegetables from hawkers who will come into the Camp. We are to have two meals a day, from the Camp kitchen, now merely a large rice caldron set up on some cement blocks in an area-way on the ground floor of our Block. Our cooks in this general kitchen seem to be some stranded American sailors, whose captain scuttled his ship when the war began.[18]

A fortnight later, they seemed to have settled down and to have got used to the daily timetable of the camp. Their activities were the same every day, either labor or preparing the next meal:

> In addition to our daily patrol, which means a two-hour shift during the day and night, we also have other activities. Some work a few hours at manual labor, helping in the kitchen, carrying cement blocks, cutting wood, getting the daily rations from "The Hill" and general cleaning up around the place . . . . At the present time when the clarion call for "chow" sounds, each one picks up what container he had managed to get and proceeds to the kitchen where he stands in line with about two hundred others and waits his turn until he reaches the table where the cooks dish out the rice, gravy and vegetables. Each gets the equivalent of a bowl of rice, about a cupful of, or rather ladleful of, gravy and another large spoonful of vegetables. And this, twice a day. This he

> takes back to his room and sits on the edge of his camp cot, if he happens to have one, and with a spoon or his fingers, does justice to his meal.[19]

In early February, there were an estimated 2,400 British, over 300 Americans, and about 60 Dutch in the camp.[20] The buildings in the camp were soon identified as either the British blocks, the American blocks, and the Dutch blocks, into which the different communities were separated.

As time passed, people fell into a routine and found their own responsibilities. They grouped themselves into work teams and made themselves useful in the camp. As someone said, "after a while, things began to get organized"; and there were the washing squads, mending squads, and repairing squads. There were always duties to perform. Internees labored endlessly building stoves and kitchens, taking bricks from fallen walls, and using red clay for cement. They even destroyed air raid shelters and used the materials for repair tasks; others gathered grass from surrounding hillsides to add to the supply of firewood. Volunteers were also needed for daily work in the kitchens and for sanitation.[21]

THE HEALTH SITUATION (PHYSICAL AND MENTAL) IN THE CAMP

Although the camp was situated on a small peninsula, internees were crammed into a limited space behind barbed wire, and had to obtain permission if they wanted to get access to the beach. In some respects, a better site could not be found, as Stanley had an excellent climate and was surrounded by excellent scenery, both important as a means of maintaining the health and morale of internees. Far away from the city, it was the place least affected by infectious diseases; close to the ocean, it benefited from cooling breezes in the hot summer months. On the other hand, the people who found themselves in this enclosed environment faced acute sanitary problems and were plagued by mosquitoes. Crowded living conditions posed a constant threat to the health of internees, and many of the sick did not receive adequate medical treatment. Within the camp, fly-breeding was suspected to be the cause of outbreaks of intestinal disease.[22] On balance, however, the location and environment of the camp had advantages; if another site had been chosen, the conditions of the internees could well have been much worse.

In the early months of internment, the general living situation was poor, and food was to be the main problem. Not only was the supply inadequate, but the food was filthy, as "rice frequently contained dust, mud, rat and cockroach excreta, cigarette ends and . . . dead rats."[23] What had hitherto been treated as inedible and was simply thrown out, became the main diet of the internees. A truck transported food to the camp on a daily basis, and each kitchen received its share. Every day the internees had a breakfast of rice soup, and two meals of rice with meat stew or fish. As one of them recollected, it was always rice or "rice slum." There were no surprises at mealtimes, and people did not expect much:

> The rice and fish diet soon told on us and we often went to bed on empty stomachs. During the five and one-half months of internment, I had nothing to eat which could not be eaten with a table spoon and out of the one sardine can, which served as a mess kit. I did not use a knife and fork in that time. Many words were coined for the various concoctions dished out by the cooks, but they all simmered down to "rice slum" in the end.[24]

In early 1942 the camp canteen opened, and long lines of people usually waited outside to buy a little extra food, which was quickly sold out. When supplies ran out, there was sometimes unrest. When people jumped the line, conflicts easily broke out. It should be added that not everyone had money to buy additional food, and even if they did, it did not add very much to their basic rations. Malnutrition was common among internees, and the problem was obvious from their declining physiques. Two and a half months after internment, they experienced dramatic weight loss, some losing up to seventy pounds. As a result, they suffered from dysentery, diarrhea, beriberi, and other diseases associated with malnutrition. Although the Japanese did not take extreme measures against the internees, the lack of attention and consideration resulted in dreadful conditions in the camp for at least the first three months.[25]

As for water, the camp managed to maintain a constant supply for most of the period of internment. Problems only occurred after November 1944 when there was a shortage of power to serve the water pumps. Water came from wells in and around the camp, as well as from piped supplies. In order to prevent diseases from being transmitted, water was either treated with chlorine or boiled. During the entire period of internment, the camp was able to obtain an adequate supply of chloride of lime, and thus the water was always treated before use. As for boiled water, each internee received about two pints per day. With these precautions, the quality of the water did not pose a health menace to internees, in the sense that water was not the source of diseases.[26]

Nevertheless, drainage was a potential source of health problems, as the drains outside the camp were occasionally choked. To combat possible outbreaks of malaria, squads were organized and allowed to work outside the compound. For the disposal of sewage, there were septic tanks, a few put outside the camp and taken care of by the anti-malaria squads. Often, the tanks were used to their fullest capacities, and when underground drains were choked there was no equipment to solve the problem. On the whole, the Japanese did not seem to pay attention to the situation.[27] Fortunately, surface drainage inside the camp was acceptable.

Because of the meager food supplies and the water and drainage situation in the camp, the greatest threat to the health of internees was the vulnerability to infectious diseases caused by malnutrition. Throughout the internment, the death rate was rather low. There were some unnatural causes of deaths: some executions, and a few bomb casualties, but the greatest numbers of deaths were caused by lack of food and malnutrition-related illness. There was a high occurrence of malnutrition-related diseases in the camp. In the first half of 1942, the number of internees was about 2,800. After the two repatriations of Americans and Canadians in 1942 and 1943, the number dropped to about 2,400–2,500. Death rates for the years concerned were: 1942, 11.3 deaths per 1,000; 1943, 7.2 deaths per 1,000; 1944, 16.0 deaths per 1,000; and in the eight months in 1945, 11.2 deaths per 1,000.[28] Those who died in 1943 included internees who were executed, while the death rate of 1945 did not take into account those killed by a bomb in an American air raid. The statistics show that, despite the terrible living environment and the dreadful food supplies, most of the internees survived.

Nevertheless, infectious and insect-borne diseases were common in the camp, and these included diarrhea, dysentery, typhoid, tuberculosis, typhus, and malaria. In the early months, there were many cases of diarrhea and dysentery as internees had already been infected in the hotels and brothels where they had been temporarily interned before they arrived in Stanley. Overcrowded living conditions facilitated the spread of disease, while poor diet and bad cooking also contributed to the problem. The first three months of internment recorded the largest number of dysentery cases, 350. Though things improved as the year progressed, the total number of cases in 1942 was 410. In 1943, 1944, and the first eight months of 1945, the numbers of dysentery cases were 191, 172, and 67 respectively.[29] Nevertheless, during the entire period of internment, only two deaths were directly blamed on dysentery. As regards typhoid, internees were inoculated against the disease before they arrived in Stanley or shortly after internment, and were inoculated again in 1943 and 1944. There were fourteen typhoid cases in the entire internment, resulting in only one death.

Many internees brought tuberculosis with them to the camp. There were thirty-three such TB cases in 1942. Malnutrition and overcrowded living conditions facilitated the spread of the disease, though the open environment tended to prevent it. Only fifteen TB patients were receiving hospital treatment at the time of release, although TB was the cause of seven deaths.[30] During the entire internment, there was only one case of diphtheria, and it occurred in 1942. As for typhus, there were nine such cases resulting in four deaths. In 1942 the spread of malaria became serious in the camp, and eventually antimalaria squads were organized under the supervision of the Japanese, taking care of grass-cutting, drainage, and the filling of holes. Almost half of the internees did not have mosquito nets, and this did not help efforts to control malaria, but the Japanese did not provide adequate supplies. There were 143 malaria cases in 1942, 331 cases in 1943, 151 cases in 1944, and 57 cases in the first eight months of 1945.[31]

Overcrowding remained the norm in the camp. Internees suffered severe hardship as a result of a lack of privacy, causing ongoing friction and nervous stress.[32] Many of them "could not adapt themselves to this strange existence; quarrels, accusations, petty meannesses and suspicion were starkly manifested."[33] As John Stericker, who took up responsibility for managing matters within the British community, recalled, a so-called barbed-wire disease already erupted in the camp in its early months. This mental condition was characterized by a "lack of initiative, inertia, failure of the powers of concentration, loss of memory, insomnia, and extreme irritability."[34] Illusions and nightmares were commonplace, and the following story was recorded by one of the internees: "Here it must be added that people had the most extraordinary dreams. The wife of a naval commander once dreamed that there was a large insect in her bed, or possibly a scorpion. She grabbed it, rushed to the window, and threw it out. Next morning, after enquiries, her dental plate was returned to her."[35] Certainly, there was also nostalgia for the old days and the comfortable life before internment. Another story went thus:

> Another instance, of which the hero was, again, a dental plate, was the dream of a senior banker. As he dreamed he saw a dear little dog sitting

> beside his bed. Then it begged for food. Being an animal-lover, and having a precious piece of pre-war toast handy, he broke the latter into small pieces and fed it to the dog. The dog accepted it readily and greedily. Next morning he was both surprised and annoyed to find his dental plate lying in small pieces on the floor beside his bed. As he never had anything to chew anyway he was not greatly inconvenienced. Moreover his generosity and kind-heartedness gave him a feeling of self-satisfaction, even though the dog had never existed.[36]

Being isolated and confined, there was not much that they could take an interest in. Memories of the good old past provided the only consolation for the internees in such extreme circumstances. It must be added here that although they faced the greatest test of their lives, they were able to avoid making serious mistakes. There were no deaths by suicide or murder within the camp throughout the internment.[37]

Days in the Camp

In such a close community life, it might be expected that quarrels, rumors, and conflicts would be rife among internees. As a former British official commented, the general situation led to a deterioration of morale among internees, which in the worst cases expressed itself in utter selfishness, total disregard of the rights of property, and disrespect for the interests of campmates.[38] To maintain some kind of order and to create a communal spirit, internees soon organized their own groups to manage affairs and solve problems. The British elected a community council under which a number of committees were formed. Council and committee members were senior officials of the Hong Kong government before the Japanese occupation, as well as leaders of major firms in the colony.[39] As it turned out, the council operated rather successfully and was able to hold constructive discussions within the British community, despite the fact that there were always a few disgruntled members.[40] Under the council, the committees took charge of the administration of certain areas of activity, for example supplies, stores, and labor. Among the Americans, a businessman became chairperson of the community, and was responsible for handling matters with Japanese and Chinese mediators. Americans organized their own club to discuss issues of concern. They also arranged church and recreational activities in the main hall of the former prison officers' club.[41] In due course, there were some recreational activities and necessary services for internees; a school, a library, and a hospital came into being in the camp.

One of the common activities among the internees was to sit and talk for long hours in the old cemetery, which was dedicated to British soldiers and their families, and commanded a perfect view of the ocean. Occasionally, the cemetery was a spot for love affairs.[42] When the weather became hot, internees were allowed to swim from Tweed Bay Beach, with Japanese soldiers standing by to watch them and to warn them not to swim more than ten yards from the shore. In the camp, there were other ways to spend time. Auctions took place at regular intervals, usually twice a week, and because of shortages of everything, anything could be sold or bartered. Used clothes, underwear, shoes, furniture, lipstick, face powder, false teeth, smoking pipes, prams, books, blankets, pots, and pans—all might make their appearance at the auction. The auctions were attention catching, and were a good way for internees to divert themselves.

Obviously, life in the camp demanded an adjustment on the part of every individual. This was not easy, but it was necessary. As an internee said, "it took six months for life to settle into an acceptable routine."[43] Most of the time was spent repeating the same round of activities again and again. As the same internee related: "Like the rest of us my life was overshadowed by an unremitting struggle to stave off starvation, the craving for a smoke, and petty wrangling with my fellow internees brought about by boredom and the circumstances of our existence. Ninety percent of our waking hours was spent on activities connected with the next meal: queueing for it, black marketeering for it, scrounging for it, working for it, cooking it, or just plain dreaming about it."[44] Occasionally, there might be excitement of some sort: "The other ten percent went on other activities. There were the escape attempts, the operation of clandestine radios, the perverted tortures inflicted on some of us, the imprisonment and executions, the anxiety over the deteriorating health of us all, the air raids, and the occasional humorous highlights that helped to keep us sane."[45] In the camp, minor happenings could lead to major squabbles, disputes, and even heated debates. It required effort to prevent oneself from losing restraint, and the provocation could come from very tiny incidents. As an internee remembered: "Trivial matters, minor personality clashes, slight or imagined grievances all became distorted and magnified in Stanley. I wrote many things in my diary that reflected thoughts and feelings at that moment in time, in those particular circumstances, when I was depressed, angry or frustrated over something. I would not have given most of them a moment's thought in normal life."[46]

Thankfully, there were volunteers who organized functions to cater to the intellectual and spiritual needs of others. This helped at least some internees set their minds on things that were useful and, to a certain extent, fulfilling. University and school teaching staff were among the internees; they drew up courses and lectures running twice or thrice a week. Their expertise was thus put to use, giving them some satisfaction and self-esteem in this worst time of their lives. In this way, both teachers and students were able to find better ways to spend their time. Class schedules were posted very casually, for example, notices were put up announcing events, such as, "Economics this afternoon under paw-paw trees," "French class, east corner, cemetery, 4.30 p.m." and "Professor Smith will lecture on Bird Life at 5.30. Rendezvous on grass bank near septic tanks."[47] There were doctrine classes from Church personnel, who were also interned. Religious services were allowed to continue in the camp. People came from a great variety of groups, including the Church of England, the Church of Ireland, and the Church of Scotland. There were American Southern Baptists, New Zealand Baptists, members of the Reformed and Evangelical Churches. There were Lutherans, Seventh Day Adventists, Brethren, members of the American Episcopal and Methodist Episcopal Churches. There were English Methodists, members of the Salvation Army and the Society of Friends, American, Irish, and New Zealand Presbyterians, members of the Canadian Assemblies of God and the Christian Missionary Alliance, Congregationalists, Christian Scientists, and Roman Catholics.[48]

Internees could celebrate festivals, such as Easter and Christmas, making use of their limited resources. The Maryknoll priests remembered well the first festive event, Easter, 1942, when people attended services and even managed to give out Easter eggs and to have coffee and cocoa. The schedule for Good Friday to Easter Sunday that year was as follows:[49]

> [April] 3—Good Friday. Mass of the Pre-sanctified at 8:30 with Father Murphy as celebrant. Stations of the Cross and Sermon in the afternoon, the latter being given by Father Haughey. . . .
>
> 4—Holy Saturday. Solemn services at 8:00 a.m. with Fathers Hozen, Dutch Salesian, Father O' Connor, Vincentian and our own Father Gaiero as ministers. The Paschal candle (made up of two vigil lights) was blessed. . . .
>
> 5—Easter Sunday. Solemn Mass at 9:30 on the verandah of the Prison Officers' Club, with the congregation assembled on the lawn. Fathers Meyer, McKeirnan and Siebert, ministers of the Mass, with

> Bishop O'Gara preaching. At noon, a children's party was held on the lawn between the American and British blocks, and each child received three eggs, a doughnut or two and some coffee or cocoa. In the afternoon at St. Stephen's, Rosary, Litany, Sermon and Benediction.

Under the harsh circumstances, religious classes and services provided spiritual and community support to internees, helping them to make sense of their life and keeping them within some moral confines. During Christmas, exchanges of gifts (which could be a small bar of soap) could make a person overjoyed. People tried to contribute, using their gifts. On camp days, internees became amateur playwrights, songwriters, and composers. Their talents were well used in celebrations and parties, providing entertainment to their campmates.

Despite the destitution and the dreadful conditions, life went on in the camp. There were births and deaths; children grew up to become adolescents. Some internees kept records of babies being born, others kept records of funeral services and burials. The following was noted on April 14, 1942: "*Born*, at Stanley Camp: a baby girl, to Mr. and Mrs. Owens, 7–1/2 lbs., Madeline Jeannette Owens, who has the distinction of being the first American born in the Stanley Camp."[50] On April 23: "Funeral Mass at 8:30 for Mr. Simmons. Burial service at 6 p.m. in the cemetery, conducted by the Rev. Mr. Martin, former Head Master of St. Stephen's College." The following day, "Bishop O'Gara, preached a eulogy this morning at a Requiem Mass, said by Father Hessler, for those whose remains were buried last evening. Another death among the British, of cancer."[51]

The children who grew up in the camp had an unforgettable childhood. They easily mingled with those of other nationalities, and had very little comprehension of the concept of class. Their world was bounded by the barbed wire:

> By the time the war ended many of the small babies had become children, the children had become adolescents, and some of the adolescents had become grown-ups. The smaller children, born and bred behind barbed-wire, had known little of normal life. They rarely saw a car, and the arrival of the ration lorry was a never-ending delight. They preferred rice to most of the small luxuries that their parents sometimes procured, and turned their noses up at chocolate when a little of it arrived in some Red Cross parcels. . . . They were undisciplined children and quite without class-consciousness. Their friends were of all colours, and their vocabularies were unprintable.[52]

The children's conversation revolved around the goings on in the camp, and their expectations for the future were all related to what they saw there. "On one occasion, two small boys were overheard discussing the all-important subject of the choice of a vocation for their later years. 'When I grow up,' said one, 'I'm going to join the ration party.' 'Oh, I'm going to join the kitchen staff,' said the other."[53]

Internees had to adjust to weather conditions, and learned to live in extreme poverty. Food was one problem, clothing was another. Few of them had brought enough clothing to the camp, and many had to sleep for months on concrete floors.[54] The winter of 1942 was their first test. The winter of 1944–1945 was another, as there was no fire, no artificial heating, and an acute shortage of warm clothing and blankets in the camp. Many of them had only one blanket to hold onto, and they used anything available, such as old hessian sacks.[55] Naturally, most internees put on everything they had, both day and night. A dressing gown doubled as an overcoat, and a blanket was made into a pair of trousers. At night, "certain warmth could be derived by the primitive process of closing all windows and huddling together in unhealthy airlessness."[56] Footwear was another concern, and the problem got worse in winter and in times when there were no materials for repairs, as internees had only one pair of shoes. "If the uppers were strong enough, soles made from old motor tyres were magnificent, and far outlasted any known sole of pre-war days."[57] For children, the situation was more serious, and many shivered through the cold winter months. The International Red Cross provided additional clothing, footwear, and bedding, but the supplies were never enough.[58]

Internees found the summer conditions more bearable, as the camp enjoyed sea breezes that helped to reduce the heat. They wore very little. "The men usually wore shorts, with or without shirt. The women followed suit, but just within the bounds of decency; their so-called sun-tops, made from two pocket-handkerchiefs, or any odd piece of material, were as analogous to the male lack of shirt as modesty would allow."[59] Many people did not have shoes to wear, and they made up for this lack with inventions of different kinds. "Amongst the men, light canvas shoes were fashionable. Most had at least two toes sticking out, and a piece of oft-replaced cardboard in the sole. The women favoured wooden sandals. These comprised a piece of wood in the rough shape of a foot. They were kept on by a single band of any available material across the top. The nails that kept the bands on had a habit of falling out or tearing the material."[60] In this way the women got more suntan than they wanted, and the men had nothing but shorts throughout the summer.[61]

Life in Stanley was dull except for the underground activities that were carried out within the camp. A small group of British internees had brought secret wireless equipment with them. Members of the group included the Defense Secretary of the Hong Kong government, J. Fraser, and personnel from the local Cable & Wireless Company.[62] The Company employees hid wireless sets in their baggage and smuggled them into the camp when they arrived in January and February 1942. At night, British internees secretly listened to broadcasts from Zhongqing (China) and New Delhi (India), using headphones rather than loudspeakers, and then jotted down notes that were later typed. Information collected was sent out during the first repatriation of Americans, who hid messages in shoes and with crockery. However, not long after this repatriation, the small group—the "inner wireless circle"—decided, for safety reason, to bury some of the wireless equipment. Around March 1943, the Japanese began an investigation into secret activities, and although some members of the group prepared for escape, the plan never materialized. Almost all members were subsequently arrested by the Japanese. Some were released. Others were executed.

Repatriation of Americans and Canadians; the Later Stage of Internment

Eventually, after rumors about repatriation had been circulating among internees for quite some time, it actually happened. On June 29, 1942, Americans and Canadians left the compound, and boarded the Japanese ship *Asama Maru*, which was anchored just outside Stanley. It was the first repatriation in the camp, Americans and Canadians being released in exchange for the repatriation of Japanese internees in other countries. The internees were in a rush, and had no time to think about what to take. Their location meant they were denied a last look at Hong Kong as they got under way:

> The day of sailing our baggage was taken over to be looked over by the gendarmes. At first they were very particular but towards the end they became quite tired and so didn't look at much of anything. It's better to get at the end of a line in inspection as the police are not tired enough to be cross but just tired enough not to want to bother about much of anything. . . . The diplomats had boarded in the morning and any Americans who had not been interned in Stanley, also boarded in the morning. The *Asama Maru* was anchored outside of Stanley, which gave us a slight disappointment in that we did not see Hong Kong before leaving. . . .[63]

The ship sailed to Lourenco Marques, East Africa, where the Americans and Canadians were exchanged for Japanese. The North

Americans then boarded the Swedish ship *Gripsholm* that sailed all the way to the United States:

> At Singapore or thereabouts we crossed the Equator and were quite aware that it was an equatorial zone. We anchored about forty miles from Singapore, . . . Flags were posted near key mines. No boats came out to sell fruit or oriental varieties as they had at Saigon, which gave the place a real atmosphere of war. A few tankers passed us with straw covered packages of dynamite. We passed quite near a tilted sunken vessel which would have been dangerous at night. . . .
>
> At Lourenco Marques we pulled up along side the Gripsholm, and stared at the Japanese passengers aboard who were to be exchanged with us. They stared back. The Japanese crew on our boat cheered them. The Swedish crew on their boat cheered us, but all aboard either ship did not cheer together.[64]

On August 25, the *Gripsholm* arrived at Hoboken, New Jersey. After the first repatriation, there were about twenty Americans left in the camp. The second repatriation took place in September 1943, mostly of Canadians. With the departure of Americans and Canadians, other internees, principally the British, were hoping that repatriation would soon apply to all those left in the camp.[65] Not knowing how much longer they were to be confined, the British internees longed for the day when they could end the internment, but their wish did not come true at that time. The fact that Hong Kong was a British colony made any repatriation of the British extremely unlikely. Though they were being urged to petition for the repatriation of their fellow countrymen, the British officials of the Hong Kong government refused to do so, as they did not want to appear to be deserting their own colony, so creating embarrassment for Britain. If the British were to abandon Hong Kong, the officials thought, it would provide useful material for Japanese propaganda, and would make the retention of Hong Kong as a British colony very difficult in the future.

Starting in January 1944, the camp was no longer under civil authorities, but was under military command. The situation got even worse as many internees had to struggle hard just to survive. They said, "the next six months proved some of the hungriest for many of us":[66]

> We were put on Japanese army rations which meant that in place of bread and meat, we were given an extra 4 ozs. of rice per day and an issue of 4 ozs. of peanut oil every ten days. The men, especially, found this extremely hard, (I should have mentioned before, that the daily ration of an infant a day old, equalled that of a grown man),—so that

> any not already down to their minimum in weight, soon reached that stage. Things were looking extremely bad when we got news of our second supply of food from the Red Cross. This time, each person was issued with three comfort parcels but there were no bulk supplies. The hospital received urgently needed drugs and vitamins which were immediately put to use. I think for twelve weeks, we had a quarter of a thiamin tablet each for four days of the week, and a vitamin capsule on two days, leaving Sunday a day of rest.

By January 1945 the situation had become hopeless. Food supplies dwindled and people continued to suffer from acute malnutrition.

From late 1942 onward, there had been a growing number of American air raids. The situation worsened in the second half of 1943, resulting in a policy of total blackout in the colony. In January 1945 a three-hour American air raid over Stanley caused fourteen deaths and four injuries, the worst incident in the entire period of the internment.[67] The air raids nevertheless raised the hope that the Allies would soon win the war, and peace rumors spread quickly within the camp. In mid-August the camp suddenly received more supplies. The internees learned about the dropping of the atomic bombs on Japan and the Japanese surrender that followed. Before the British forces arrived in Hong Kong, however, the internees were warned against making any unwanted moves, because the Japanese were still in control of the camp. On August 31, British officials arrived in the camp and the internment came to an end.

Conclusion

The internment of foreign nationals was indeed an exceptional episode in the history of Hong Kong. Antiforeignism was expressed not by local Chinese, but by Japanese who were suspicious of civilians of enemy countries, and whose aim was to maintain Japanese control of the British colony. The internees in Stanley Civilian Internment Camp did not have adequate food, clothing, and medical care, and their health and the conditions of hygiene in the camp conditions were depressing. Although they lived below bare subsistence level, the death rates during their years in the camp were rather low. Malnutrition was the norm among internees, and diseases related to malnutrition were a serious problem for them. Living in an overcrowded situation, infectious and insect-borne diseases caused some deaths, but the number was small. The location of Stanley, far from the city and close to the sea, prevented large-scale outbreaks of epidemics.

A more suitable site could not have been chosen for the camp. During internment, foreign civilians lost their freedom, lacked basic necessities, and were cut off from contact with the outside world. Of course, the Japanese had neither the will nor the motive to improve conditions in the camp. Neglect by the Japanese was the cause of the problems and sufferings of the internees.

Uncertainties about the war and the future created much psychological pressure for the internees. Life was monotonous and there were few diversions. Even very minor matters could occasion large squabbles and fighting. It required an effort to keep oneself sane, and religious and leisure activities were beneficial ways for internees to hold onto their values and to spend their time. They would never forget what they had endured during the three years and eight months of Japanese occupation. None could expect the future to bring anything worse than what they had experienced in Stanley. Throughout the period, the different foreign communities in the camp lived together, and individuals mingled without distinction of nationality and class. They lived in a world behind the barbed wire, unable to contact the people immediately outside, not to mention families and relatives in distant lands. The memoirs written by internees contained details of every kind, descriptions of their accommodation, their rations, their nightmares, and their worries. Even many years after internment, these memories remained vivid. Their time in the camp was the greatest test of their perseverance and religious faith. The period of the internment was the only time in Hong Kong's history in which foreign nationals suffered from planned discrimination, in the sense that they were suspected, confined, and left in a helpless and despairing situation. It would be difficult to imagine this event being repeated in Hong Kong. Life within Stanley Civilian Internment Camp was a unique episode in Hong Kong's history, and the records left by the foreign nationals of the time are likewise a unique and engaging testament to a one-off sequence of events.

NOTES

1. Tak-Wing Ngo, "Colonialism in Hong Kong Revisited," in Tak-Wing Ngo, ed., *Hong Kong's History: State and Society under Colonial Rule* (London: Routledge, 1999), pp. 3–6.
2. Winston Churchill's phrase reappeared in the title of Tony Banham's *Not the Slightest Chance: The Defence of Hong Kong, 1941* (Hong Kong: Hong Kong University Press, 2003).
3. Banham, *Not the Slightest Chance*, pp. 26–64.

4. Geoffrey Charles Emerson, "Behind Japanese Barbed Wire: Stanley Internment Camp, Hong Kong 1942–1945," *Journal of the Hong Kong Branch of the Royal Asiatic Society*, vol. 17 (1977), p. 30.
5. George E. Baxter, "Personal Experiences during the Siege of Hong Kong, December 8th–25th, 1941; Internment by the Japanese, January 5th–June 29th, 1942; Trip Home and Exchange Civilian Prisoners, Laurenco Marques, P.E.A., June 30th–August 26th, 1942" (Hong Kong: United Press Association, n.d.), p. 20 (Xerox copy kept at Hong Kong Collection, University of Hong Kong Main Library).
6. Lewis Bush, *The Road to Inamura* (London, Robert Hale, 1961), p. 157.
7. Emerson, "Behind Japanese Barbed Wire," p. 31.
8. Baxter, "Personal Experiences during the Siege of Hong Kong, December 8th–25th, 1941; Internment by the Japanese, January 5th–June 29th, 1942," p. 29.
9. G. B. Endacott, *Hong Kong Eclipse*, edited and with additional material by Alan Birch (Hong Kong: Oxford University Press, 1978), p. 198.
10. Ibid.
11. Jean (Hotung) Gittins, *I Was at Stanley* (Hong Kong: n.p., 1946), p. 7.
12. Ibid., pp. 7–8.
13. Emerson, "Behind Japanese Barbed Wire," p. 32.
14. "The Story of the Internment Camp," n.d., p. C-3, Folder 9, Box 1, Personal Narratives of WWII—South China, Maryknoll Mission Archives, Maryknoll, New York.
15. Reverend James Smith and Reverend William Downs, "The Maryknoll Mission, Hong Kong 1941–1946," *Journal of the Hong Kong Branch of the Royal Asiatic Society*, vol. 19 (1979), p. 78.
16. Ibid., pp. 71–73.
17. Ibid., p. 72.
18. Ibid., p. 73.
19. Ibid., p. 77.
20. Ibid., Emerson, "Behind Japanese Barbed Wire," p. 33; Baxter, "Personal Experiences during the Siege of Hong Kong, December 8th–25th, 1941; Internment by the Japanese, January 5th–June 29th, 1942," p. 30.
21. Gittins, *I Was at Stanley*, p. 10.
22. N. C. Macleod, Deputy Director of Health Services, Hong Kong, "Civilian Internment Camp, Stanley, Hong Kong, Health Report," March 6, 1946, p. 1, HKRS 163-1-81 "Miscellaneous Papers in Connection with Stanley Internment Camp during the Period 1941–1945," Public Records Office, Hong Kong.
23. Emerson, "Behind Japanese Barbed Wire," p. 34.

24. Baxter, "Personal Experiences during the Siege of Hong Kong, December 8th–25th, 1941; Internment by the Japanese, January 5th–June 29th, 1942," p. 30.
25. A. D. Blackburn, "Hong Kong, December 1941–July 1942," *Journal of the Hong Kong Branch of the Royal Asiatic Society*, vol. 29 (1989), pp. 82, 88–89.
26. Macleod, "Civilian Internment Camp, Stanley, Hong Kong, Health Report," pp. 1–2.
27. Ibid., pp. 2–3.
28. Ibid., p. 3.
29. Ibid., pp. 12–13.
30. Ibid., p. 13.
31. Ibid., pp. 14–15.
32. Blackburn, "Hong Kong, December 1941–July 1942," p. 88.
33. Endacott, *Hong Kong Eclipse*, pp. 200–01.
34. John Stericker, *A Tear for the Dragon* (London: Arthur Barker, 1958), p. 190.
35. Ibid.
36. Ibid.
37. Macleod, "Civilian Internment Camp, Stanley, Hong Kong, Health Report," p. 3.
38. Letter from Franklin Charles Gimson (Colonial Secretary in Hong Kong before Japanese occupation) to Colonial Office in London, n.d., p. 8, HKRS 163-1-81 "Miscellaneous Papers in Connection with Stanley Internment Camp during the Period 1941–1945," Public Records Office, Hong Kong.
39. Bush, *The Road to Inamura*, pp. 158–61; Letter from Gimson to Colonial Office, p. 6.
40. Letter from Gimson to Colonial Office, p. 14.
41. Cindy Yik-yi Chu, *The Maryknoll Sisters in Hong Kong, 1921–1969: In Love with the Chinese* (New York: Palgrave Macmillan, 2004), pp. 53, 55.
42. Bush, *The Road to Inamura*, pp. 158–59.
43. George Wright-Nooth (with Mark Adkin), *Prisoner of the Turnip Heads: Horror, Hunger and Humour in Hong Kong, 1941–1945* (London: Leo Cooper, 1994), p. 93.
44. Ibid.
45. Wright-Nooth, *Prisoner of the Turnip Heads*, pp. 93–94.
46. Ibid., p. 94.
47. Stericker, *A Tear for the Dragon*, p. 185.
48. Ibid., pp. 185–86.
49. Smith and Downs, "The Maryknoll Mission, Hong Kong 1941–1946," p. 91.
50. Ibid., p. 95 (italics his).
51. Ibid., p. 97.

52. Stericker, *A Tear for the Dragon*, p. 165.
53. Ibid.
54. Macleod, "Civilian Internment Camp, Stanley, Hong Kong, Health Report," p. 7.
55. Stericker, *A Tear for the Dragon*, p.162.
56. Ibid.
57. Stericker, *A Tear for the Dragon*, p. 163.
58. Macleod, "Civilian Internment Camp, Stanley, Hong Kong, Health Report," p. 7.
59. Stericker, *A Tear for the Dragon*, pp. 162–63.
60. Ibid., p. 163.
61. Macleod, "Civilian Internment Camp, Stanley, Hong Kong, Health Report," p. 7.
62. "Report on Wireless Activities and Escape Plans in the Civilian Internment Camp, Stanley," November 27, 1945, pp. 1–6, HKRS 163-1-81 "Miscellaneous Papers in Connection with Stanley Internment Camp during the Period 1941–1945," Public Records Office, Hong Kong.
63. Sister Frances Marion Gardner, "HongKong War Experience," n.d., pp. 12–13, Folder 9, Box 1, Personal Narratives of WWII—South China, Maryknoll Mission Archives, Maryknoll, New York.
64. Ibid., pp. 13–14.
65. Letter from Gimson to Colonial Office, p. 17.
66. Gittins, *I Was at Stanley*, p. 11.
67. Endacott, *Hong Kong Eclipse*, pp. 215–16.

Chapter 8

Migrants from India and Their Relations with British and Chinese Residents

Caroline Plüss

Introduction

This chapter discusses the relations that Indian migrants established with the Chinese and British residents of Hong Kong. Its focus is on the changing economic and social relations between migrants from India on the one hand, and the Chinese numerical majority and the British political majority in Hong Kong on the other hand. The period examined runs from the second half of the nineteenth to the mid-twentieth century. Four groups of migrants from India are investigated: the Parsees, the Muslims, the Sikhs, and the Hindus. The primary sources for this chapter are the results of archive research, material provided by the different associations these migrants founded, interviews with members of the four groups, and written documents provided by interviewees. The communications with interviewees are treated as having been made anonymously. Secondary sources are historical accounts of Hong Kong society, often pertaining to the economic activities in which individuals of Indian origin were engaged.[1]

Migrants from India started settling in Hong Kong from the time when the British took the island in 1841 as a result of the Opium War (1839–1842).[2] Among the first Indians who came to Hong Kong were soldiers serving in the British army, many of whom were Muslims.[3] A few years later, the British army recruited Sikh soldiers, and Sikhs were also recruited by the Hong Kong police force. It was a common policy in the British Empire to transfer security personnel from India to its new possessions, and these security force personnel were transferred from India to Hong Kong. Also, since Hong Kong's earliest colonial days, Parsees and Bohra Muslim traders from India opened offices in the territory, taking advantage of the economic opportunities and political stability this new British territory provided. A number of these merchants had already been trading in the Chinese city of Guangzhou (Canton), close to Hong Kong and connected to the South China Sea by the Pearl River. Some of these traders also had experience in trading in the Portuguese enclave of Macau, near Hong Kong.[4] In addition, other entrepreneurs of different ethnic origin moved from India to Hong Kong to trade in opium, silk, and cotton, or opened stores supplying provisions to the soldiers of the British garrison.

In the second half of the nineteenth century, the number of individuals of Indian origin in Hong Kong fluctuated considerably, because of the stationing and withdrawal of Indian soldiers. Excluding the soldiers, there appear to have been no more than 1,500 individuals of Indian origin at this time. In 1898, for example, the census report counted 1,348 Indians. This number included the members of the Indian contingent of the police force, but excluded the Indian soldiers, who numbered 1,454.[5] In the twentieth century, however, the number of individuals of Indian origin in Hong Kong increased significantly. The 1906 census counted 4,299 Indians in the colony, most of them being employed males.[6] In the early 1930s, there were over 7,000 Indians in Hong Kong. By the 1960s, their estimated number was over 20,000.[7]

In the middle of the twentieth century, a larger number of Indians arrived from the Sind and Gujarat provinces of India, and most of them were Hindus.[8] Sindhis generally were traders, or the employees of traders. These merchants had widespread diasporic trading networks with the Sindhi communities in Africa, the Middle-East, India, and Pakistan.[9] Despite being a small minority of Hong Kong's population, migrants from India had been important to Hong Kong's economy, supporting its trade with other geographical regions. They established a significant number of businesses throughout the period examined in this chapter.[10]

PARSEES: MIDDLEMEN ORIGINS AND COSMOPOLITAN IDENTIFICATIONS

To understand how Parsees interacted with British and Chinese residents in Hong Kong, it is first necessary to take a brief look at

Parsee history. Following the Muslims' invasion of Persia, the adherents of the then-dominant religion in Persia, the Zoroastrians, were forced to convert to Islam, and many of them fled. From the eighth century onward, a number of Zoroastrians settled in Gujarat Province on the western coast of India, where they came to be known as Parsees, or Parsis.[11] The origins of the name "Parsee" are not entirely clear, but it has been suggested that the name indicates they came from the Pars (or Fars) province in Persia.[12] Perhaps they chose this name to deflect attention from their distinctive religion.

Even though Parsees were allowed to live in India, a number of restrictions were placed on them. For example, Parsee women had to change their dress and wear traditional Indian saris. Parsee wedding ceremonies were required to be conducted in part in the Sanskrit language, and could only be performed in the evening, when they were less noticeable. Parsees were not allowed to carry arms, or to convert people to Zoroastrianism.[13] Their subordinate position in Indian society was one of the reasons why the Parsees were keen to engage in trade with outsiders, first with the Portuguese, and then with the British, after the latter two groups settled in Bombay (now Mumbai). Parsees acted as middlemen between the Indian population and the foreign traders. This promoted them into prominent trading positions.[14] They prospered as merchants, and gained a solid reputation as bankers and financiers. They also became famous for building and owning ships, which they were willing to deploy to the British for trade in their Empire. Westernization supported the Parsees' economic and social ascendancy in India. Parsees began to speak English, learned Western manners, and became very loyal to the British. Beginning in the eighteenth century, the British valued the Parsees for the help they provided with establishing trade in India, as well as their help with trade between India and China. Emphasizing their willingness to help the British, a number of Parsees adopted English names that indicated their professional specialization, such as Captain, Readymoney, or Engineer.[15] After they came to Hong Kong in the second half of the nineteenth century, many Parsees continued the process of Anglicization. For example, in the twentieth century, members of the Kotwaj family in Hong Kong changed their surname to Kotwall.[16] In addition to being traders, some Parsees became investors in real estate and stocks.[17]

Throughout the twentieth century, the importance of the Hong Kong Parsees' links with India decreased. Nevertheless, their social connections with coreligionists in the Indian subcontinent remained important, and they turned to the much larger Parsee communities in

India for spouses. Their number in Hong Kong was small. In the early 1950s, for example, there were only about eighty to ninety Parsees in Hong Kong.[18] Since many of these had moved to Hong Kong from Shanghai in the late 1940s, it seems that their numbers in Hong Kong may have been significantly smaller in the early part of the twentieth century. The small community size and the wish to maintain tradition explained why Hong Kong Parsees looked for spouses in Bombay, which had a much larger Parsee community. The close links between these two communities are evident in the comment made by a Hong Kong Parsee, explaining that "all Hong Kong Parsees have relatives in India."[19] Parsees frown upon marriages with non-Zoroastrians, do not allow conversions, and continue to be very strict about maintaining the distinction between who is, and who is not, a Zoroastrian: only children born to a Zoroastrian father are considered Zoroastrians.

Being a minority community, they are worried that exogamy threatens its survival. If a Parsee man marries a non-Parsee woman, this is less damaging for the number of Zoroastrians than if a Parsee woman marries a non-Parsee man. Nevertheless, Parsees are not keen on their men marrying non-Parsee women because they believe that the passing on of Parsee tradition is predominantly the role of women.[20] Perhaps the British exclusion of Parsees in Hong Kong from close social interaction until the latter part of the twentieth century further motivated the Parsees' transregional marriages. Marriages between Parsee men and Chinese women in Hong Kong existed both in the nineteenth and in the early twentieth centuries. Homaje Kotwaj, and then his son Samuel Kotwall, both had spouses who were ethnically Chinese.[21]

The Ruttonjee family is a good example of how prominent Parsee families established themselves in Hong Kong.[22] In 1886, Hormusjee Ruttonjee came to Hong Kong from India and started a business as a wine merchant.[23] With the help of his son Jehangirjee, he established the Hong Kong Brewery. Jehangirjee Ruttonjee prospered further through investing in property in Hong Kong. An idea of his character can be gained by looking at the groups of people to whom he directed his philanthropy. Jehangirjee Ruttonjee's biggest project was establishing an antituberculosis sanatorium in Hong Kong in 1948. With help from the Hong Kong government, it became the Ruttonjee Tuberculosis Sanatorium, to which Ruttonjee continued to make donations. By supporting the sanatorium, Jehangirjee Ruttonjee indicated that he helped Hong Kong society as a whole, without favoring any particular group. This demonstrated his cosmopolitan characteristics. This is not to say that he wished to distance himself from his coreligionists, for whom he often acted as a leader. For example, during the Second World War (1939–1945) he housed nearly the entire Parsee community in his residence in Duddell Street, Dina House.[24] At the same time, he also supported Indians, who were interned during the Japanese occupation of Hong Kong (1941–1945), helping to smuggle in food parcels to them.[25]

Cosmopolitan characteristics were also evident in Jehangirjee Ruttonjee's son, Dhunjisha (Dhun) Ruttonjee. Born in Hong Kong in 1903, he built friendships with both prominent Chinese and British residents. For example, he played poker regularly with the financiers George Kwok and Noel Croucher.[26] His efforts in relating to ethnically different groups of residents in Hong Kong earned him political acceptance by the British administration, which became increasingly willing to include individuals of non-British origin into the running of its institutions. Dhun Ruttonjee was elected to the Urban Council from 1950 to 1957, and to the Legislative Council from 1953 to 1968.[27] A further indication of his cosmopolitan nature was his marriage to an ethnically Chinese woman. Such marriages continued to constitute a break with Parsee orthodoxy. But in his case, it did not prevent his appointment as President of the Incorporated Trustees of the Zoroastrian Charity Funds of Hongkong, Canton, and Macau.[28] On a religious level, however, Parsees did not redefine their group boundaries. They remained strict about excluding non-Zoroastrians from these activities.

MUSLIMS: TOWARD ECONOMIC IDENTIFICATION

The Muslims who migrated from India to Hong Kong included both Sunnis and Shi'ites, the two main groups in Islam. The large majority of the Shi'a Muslims in Hong Kong were Bohras. They maintained close links with their coreligionists in the Gujarat province in India. Sunnis migrated to Hong Kong from both the northern and southern regions of the Indian subcontinent. In the second half of the nineteenth century, economic connections with India were strong elements in defining the identities of the Bohras and Sunnis who came to Hong Kong as traders or as traders' employees.[29] These connections supported their trade. Significant changes in how the Sunnis came to think of themselves took place in the early twentieth century. A number of them started to accentuate their business links with various groups of people in different geographical regions. For example, in 1905 they founded an association called the Islamic Union of

Hong Kong.[30] The aim of this organization was to promote trade with China.[31] Comparing the name of the association with its purpose indicates that Sunnis accorded a similar importance to their religious and economic interests.

The fact, that the Sunnis' identities became increasingly defined by their economic activities, was also evident in how they chose representatives in the early twentieth century. In the 1850s, Sunni Muslims had founded the association called the Trustees of the Islamic Community. Its aim was to give the Hong Kong government assurances regarding the appropriate use of a piece of land, which had been given to the Muslims for the construction of a mosque. When new trustees needed to be appointed in 1911, they were selected so as to represent the main religious groups among the Indian Muslims. Four Sunni Muslims and two Shi'ites were appointed. The Sunni Muslim representation was further broken down according to whether or not they were engaged in trade with China, that is, whether or not they were members of the Islamic Union.[32] Economic characteristics hence created a new distinction among the Sunnis.

After arriving in the territory, Sunni traders and employees established social links with Chinese residents by marrying Chinese women.[33] It is interesting to observe that, although Indian Muslims in Hong Kong increased their trading connections with China, they did not establish significantly closer social or economic relations with the growing numbers of Muslims from China who came to live in Hong Kong.[34] Perhaps there was distrust felt toward Islam by British and Chinese non-Muslims, and this might explain why neither Indian nor Chinese Muslim traders thought they could gain much by establishing closer business relations with each other.

Toward the middle of the twentieth century, Muslims in Hong Kong of Indian origin diversified into a wider range of economic activities, and they became less dependent on working for trading firms owned by coreligionists. This was one of the reasons why some of them relinquished elements of the Islamic lifestyle that they perceived as hindering economic activities. Examples include the adherence to Islamic dietary prescriptions (especially abstinence from alcohol) and visits of the mosques, both of which tended to complicate their interaction with non-Muslim colleagues and clients. However, Muslims of Indian origin became concerned that their coreligionists might lose sight of their Islamic traditions in Hong Kong. They were also unhappy that there was little Islamic teaching available for Muslim children.[35] Their minority position in Hong Kong society, and especially in the case of the Sunni Muslims, the declining connection between religious characteristics and economic activities, decreased some Muslims' assertion of their distinct traditions.

THE SIKHS: DEPENDENT ROLES

Most Sikhs migrating to Hong Kong came from the Punjab province. Before the partition of India and Pakistan in 1947, this was in Northern India, and thereafter became part of Pakistan.[36] Sikhs follow the religion of Sikhism, which established itself in the sixteenth century. Described by the British in India as "more warlike than the Southerners [Southern Indians]," Sikhs were appreciated as soldiers and policemen in India. The colonial administration in Hong Kong also sought their services.[37] Sikh soldiers arrived in the territory in the early 1890s, after the Colonial Defence Committee in Hong Kong had proposed that if no British Army unit was available to be added as an extra battalion to the garrison of Hong Kong, a corps of soldiers was to be recruited in Punjab.[38] Relations between Indian soldiers and the Chinese residents in Hong Kong were strained. The soldiers defended the interests of the British administration, which included controlling Chinese residents, especially in the rural areas of the colony, called the New Territories.[39] There were also tensions between Sikh soldiers and the Western residents, stemming not least from the two groups' unequal access to resources. Hong Kong newspapers reported occasional brawls between members of these different ethnic groups. For example, in 1892 a Hong Kong daily newspaper reported that Indian soldiers, while off-duty, wounded a European police constable and a number of Chinese residents.[40]

The police force in colonial Hong Kong was keen to employ Sikhs because it had difficulties with using Chinese constables and with finding suitable Westerners. Chinese constables were judged corrupt and prone to taking bribes. In 1848, when the police had vacancies for twelve European constables, it was "exceedingly difficult to procure sober well-conducted Europeans."[41] One account explains that positions for Chinese and European constables were "too lowly paid to attract decent people," but that the Sikhs and Muslims from India were not too dissatisfied with the remuneration they could receive in Hong Kong, given the relatively worse economic situation in India.[42] Instead of recruiting the twelve European constables as planned, the Hong Kong police decided to recruit twenty constables in India, emphasizing that doing so would save £67.10 per year.[43]

In 1848, fifty Sikhs and Muslims were recruited from the Punjab province for police work in Hong Kong.[44] By 1870, the Armed

Constabulary Section of the Hong Kong police force was made up mainly of Sikhs.[45] In 1898, there were 630 policemen in the colonial police force, consisting of 112 Europeans, 292 Chinese, and 226 Indians.[46] In 1909, the police force consisted of 128 Europeans, 511 Chinese, and 411 Indians, and most of the Indians were either Sikhs or Muslims.[47] The constables from India were allowed to carry firearms, whereas initially the Chinese constables were not allowed to do so; an indication of the greater trust placed by the colonial administration in the Sikh constables. Nevertheless, the Sikhs did not have much control over the terms of their employment.

The conditions in which Sikhs lived in Hong Kong were at times precarious. A letter written by the Chief Magistrate of Hong Kong expanded on the case of an Indian woman, presumably Sikh, whose husband had worked for the police. He had been dismissed and had then died. The widow and their infant became completely destitute, living in an empty cell in the North Point police station. The letter explained that the only support she had was from those Indian constables who, like her, wished to return to India.[48] This letter was written to the Colonial Office in London in order to secure money to fund the passage of the woman and her child back to India; they finally received the money.

Disciplinary actions taken by the superintendent of police indicate that the Indian constables' working lives were not without considerable strain. In 1909, Indian constables were reprimanded more often for drinking offences than were European or Chinese constables: twenty-nine Indians, eight Europeans, and two Chinese were punished. That same year, Indians were also fined more often than constables from the other two groups for the offenses of disorderly conduct, neglect of duty, and absence from duty. In comparison with the Indian constables, the Chinese constables were more frequently disciplined for minor offences, or for being asleep while on duty.[49]

The colonial framework imposed limits on the extent to which Sikhs could rise in the ranks in British employment. The wish to better their economic prospects motivated some Sikhs to leave the police force, finding other employment in Hong Kong or moving elsewhere. In 1907, an unspecified number of Sikhs traveled from Hong Kong to Peru, where they became destitute. It is not known how many of these Sikhs were former police employees.[50] Worries over the possibility that Indians whom the British had trained as soldiers and policemen would serve employers of non-British nationality in China prompted the Colonial Office in London to instruct the Hong Kong police to stop recruiting Indians for police work in Hong Kong, and instead to recruit policemen from the ranks of the Indian Army in India, which the British controlled.[51] The idea was to make it more difficult for Sikhs to find employment in the Far East after their services with the police, or army, ended.[52] In 1908, the Governor of Hong Kong even suggested repatriating all Indians who had been employed by his administration. He wrote in a letter to the Colonial Office in London:

> It is feasible . . . for me to undertake to repatriate all men who have completed their services under this Government . . . to secure this it is necessary to take measures which shall prevent a man who has been provided with a passage to India from disembarking at Singapore. . . . and that men who actually land in India do not return. . . . I should also be glad to co-operate in making known the liabilities incurred by a British-Indian subject who should take service against His Majesty's Troops in time of war.[53]

In practice, it was difficult to implement a policy that prevented former soldiers and police constables from serving non-British employers in the Far East. Attaining such a degree of control would not only have proved very costly, but would also have risked straining even further the relations between the British representatives and the representatives of other European nations in China. In 1915, for example, the British consul general in the Chinese city of Hankou informed the Governor of Hong Kong that he did not wish to withdraw former Indian policemen who were working in the German concession in that city:

> Their withdrawal would almost certainly be followed by retaliatory action on the part of the German authorities who would most probably order all Indian watchmen to leave their Concession, thereby causing two important British establishments, the International Export Company and the British Cigarette Company, serious inconvenience. Moreover, the withdrawal of the police and probable expulsion of watchmen [from the German Concession] would leave some 40 to 50 unemployed Indians on my hands, for whom. . . . I should have to provide maintenance pending their repatriation.[54]

The fact that many Indians resided in Hong Kong played a role in the migration of Indians from Hong Kong and the Indian subcontinent to North America. Rumors circulated in Hong Kong about the fortunes made by Indians in Canada. Some Indian soldiers had previously discharged themselves from service in the territory and moved to Canada, where they indeed found more gainful employment. Reports on the success of these migrants reached Punjab, and Punjabis from different age groups, often without English language skills, traveled to Canada. The Canadian authorities were not keen on receiving these migrants, and many were turned away.[55] Between August 16, 1907 and September 10, 1912, 623 Indians passed through Hong Kong en route to Victoria in British Columbia.[56] The Governor of Hong Kong declined to take responsibility for these migrants, responding to the complaints of the Canadian authorities that they were not residents of Hong Kong, but that they had bought their passages to Canada in India.[57] Indians also traveled through Hong Kong on their way to the Philippines, where they stayed for six months in order to establish residence, which then permitted them to enter the United States.[58]

Despite the occurrences of economic, social, and political tension, Indians in Hong Kong generally were loyal to the British residents. For example, during the First World War (1914–1918), civilians in Hong Kong could enter the police force to help in the Special Police Reserve. These volunteers were divided into three groups: British and Indian individuals formed one group, Chinese individuals the second, and Portuguese individuals the third.[59] During the Second World War, Sikh and other Indian soldiers defended the New Territories against the invasion of Japanese forces. In 1940, more than 1,000 Indian soldiers lost their lives fighting for the British.[60] Only a small number of Indian soldiers later collaborated with the Japanese during the occupation, hoping that this would help India become independent from Britain. After the liberation of Hong Kong from Japanese occupation in August 1945, the colonial administration employed Indian soldiers to help with civilian causes. Two hundred and sixty Indians, for example, operated the telephone exchange.[61] These soldiers returned to India in 1947, when India gained independence from Britain. Gurkha soldiers recruited in Nepal replaced them.[62] From the 1950s onward, the police gradually replaced Sikh constables with Chinese ones. A number of Sikh former policemen remained in Hong Kong as security guards, and some opened their own businesses.

The Hindus: Diasporic Traders

In the early colonial days, the most prominent traders from India were Parsees and Bohra Muslims. In the second half of the twentieth century, Hindus became the largest group of Indians in Hong Kong, and they specialized in importing and exporting a wide variety of goods.

The largest group of these entrepreneurs was the Sindhis, who traded often through their widespread diasporic links. Sindhis come from the Sind province, which lies in what was Northern India before the partition of India and Pakistan in 1947. Thereafter, the largest parts of this province became part of Pakistan. One of the most prominent Sindhi families in twentieth-century Hong Kong was the Harilelas. Their economic history was not typical of Sindhi traders in Hong Kong, most of whom started their ventures by trading in silk.[63] Naroomal Mirchandani and his family moved to Hong Kong after having traded in the nearby Chinese city of Guangzhou, where he had moved at the beginning of the twentieth century. In Guangzhou, he made a fortune dealing in curios and camphor, trading mainly between China and the United States. With the recession in the United States, he lost his entire fortune. The family moved to Hong Kong in 1934 as paupers.[64] For family reasons, Naroomal changed his surname to Harilela, constructing it out of the first names of his parents, Haribai and Lilaram.[65]

The Harilelas prospered again, but only by breaking with Hindu ideals regarding the status of various professions. For Hindus, tailoring is considered an occupation with low social prestige (it is only a little more acceptable than working with leather, which is regarded as a lower-caste activity). Naroomal's son, Hari Harilela, recounted that he had to give up school in Hong Kong in order to contribute to the family's upkeep by hawking for the British armed forces. It was through his contacts with the British army that he met Muslims from India who were tailoring uniforms for the soldiers. He learned tailoring from these Muslims, and then started his own tailoring business. The Harilelas used this tailoring expertise and launched themselves into mail-order tailoring, at times employing up to 600 tailors.[66] Having become prosperous, the family started to invest in numerous Hong Kong-based ventures. Their economic success and close ties with the territory explained why the Harilelas became leading members of the wider Indian community in Hong Kong.

The economic trajectory of the Gidumal family was more typical of Sindhi traders in Hong Kong. Mohan Gidumal arrived in the colony around 1910 to work as an assistant for a Sindhi company called Pohoomull Brothers, which had set up provision stores in several ports of the British Empire. Among younger Indian migrants to the Far East, it was common to work first as an assistant in companies owned by members of their ethnic group, often for relatives. Once they had gained some experience, they often opened their own companies. The Gidumals opened Gidumal and Watumull Ltd. in 1927, and Gidumal & Sons in 1949, initially making use of their networks with the Sindhi trading diaspora.[67] One characteristic that distinguished Sindhi trading firms from the larger British firms was that the former could not afford to employ middlemen to communicate with Chinese clients. Sindhi traders often learned to speak Cantonese (*Guangdonghua*), which made it easier for them to do business with the Chinese population. Nevertheless, social integration with Chinese residents remained low. Both groups have been described as conservative about maintaining their own cultures. Neither Sindhis nor Chinese were in favor of intermarrying.[68]

The Sindhis had become the largest group of Indian traders in Hong Kong by the second half of the twentieth century, and consequently took the leading role in representing the interests of all traders of Indian origin in the territory. In 1952, Sindhi traders were instrumental in founding the Indian Chamber of Commerce in Hong Kong.[69] Their widespread trading connections were important to Hong Kong's economy, and the government recognized this by giving the chamber permission to issue certificates of origin for the export of products manufactured in Hong Kong. This strengthened both the economic position of the Indian traders in the territory, and Hong Kong's exports to places where Indians had access.

Conclusion

In this chapter we have discussed the relations between four groups of Indians and the British and Chinese residents in Hong Kong. These relations differ depending on whether the Indians were brought to the territory by the colonial administration, or migrated as more independent entrepreneurs. Sikh soldiers and policemen did not have much bargaining power in relation to their British employers, and the latter had a high degree of control over the economic prospects of Sikhs in these positions in the territory. The Sikhs' relations with the Chinese population were strained because the Chinese perceived them to be largely auxiliaries of the British, brought to the territory to defend British interests. Traders from India, such as Parsees, Muslims, and Hindus, had more power to determine their interactions with the British and the Chinese residents. Although their economic position provided them with a little more social acceptance, they nevertheless wished to preserve their core cultural characteristics in relating to both. For example, the Parsees largely refrained from marrying non-Parsees, although Parsees became highly Westernized and loyal to the British. The fact that the social acceptance the Parsees received from

British and Chinese residents remained limited has probably contributed to their continued reliance on the Parsee communities in India (especially in Bombay) to find spouses.

At the beginning of the twentieth century, many Muslim traders of Indian origin shifted the focus of their economic activities from India to China, but this did not perceptibly change their economic and social relations with Chinese residents in Hong Kong. This indicates that the Muslims' position in the economic networks established among Chinese individuals in the territory was marginal. Prejudices against race and religion explain why the relations of the Muslims with British residents also remained distant. However, the Sunni Muslims were less restricted by their religion than were the Parsees when it came to redefining group boundaries, so it was not uncommon for them to intermarry with Chinese residents, especially women, giving rise to mixed descendants. These "local boys" (and girls) were closely integrated into Chinese culture.

The strength of the diasporic trading networks of the Sindhis, a more recent group of immigrants, explains their advantage in dealing with the colonial administration. In the mid-twentieth century, and under the leadership of Sindhi entrepreneurs, migrants from India managed to gain access to key economic resources in Hong Kong. However, the Sindhis' desire to maintain their own culture largely hindered them from establishing closer social relations with Hong Kong's Chinese residents.

NOTES

The author would like to thank The Hang Seng Bank Golden Jubilee Education Fund and The Lord Wilson Heritage Trust for their grant contributions to the research on which this chapter is based.

1. Archive research was done in the Hong Kong Collection of the Main Library of the University of Hong Kong, in the archives of the Islamic Union of Hong Kong, and in the private collection of a member of the Parsee community in Hong Kong. Material stemming from sixty-two oral history interviews with individuals of Indian origin in Hong Kong is also used.
2. Frank Welsh, *A History of Hong Kong* (London: HarperCollins Publishers, 1997), pp. 120–25.
3. Two thousand and seven hundred Indian troops witnessed the raising of the British flag in Hong Kong. Since their stationing was temporary, they are not counted as residents of the territory. See in: Kanwal Narain Vaid, *The Overseas Indian Community in Hong Kong* (Hong Kong: Centre of Asian Studies, University of Hong Kong, 1972), p. 12.

4. Carl Smith, "The Establishment of the Parsee Community in Hong Kong," in *A Sense of History: Studies in the Social and Urban History of Hong Kong* (Hong Kong: Hong Kong Educational Publishing Co., 1995), p. 390.
5. Elizabeth Yuk Yee Sinn, *Index to CO 129 (1842–1926)* (Hong Kong: Department of History, University of Hong Kong, 1997, computer file), CO 129/292, p. 243.
6. Sinn, *Index to CO 129*, CO 129/341, p. 444.
7. Vaid, *The Overseas Indian Community in Hong Kong*, p. 20.
8. The Gujarati immigrants, migrating to Hong Kong from Gujarat province in north-western India from the middle of the twentieth century onward, were predominantly Hindus, but consisted also of a smaller number of Jains and Parsees. (Jainism is a religion that is perceived to have more similarities with Buddhism than with Hinduism.) (Anonymous communication)
9. Anonymous communication.
10. Vaid, *The Overseas Indian Community in Hong Kong*, pp. 85 and 95.
11. Ninian Smart, *The World's Religions: Old Traditions and Modern Transformations* (Cambridge: Cambridge University Press, 1989), p. 411.
12. Anonymous communication.
13. Anonymous communication.
14. I have discussed this point in: Caroline Plüss, "Globalizing Ethnicity with Multi-local Identifications: The Parsee, Indian Muslim and Sephardic Trade Diasporas in Hong Kong" in Ina Baghdiantz McCabe, Gelina Harlaftis, and Ioanna Pepelasis Minoglou, eds., *Diaspora Entrepreneurial Networks: Four Centuries of History* (Oxford: Berg Publishers, 2005), pp. 245–68.
15. See also in: Caroline Plüss, "Transnational Identities: The Hong Kong Indians," *International Scope Review*, vol. 2 (2000), p. 4.
16. Peter A. Hall, *In the Web* (Wirral, U.K.: Peter A. Hall, 1992), p. 188.
17. Anonymous communication.
18. Harold W. Ingrams, *Hong Kong* (London: Her Majesty's Stationery Office, 1952), p. 248.
19. Anonymous communication.
20. Anonymous communication.
21. Hall, *In the Web*, p. 188.
22. I used the Ruttonjee example in: Plüss, "Globalizing Ethnicity with Multi-local Identifications." I also mentioned the Ruttonjee family in: Caroline Plüss, "Constructing Globalised Ethnicity: Migrants from India in Hong Kong," *International Sociology*, vol. 20, no. 2 (2005) pp. 203–26.
23. Jamshed K. Pavri, "Honourable Dr. Dhunjishah J. H. Ruttonjee O.B.E., C.B.E., J.P. of Hong Kong," (n.d., photocopy), p. 1.
24. Pavri, "Honourable Dr. Dhunjishah J. H. Ruttonjee," p. 1.
25. Anonymous communication.

26. Anonymous communication.
27. Pavri, "Honourable Dr. Dhunjishah J. H. Ruttonjee," p. 1.
28. This association of the Parsees in Hong Kong is called the Incorporated Trustees of the Zoroastrian Charity Funds of Hongkong, Canton, and Macau.
29. Caroline Plüss, "Hong Kong's Muslim Organisations: Creating and Expressing Collective Identities," *China Perspectives*, no. 29 (May–June 2000), p. 20.
30. Incorporated Trustees of the Islamic Community Fund of Hong Kong, *ITICFHK* (Hong Kong: By the author, 1985), p. 8.
31. Plüss, "Hong Kong's Muslim Organisations," p. 23. I also mentioned this example in: Plüss, "Globalizing Ethnicity with Multi-local Identifications."
32. Joel Toraval, "Zhangli yu qidao anpai: Xianggang musilin jijin zonghui lishi gaimao" (Managing Death and Prayer: A Historical Sketch of the Board of Trustees of the Hong Kong Muslim Community), *Guangdong minzu yanjiu luncong* (The Collection of Studies of Ethnic Groups of Guangdong), vol. 5 (1991), p. 225.
33. Most of these marriages were with Chinese women who were not Muslims, but who took up the religion before they married. See in: Anita Weiss, "South Asian Muslims in Hong Kong: Creation of a 'Local Boy' Identity," *Modern Asian Studies*, vol. 25, no. 3 (1991); and Plüss, "Globalizing Ethnicity with Multi-local Identifications."
34. Tang Kaijian and Tian Yingxia, "Xianggang yisilanjiao de qiyuan yu fazhan" (The Origins and Development of Hong Kong's Islam), *Dongnanya yanjiu* (Southeast Asian Studies), vol. 6 (1995), p. 51.
35. Anonymous communication.
36. Sikhs follow the religion of Sikhism, which was established in the sixteenth century. Smart, *The World's Religions*, p. 98.
37. Alan G. Harfield, *British and Indian Armies on the China Coast, 1785–1985* (London: A. & J. Partnership, 1990), p. 185.
38. Ibid.
39. Harfield, *British and Indian Armies on the China Coast*, p. 199.
40. *China Mail*, May 28, 1892. Quoted in: Harfield, *British and Indian Armies on the China Coast*, p. 187.
41. Sinn, *Index to CO 129*, CO 129/23, p. 66.
42. Kevin Sinclair, *Asia's Finest: An Illustrated Account of the Royal Hong Kong Police* (Hong Kong: Unicorn Books, 1983), p. 30.
43. Sinn, *Index to CO 129*, CO 129/23, p. 67.
44. Sinclair, *Asia's Finest*, pp. 27–28.
45. Harfield, *British and Indian Armies on the China Coast*, p. 185.
46. Sinclair, *Asia's Finest*, p. 35.
47. Ibid., p. 39.
48. Sinn, *Index to CO 129*, CO 129/23, p. 77.
49. Sinclair, *Asia's Finest*, p. 39.
50. Sinn, *Index to CO 129*, CO 129/341, p. 444.

51. Ibid., CO 129/354, p. 11.
52. Ibid., CO 129/346, p. 217.
53. Ibid., CO 129/346, pp. 220–21.
54. Ibid., CO 129/427, p. 410.
55. Ibid., CO 129/341, p. 447.
56. Ibid., CO 129/341, p. 446.
57. Ibid.
58. Sinn, *Index to CO 129*, CO 129/395, p. 360.
59. Kevin Sinclair, *Royal Hong Kong Police: 150th Anniversary Commemorative Publication, 1844–1994* (Hong Kong: Police Public Relations Branch, Royal Hong Kong Police Force, 1994), p. 9.
60. Harfield, *British and Indian Armies on the China Coast*, p. 445.
61. Ibid., p. 459.
62. Ibid., p. 464.
63. Anonymous communication.
64. Anonymous communication.
65. Reportedly very upset about the fact that his family cremated his mother before he could return to India, Naroomal chose this new family name. See in: "Meet Hong Kong's Harilelas," *Hinduism Today*, November 1994 <http://www.hinduismtoday.com>.
66. Anonymous communication.
67. Anonymous communication.
68. Anonymous communication.
69. Indian Chamber of Commerce in Hong Kong, *Directory of Members. Reunification Edition 1997–98* (Hong Kong: By the author, 1998), p. 7.

Chapter 9

American "China Hands" in the 1950s

Chi-kwan Mark

Introduction

Americans have long played a part in the making of modern Hong Kong, beginning in 1842. Early that year, an American Protestant missionary, Jehu Lewis Shuck, came from Macau and founded the island's first Christian church on Queen's Road (named the Queen's Road Chapel).[1] In 1843, United States officials arrived to open the first foreign consulate in the colony. American merchants were likewise attracted to the free port, establishing one of the largest trading firms there, Russell & Company.[2] Nevertheless, until the second half of the twentieth century the American community in Hong Kong remained small, and their interests and influence were limited. Indeed, it was mainland China, rather than Hong Kong itself, that caught the imagination of most American sojourners. Hong Kong was seen primarily as a springboard to China, a country in which there were more Chinese to convert, more economic opportunities to exploit, and more political interests to protect.[3]

The intensification of the Cold War in Asia brought significant changes in Washington's perception of Hong Kong and its policy toward American nationals there. Following the establishment of a Communist regime in mainland China in 1949, U.S. consular officers moved their operations to Hong Kong, and subsequently those operations became more important than ever and called for a larger official presence. American missionaries also withdrew from the mainland to Hong Kong, which became flooded with tens of thousands of Chinese refugees awaiting assistance from the colonial authorities and voluntary organizations.[4]

It was American businessmen who constituted the largest sector of the American community in a rapidly changing Hong Kong. As Hong Kong, from the mid-1950s onward, transformed itself into a world manufacturing and financial center, it also became an attractive place for American companies to invest and establish their regional headquarters. By 1972, when relations between China and the United States were normalized, the Americans had become an integral part of Hong Kong society, their lives and fortunes being inextricably tied to Hong Kong's prosperity and stability. Only then did the Americans fully come to value the intrinsic importance of Hong Kong.[5]

This, in brief, is an overview of the American presence in Hong Kong since 1842. This chapter, however, focuses on one sector only of the American community—the U.S. consular establishment; on one aspect of their life—their working relationship with the colonial authorities; and on one decade—the 1950s. It examines the roles, identities, and activities of U.S. consular officials, whom I call the American "China Hands,"[6] who sojourned in Hong Kong to assist in the implementation of Washington's Cold War policy. While it is well-known that the Americans—and indeed the Chinese, Communists, and Nationalists alike—used Hong Kong for intelligence gathering and other Cold War purposes, it is not clear to what extent U.S. officials on the ground enjoyed the support of the British colonial authorities, who were highly sensitive about provoking Beijing.[7] It is an exaggeration to say that the Americans were launching an unrestrained anti-Communist crusade in Hong Kong, as some scholars seem to have suggested.[8]

This chapter examines the dilemmas and difficulties faced by U.S. consular officials in Hong Kong in their day-to-day operations in the 1950s, the period when American–Chinese confrontation was at its height. It focuses on the interactions among U.S. officials on the spot, the British colonial authorities, and the U.S. administration. It also assesses the role of this distinct sector of the American community in Hong Kong society. This chapter puts a "human face" to what would otherwise be treated in a strictly "impersonal" way, U.S. policy in Hong Kong, thereby bridging the gap between American diplomatic history and Hong Kong social history.

THE NEW "CHINA HANDS": BETWEEN PATRIOTISM AND PRAGMATISM

After the founding of the People's Republic of China in 1949, the Americans were forced to close all their embassies and consulates on the mainland, and to move their operations to the peripheries of China, such as Hong Kong and Taiwan. Gradually, this resulted in the presence of a disproportionate number of U.S. consuls and vice-consuls, economic officers, and information officers in the U.S. consulate general in Hong Kong, where they engaged in intelligence gathering, export controls, and overt propaganda. In October 1949, the American consulate, including the United States Information Service, the armed service attachés and their support staff, as well as representatives of other U.S. agencies, such as Agriculture and the Treasury, had only two consuls and six vice-consuls. By September 1951, the number had increased to five and no less than twenty-four respectively, bringing the total number of U.S. personnel (excluding the local staff) to ninety-six. At that time, the size of the American community in Hong Kong scarcely exceeded 1,000. In 1956, the number of U.S. officials reached 160, presumably taking care of approximately 1,800 American nationals in the territory.[9] The American consulate in Hong Kong became one of the largest U.S. consulates in the world, comparable to such U.S. embassies as the one in Burma but with a more important function.[10]

Unlike the "Old China Hands" in treaty port China, successive U.S. consuls general in 1950s Hong Kong, such as Karl Rankin (September 1949–August 1950), Walter McConaughy (November 1950–June 1952), and Julian Harrington (July 1952–December 1954), had not been born into missionary families. They were not China specialists in a real sense: none of them had received formal Chinese language training.[11] The only U.S. consul general in Hong Kong who had served in China long enough to deserve the status of a veteran "China Hand" was Everett Drumright (December 1954–March 1958). Nevertheless, within the American consulate, there were a number of consuls, vice-consuls, and political and economic officers who were knowledgeable about things Chinese, for example Ralph Clough, Larue Lutkins, Arthur William Hummel, Jr., John Holdridge, and Lindsey Grant, to name just a few. They served in such capacities as chief of the Political Division, public affairs officer of the United States Information Service, head of the Press Monitoring Unit, and so forth.[12] Formal Chinese language training, together with field experience on the mainland prior to 1949, made them China experts within the U.S. consulate in Hong Kong. These American "New China Hands" valued the experience they gained from their service in Hong Kong, regarding the colony as the most interesting and important post for the observation of Communist China.[13]

In Hong Kong, the American "China Hands" played diverse, and at times conflicting, roles as China watchers, policy implementers, and supporters of the colonial authorities. In their day-to-day operations, they were constantly caught between the conflicting demands of professional reporting on China, staunch support for Washington's policy, and sympathetic concern over Hong Kong's problems. They had to strike a balance between their American identities and the perspectives they picked up as residents in the colony, between patriotism and pragmatism. On the one hand, in an all-embracing Cold War conflict, American nationals abroad had to demonstrate their patriotism by identifying with the anti-Communist cause of their home government. As obedient public servants, U.S. consular officers in Hong Kong had to constantly bear in mind that the national interests of the United States should always come before the local needs of the colonial authorities. On the other hand, U.S. officials on the ground came to sympathize with the precarious position of Hong Kong, existing as it did in the shadow of China. They became convinced, through their close contact with the host government, that a confrontational approach on the part of the United States would provoke Beijing into retaliation against Hong Kong itself. Through close range observations of the People's Republic, the American "China Hands" in Hong Kong gradually developed a more realistic understanding of Communist China than that of the decision-makers in Washington. However, their pragmatic, forward-looking views on Beijing ran ahead of government policy, at a time when anti-Communism was running high in the United States. In short, multiple roles and competing loyalties meant that the American "China Hands," in carrying out Washington's policy, were pulled in different directions, by their home government on one hand, and their host government on the other.

CHINA WATCHING

After 1949, Hong Kong became a principal listening post for the Americans because of its proximity to the mainland, the difficulties of running human agents in a totalitarian state, and, more importantly, the availability in the territory of Chinese refugees with first-hand experience of what was happening on the mainland. Intelligence on developments in Communist China was obtained by interrogating refugees from the mainland, by monitoring the Chinese mainland press and broadcasts, and by covert means. To the American China watchers in Hong Kong, reporting events as truthfully as they saw them was their professional obligation. As Consul General Rankin wrote in June 1950, "[W]e often have a contribution to make [in U.S. policy making]. Certainly, I have not hesitated to express to the Department my opinions on the Far Eastern situation, and in considerable detail."[14] Rankin wrote this at a time when the situation in Asia was deteriorating rapidly, as North Korea invaded the South. The escalation of the Cold War in Asia, together with domestic political factors, created strong anti-Communist feeling in the United States, culminating in McCarthyism in the early 1950s. Such "Old China Hands" as John Carter Vincent and John Paton Davies were purged by the administration. For U.S. Foreign Service officers at that time, a sympathetic report on the Chinese Communists, or even a critical one on the Chinese Nationalists, might spell the ruin of their career.

During the 1950s, three U.S. consuls general in Hong Kong were staunch supporters of a hard-line U.S. policy toward Communist China, namely Rankin, Walter McConaughy, and Everett Drumright. But their anti-Communism derived more from their own conviction than from their fear of McCarthyism. Indeed, the American "China Hands" in Hong Kong were not specifically singled out for criticism by McCarthy and his supporters (except during the most intense phase of the Korean War, the war itself from 1950 to 1953), not least because none of them were "in responsible positions at the time that China was lost."[15] This new generation of China experts felt free to report on China on the basis of their own judgment and ethics. The freedom enjoyed by these China watchers and their pragmatic reporting also owed much to the attitude of the "China watchers' watcher," the consul general. As most of the U.S. consuls general in the 1950s were not China experts themselves, they were quite willing to give their subordinates—political and economic officers/consuls—"a relatively free hand in their work, while according them maximum support, and useful guidance."[16] Thus, Ralph Clough, Chief of the Political Division between 1950 and 1954, considered the anti-Communist McConaughy "a very good boss," who "very rarely made any changes in the things that I wrote for reporting to Washington."[17] Likewise, John Holdridge, who was an interrogation officer and Head of the Press Monitoring Unit in the mid-1950s, recollected that Drumright "may have added his own comments somewhere else, but at the same time, he did not move in the direction of trying to influence our reporting in any way."[18]

Over time, the American China watchers in Hong Kong developed a realistic understanding of the strengths and weaknesses of Communist China. Whereas hard-line U.S. decision-makers such as Secretary John Foster Dulles regarded the Chinese Communist regime "only as a temporary aberration," Holdridge and his team held the view that "the Chinese Communists were there to stay."[19] Lindsey Grant, a political and economic officer in the American consulate, believed that "it was our obligation to tell Washington that what we were seeing was a regime that was establishing itself very effectively in power, even though it was not a very attractive one in many ways." Despite the belief of a monolithic Sino-Soviet threat held by most hard-liners at Washington, Grant was convinced by his field experience that the Chinese Communists "were pretty cautious. The longer I watched them, the more I was aware of this Chineseness."[20] In short, American consular officers trained in Hong Kong were some of the first to advocate a constructive approach toward the People's Republic, the approach that culminated in the Sino-American rapprochement in 1972.[21] Such a realistic understanding of China (if not necessarily an admiration for the Communist regime) also made them more conscious of the precariousness of Hong Kong.

In intelligence gathering, U.S. consular officers generally enjoyed good working relations with British officials in Hong Kong. As the Cold War intensified in Asia, both Washington and London had a great need for information on China, and they realized that they would benefit from a pooling of expertise and resources. The Hong Kong government (the Hong Kong Police Special Branch and the British Secret Service in particular)[22] interrogated most of the Chinese refugees, who came mainly from south China. Unless by special arrangement with the British, the American consulate was not allowed to interrogate Chinese nationals on a large scale; its proposals for a joint interrogation team were consistently rejected. The only Chinese interviewed by U.S. consular officers were some incidental "walk-ins," who voluntarily approached them to offer information. The American consulate interrogated mainly Westerners who were allowed to leave the mainland, such as missionaries, travelers and journalists, and exchanged copies of interrogation reports with the British.[23] As John Holdridge, an interrogation officer, recollected, the consulate had "a good working arrangement with the Brits," and there was "a healthy exchange" of intelligence.[24] On the other hand, the Hong Kong station of the Central Intelligence Agency (CIA) was secretly involved in interrogating Chinese refugees, although direct evidence of this is scarce.[25]

With regard to intelligence collection from open sources, U.S. consular officers also enjoyed close cooperation with the British. The Press Monitoring Unit within the U.S. consulate translated into English and published a daily digest of the Hong Kong Chinese language press, the *Survey of China Mainland Press*, and the *Current Background Series.* The Americans then exchanged their monitoring output with the translation service of the Hong Kong branch of the British Regional Information Office,[26] which was much smaller in scale.[27]

If Anglo-American cooperation in the interrogation of refugees and the monitoring of the press was generally close, the relationship was less comfortable when it came to intelligence gathering by covert means. The Hong Kong government had serious reservations about the running of secret agents by the Americans in the territory. For example, in a number of surprise raids against both Communist and Nationalist organizations in early 1951, the Hong Kong Police incidentally uncovered a previously unknown Chinese contact of the American consulate, and detained him for "intensive questioning." As the State Department assessed it, this showed "the sensitiveness with which the British view our several activities in Hong Kong and their concern over what they may suspect we may or would like to undertake."[28] The Hong Kong government was sensitive to American activities that were secret and unilateral in nature, fearing that the U.S. intelligence service would turn the colony into a base for subversion against China. In this regard, the Chinese Communist propaganda machinery often criticized the ever-growing U.S. consulate in Hong Kong for engaging in clandestine activities against Beijing.[29] The size of the U.S. establishment in Hong Kong became a source of embarrassment for the Hong Kong government throughout the 1950s. On more than one occasion, the British had to raise the issue at the diplomatic level, urging the U.S. administration to limit the size of the American consulate.[30]

The Hong Kong Governor, Alexander Grantham, "took a poor view of it [the consulate]—the largest anywhere in the world"—saying that it was "at enmity with the lawful government of mainland China." The CIA in particular, he claimed, was "extremely ham-handed at one time until we had to take a very strong line to stop them being so stupid."[31] What can be discerned from this is that Grantham made a distinction between the American consulate and the CIA station, between the operations of the American "China

Hands" and those of the U.S. secret agents. Despite his reservation about its "very large" size, Grantham did say in his memoirs: "We should, however, remember that the consulate-general in Hong Kong was the regional headquarters for many of their agencies in the Far East, such as information. Large staffs were also necessary for translations of newspapers and other publications coming out to China . . . and for screening Chinese who wished to go to the United States."[32] At a personal level, Grantham regarded successive U.S. consuls general as "men of high calibre," who, in carrying out the instructions of their home government, "appreciated the trickiness of Hong Kong's situation."[33] By the same token, Rankin had "great admiration" for the Hong Kong Governor, who was "extremely well informed" and "ready to appreciate both sides of a question."[34] Drumright, too, enjoyed "the most cordial, friendly and cooperative relations with the Granthams." (It is worth noting that Lady Grantham was American-born and, in Rankin's words, "an exceptionally charming and able hostess.")[35]

The American "China Hands" realized that their host government's concerns had to be addressed, if they themselves were to be allowed to operate in Hong Kong. Throughout the 1950s, the U.S. administration attempted to hold the size of the consular establishment "at the absolute minimum."[36] Disputes with the British over the size (and operations) of the American consulate remained, but none was serious enough to disrupt their overall good working relationship. Even the U.S. intelligence service saw the need to show restraint. Notwithstanding some (abortive) attempts to use Hong Kong as a base of operations against China during the Korean War, the CIA station was quite willing to follow "the rules of the game in intelligence work in Hong Kong."[37] The tacit understanding was that the politically precarious Hong Kong was to be used mainly for intelligence gathering, rather than as a base for subversion against China.[38]

Export Controls

In addition to China watching, the second main area of U.S. operations in Hong Kong during this period was export control. After the outbreak of the Korean War in June, and the massive Chinese intervention in November 1950, the United States secured the support, first of its Western European allies, and then of the United Nations, to impose an embargo on the export of strategic goods to China. Owing to its proximity to the mainland and its traditional role as an entrepôt, Hong Kong was seen as the main loophole through which embargoed strategic goods would find their way into China.[39] The American consulate in Hong Kong was charged with responsibility for supervising export controls in the territory. U.S. economic officers were heavily involved in approving applications for export licenses, identifying the origin of goods, investigating Hong Kong's import requirements, preventing smuggling, and so forth.[40]

For the successful enforcement of the embargo, Washington needed the cooperation of the Hong Kong government. Postwar Hong Kong depended on its entrepôt trade with China (although to a lesser degree than it had done previously) and with the outside world. Any attempt to restrict trade with China would put Hong Kong in jeopardy. No contemporary official or businessman could have predicted then that the Korean War embargo would turn out to be a blessing in disguise for Hong Kong, helping speed up (if not initiate) its industrialization. More importantly, the main worry was that the U.S. administration, propelled by both the military twists and turns in Korea and domestic politics at home, would escalate the economic warfare against China—from an embargo on strategic goods *only* (which the Hong Kong government reluctantly accepted) to a total embargo on *all* trade with China (which would have serious economic and political consequences for Hong Kong). This possibility constituted the greatest threat to Hong Kong during the Korean War.[41]

Here again, the American "China Hands" played an important mediating role between the U.S. administration and the Hong Kong government in the functioning of the embargo regime. They were sympathetic toward the difficulties faced by Hong Kong in the enforcement of export controls. They attempted to minimize the negative impact of the Korean War embargo on Hong Kong, while ensuring that the colonial authorities would be as cooperative as possible with regard to the achievement of U.S. policy objectives. Such a balancing act would not be an easy one for U.S. officials in Hong Kong, given both the intense feeling in the United States against Communist China on one hand, and the perceived British preoccupation with trade with China on the other.

There were many instances in which the American "China Hands" faced difficulties with the Hong Kong government as a result of the Korean War embargo. On December 3, 1950, in response to the Chinese intervention, the U.S. Department of Commerce announced that validated licenses were required for all U.S. shipments to mainland China, Hong Kong and Macau, the latter two being included because of their "importance [as] possible transshipment points."[42] Applications for U.S. shipments to Hong Kong would still be considered on a case-by-case basis, but given the tense situation in Korea, and pending the establishment of effective export controls in the territory, the United States imposed a de facto embargo on Hong Kong for the time being. The U.S. announcement created much uncertainty in Hong Kong, which depended heavily on U.S. raw materials, such as tinplate, blackplate, and especially raw cotton, for its domestic industry and reexports.[43] Concerned that the supply of essential U.S. raw materials would be cut off, the Hong Kong government immediately demanded greater clarification of the licensing procedure by the U.S. administration. Responsibility for explaining U.S. policy to a worried government fell on the American consulate in Hong Kong.[44]

However, the U.S. consuls for economic affairs were themselves as confused about the Commerce Department's licensing policy as were the Hong Kong public. Shortly after the announcement of the new policy, Ralph H. Hunt noted that both the English and pro-Nationalist Chinese press in the territory were no more than "moderately critical" of U.S. action and "withheld full attack," mainly because the American consulate had promised full particulars from the Commerce Department as soon as they became available. By mid-December, Hunt's inability to furnish information about the criteria for U.S. licensing to Hong Kong was causing the consulate "some embarrassment with local elements," especially the Hong Kong government, which now requested London to make a "strong protest to Washington." Worse still, Hunt found it "[e]specially unfortunate" that all sections of the Hong Kong press were giving extensive coverage to an interview with U.S. Commerce officials in Washington, who "allegedly indicated that new machinery would 'decide whether H[ong]kong shall be allowed to continue under minimum economic standards or will be reduced to austerity' and that in either case 'the future of the Colony looks pretty grim.' " To Hunt, this "immediately nullified" the consulate's earlier successful efforts to "prevent outspoken comment until all elements possessed accurate facts [of] new US export policy."[45]

From Hunt's reports, it is clear that the consulate had an important role to play in reassuring the Hong Kong public that the Americans would take full account of the colony's concerns in drawing up the new licensing policy. However, U.S. officials in Hong Kong felt that their efforts were being undercut by the Department of Commerce, whose main concern was the prevention of U.S. exports to China, rather than the maintenance of confidence and economic well-being in the colony. In a word, the American "China Hands" were caught between the immediate needs of Hong Kong and the national interests of the United States.

What really put U.S. consular officers' relations with their host government to the test were the Congressional hearings about the dismissal of General Douglas MacArthur as the Commander of the United Nations forces in Korea in May–June 1951. When testifying before the Senate Armed Services and Foreign Relations Committees on May 3–4, MacArthur criticized Britain for its "token" contribution to the United Nations war effort and its continued trading with China. Citing a report from the U.S. consulate in Hong Kong, MacArthur read out a "very compendious list" of "strategic materials," which were exported from Hong Kong to the mainland between February 19 and March 4, 1951, including chemicals, steel bars, machinery, and petroleum products. He argued that these materials, totaling HK$210 million in value, would have been of "substantial assistance to the Communist force."[46]

The Hong Kong government and the public reacted strongly to MacArthur's criticisms. Governor Grantham regarded MacArthur's statement as "a gross distortion."[47] In fact, at the Congressional hearings, MacArthur cited, out of context, the report that he had obtained from the American consulate, mentioning merely the type of "strategic materials," but saying nothing about the volume of their export to China, which was very small. Indeed, in the case of petroleum products, with the exception of paraffin wax, it was nil.[48] On this issue, the U.S. officials in Hong Kong were on the side of their host. Consul General McConaughy immediately issued a public statement denying that his officers had listed petroleum among other products in the report allegedly quoted by MacArthur. On another occasion, McConaughy further stated that the American consulate "had reported on several occasions how conscientiously Hong Kong was enforcing the ban imposed on petrol exports" since July 1950. Thus, he "could only assume that General MacArthur had been misinformed or had made an error" in alleging that Hong Kong had exported petroleum products to the People's Republic.[49]

Through their export control work, U.S. economic officers in Hong Kong were generally convinced of the colonial authorities' cooperation in preventing strategic materials from reaching China (despite the continued smuggling).[50] But the anti-Communist elements in the U.S. administration, and in Congress and among the U.S. public, were not. They criticized Hong Kong (and Britain) for trading with China; the more extreme view even portrayed the Hong Kong business community as "a bunch of pirates," who were only interested in making money at a time when U.S. soldiers were being killed in the Korean Peninsula.[51] Such anti-British and anti-Hong

Kong feeling in the United States was incited by the MacArthur hearings. The American "China Hands" in Hong Kong found themselves in a dilemma, caught between standing up for their host government and identifying with their home government.

Worse still, after the MacArthur hearings, the Hong Kong authorities suspended the supply of economic information (e.g., the *Strategic Materials Bulletin*) to the U.S. consulate. Furious that this material had been passed into MacArthur's hands and was being used for political purposes, Grantham insisted that any resumption of supply be contingent on assurances from the Americans that no classified material would be made public without his consent, or that its release should not be attributed to official British sources in the future.[52] Other disputes between the American consulate and the local authorities during this period included allegations that the former was applying pressure to foreign and Chinese business firms in Hong Kong in order to discourage them from trading with China.[53] At a time when the Chinese Communists were fighting the Americans to a standstill in Korea, and when Washington and London differed over how the war should be waged, Anglo-American differences would inevitably be manifested in Hong Kong. It is impossible to detail all their differences here. Suffice it to say that things would have been even worse had it not been for the American "China Hands" efforts to minimize the impact of the Korean War on the colony. In late 1951, the U.S. administration agreed to give assurances to the Hong Kong government regarding the future use of classified economic material. To McConaughy, the agreement on the resumed supply of economic information "eliminates a principal complaint against the Hong Kong Government and should considerably raise the level of cooperation."[54]

Overt Propaganda

The third main aspect of U.S. operations in Hong Kong was information work. The United States Information Service (USIS) in Hong Kong was responsible for the production of anti-Communist materials for overt or white propaganda. Its main publications included *World Today* (or *America Today* prior to 1952), a semimonthly magazine attributed to USIS, and *Four Seas*, a monthly pictorial that was unattributed. It also produced pamphlets, leaflets, and Chinese language scripts for the Voice of America (VOA) broadcasts from transmitters in Manila and Honolulu. Other operations included running motion picture shows and USIS libraries in the territory.[55] Although based in Hong Kong, USIS ranked the Hong Kong audience, both Chinese and British, "only third and fourth in priorities," behind overseas Chinese and mainland Chinese audiences. Although anti-Communist materials were produced in Hong Kong, they were used mainly by other USIS posts in Southeast Asia and by different agencies in the United States.[56]

The Hong Kong government had strong reservations about certain USIS activities in Hong Kong, especially those targeted at the Hong Kong audience. It was sensitive to "anti-Chinese communist propaganda."[57] U.S. information officers had been cautioned against the use of Hong Kong as "a production or distribution point for material which would in any way antagonize Communist China and, thereby, jeopardize the future safety of the Colony."[58] The Hong Kong government considered unattributed material "illegal." The USIS function, it believed, was to "explain, by overt means, American policies and American life." This caused difficulties with U.S. information officers, since "some types of propaganda are much more efficacious when they are not attributed."[59]

Throughout the 1950s, the British restricted or even opposed outright USIS activities on several occasions. In January 1951, the Hong Kong government discontinued, without prior notification, the nightly relay of VOA news programs in Cantonese (*Guangdonghua*) over Radio Hong Kong. The official explanation for the cancellation of VOA broadcasts was the need to make a wider use of the British Broadcasting Company Overseas Services news in Mandarin. But underlying it was the British concern that recent American broadcasts had taken an "extremely belligerent" turn.[60] To Grantham, the United States was "well aware of our policy not to use Hong Kong as a base for propaganda against the Central People's Government," and had expressed "full understanding of our action," if not "complete agreement." But recent VOA broadcasts on China had been taking "a line widely divergent from the policy of His Majesty's Government."[61] The U.S. administration reacted strongly to Hong Kong's decision by instructing the consulate to deliver "an aggrieved protest to the Governor about absence of prior warning." While "not question[ing] the right of the Hongkong authorities to carry out this action," Paul Frillman, the head of USIS Hong Kong, felt that "it had been done in a most uncooperative manner."[62] Despite the U.S. protest, the Hong Kong government was adamant about its decision. In the aftermath of the incident, Radio Hong Kong, as U.S. information officers observed, "remained relatively indifferent to the resources of USIS Hong Kong." The result was that USIS had no choice but to sever all relations with the two local radio outlets.[63]

In May 1953, the Hong Kong Police confiscated a truckload of USIS leaflets containing a speech by the U.S. Secretary of Labor to be distributed to local workers.[64] The Hong Kong government was always sensitive to the pro-Beijing and pro-Nationalist elements in labor unions, and would not welcome any U.S. involvement. U.S. information officers realized that the local authorities were "particularly touchy" in this sensitive field, and their operations had to be "as unobtrusive as possible." As a result, USIS Hong Kong decided to stop producing and distributing materials designed primarily for Hong Kong workers. The showing of motion pictures (together with the lending of books to union reading rooms) remained the only effective means of reaching labor.[65]

In the field of education, the Hong Kong government exercised tight control over political propaganda in both leftist and rightist schools. Leftist schools, in particular, felt that they were the main target of government repression.[66] But the colonial authorities equally did not take a hands-off approach toward U.S. propaganda, and American offers to assist in the distribution of literature to counter left-wing influence in schools were often turned down.[67] In short, the British attitude toward USIS operations targeted at the Hong Kong audience fluctuated between tacit consent at best, and outright opposition at worst.[68]

The American "China Hands" were willing to accommodate their host government. Arthur William Hummel, Jr., then head of USIS Hong Kong, was sensitive to the territory's difficulties. Born into a missionary family in 1920 China, and having lived part of his life there, Hummel was typical of the old "China Hands," who had great affection for China's great civilization. His long involvement with China and the Chinese also shaped his pragmatic attitude toward the People's Republic. In Hong Kong, Hummel worked with a team of Chinese writers and translators, a group of "talented people" whom he appreciated.[69] Thus, he was inclined not to rock the British boat. As Hummel reported to Washington in 1954, "the Hong Kong government thinks it has a vested interest in peace and quiet . . . [Thus] we have scrupulously avoided activities among the local population which might conceivably arouse alarm in the minds of the authorities, whom we know maintain vigilant surveillance over us."[70] To the American "China Hands," "Hong Kong is, after all, a British colony, and we cannot expect to carry on activities that the British find objectionable." Besides, it would be "most short-sighted to jeopardize our principal Hong Kong function, the preparation of material for Chinese audiences elsewhere, in our eagerness to reach the two million Chinese in the colony."[71] It is true that most of the anti-Communist materials produced in Hong Kong were not used locally, but by other USIS posts in Southeast Asia to influence the overseas Chinese there. Thus, after 1954, the USIS curtailed those activities designed for Hong Kong itself, and focused instead on audiences in Southeast Asia and mainland China.[72]

This policy of accommodation by USIS Hong Kong did not create much controversy within the administration. Unlike their colleagues carrying out export control work, especially during the Korean War period, U.S. information officers were fortunate that their operations in the territory were not so controversial as to attract strong criticism from other U.S. departments, from Congress, and from the American public. Even the United States Information Agency (USIA) gave its overseas staff a relatively free hand in day-to-day operations. While USIA provided firmer guidelines to the Hong Kong post in the years following early 1954, Hummel found that he still had "plenty of room for freedom of action within the range of policy directives."[73] There was no serious conflict in Hummel's mind between patriotism and pragmatism.

CONCLUSION: MULTIPLE IDENTITIES

In carrying out their intelligence, export control, and propaganda operations in Hong Kong, U.S. officials on the ground were generally willing to work within the political and legal framework laid out by the colonial authorities. This was inevitable, since the American sojourners were, after all, in a host environment. That Hong Kong was a *British* colony was not insignificant. The Americans respected Britain as a principal Cold War ally and a responsible colonial power. This respect was rooted in the American ideology of racial hierarchy, which placed the Anglo-Saxon race at the top, together with the Anglo-American community of values and of language, which facilitated close consultation and mutual understanding.[74] Although British officials in Hong Kong did not always look with favor on the activities of the American consulate, at a personal level successive consuls general such as Rankin and Drumright remained on good terms with Governor Grantham. Any differences were to be dealt with in a way that, so far as possible, accommodated both sides.

A Hong Kong posting was something that was sought after by U.S. Foreign Service officers. It served as a good training ground for a new generation of China experts, who were innovative, forward looking, and free from extreme anti-Communist pressures (Chinese

Nationalist and McCarthyite alike).[75] As a result of their field experience, the American China watchers in Hong Kong gradually developed a more realistic understanding of Communist China and acquired greater sympathy for the precarious colony than did the officers in their home administration. They held the view that the new China was there to stay, and that the United States had to deal with it positively. Although, at the time, their views were not taken seriously by decision-makers in Washington (nor even by the "China watchers' watchers" in Hong Kong), in the long run the wisdom of their course would be proven. Field experience also impressed upon U.S. consular officers the fragile coexistence between Hong Kong and Communist China. Accordingly, U.S. operations had to be as discreet and as subtle as possible, and from time to time they were willing to curtail those activities that were seen by the British as too "provocative." The American "China Hands" played an important role in mediating between the Hong Kong and U.S. governments, and in minimizing the impact of the Sino-American confrontation on the territory.

One should not go so far, however, as to say that the American "China Hands" in Hong Kong "imagined" themselves as a distinct community, ignoring the Cold War requirements of their home government. Nor should one suggest that the American sojourners abandoned their national identity and identified themselves with the indigenous population. Quite the contrary, U.S. consuls general such as Rankin and Drumright were intensely anti-Communist, each later becoming U.S. ambassadors to Taiwan and staunch supporters of Jiang Jieshi (Chiang Kai-shek). To a greater or lesser extent, U.S. officials who were posted to Hong Kong brought with them an ethnocentric worldview, with Washington at the center. Social interactions with the local people were limited to the Chinese staff within the consulate, and members of the Chinese elite in the broader society. (Of course, U.S. interrogators "interacted" with the Chinese refugees as well.) U.S. officials preserved their "Americanness" by identifying with their own institutions and traditions—for example, going to the American Club in Hong Kong (and the British clubs) and celebrating their July Fourth Independence Day.[76] In a word, however sympathetic their attitude toward Hong Kong might have become, the American "China Hands" stopped very far short of "going native."

Nevertheless, the American "China Hands" in Hong Kong were generally successful in striking a balance between their national identity and the perspectives they gained from living locally, as between the implementation of U.S. foreign policy and the maintenance of Hong Kong's stability. In a sense, they had multiple identities: they were simultaneously professional individuals in China watching, pragmatic allies of the British colonial state, and patriotic nationals of the United States. Their success in maintaining these multiple identities was due in no small part to the fact that their home government gave them a relatively free hand in their day-to-day operations in Hong Kong. This was especially the case regarding their U.S. intelligence and propaganda operations (although less so in export control work), which did not often command the attention of top decision-makers or of the American public.

Notes

1. Wang Gungwu, ed., *Xianggangshi xinbian* (Hong Kong History: New Perspectives), vol. II (Hong Kong: Joint Publishing (H.K.) Co., 1997), p. 743.
2. Liu Shuyong, ed., *Jianming Xianggangshi* (A Concise History of Hong Kong) (Hong Kong: Joint Publishing (H.K.) Co., 1998), pp. 34 and 37.
3. For an interesting account of American activities in China and Hong Kong, see Andrew Coe, *Eagles & Dragons: A History of Americans in China & the Origins of the American Club Hong Kong* (Hong Kong: American Club, 1997).
4. An American missionary institution which moved its operations from the mainland to Hong Kong after 1949 was Yale-in-China. See Nancy E. Chapman, *The Yale-China Association: A Centennial History* (Hong Kong: Chinese University Press, 2001), pp. 77–93.
5. Coe, *Eagles & Dragons*, p. 11.
6. The term American "China Hands" in Hong Kong is used here as a shorthand for all consuls general, consuls, vice-consuls, political and economic officers, and information officers within the U.S. consulate general in Hong Kong, notwithstanding their differences of background and outlook. They all shared striking similarities in their attitude toward China and U.S. operations in Hong Kong, as discussed later. The term, however, does not include covert specialists of the Central Intelligence Agency (CIA) Hong Kong station, which was attached to, but nonetheless acted independently of the American consulate. Although some American missionaries and scholars in Hong Kong could be classified as "China Hands" in this sense, they are not the focus of this chapter.
7. See e.g., Nancy Bernkopf Tucker, *Taiwan, Hong Kong, and the United States, 1945–1992: Uncertain Friendships* (New York: Twayne Publishers, 1994); Richard Deacon, *The Chinese Secret Service*, rev. and updated edn. (London: Grafton Books, 1989).
8. Johannes R. Lombardo, "A Mission of Espionage, Intelligence and Psychological Operations: The American Consulate in Hong Kong, 1949–64," *Intelligence and National Security*, vol. 14, no. 4 (Winter 1999), pp. 64–81.

9. Hong Kong to Colonial Office, 5 June 1950, FO 371/83557, FC1908/8/G; Hall to Trench, 27 September 1951, FO 371/92385, FC1905/9, The National Archives, formerly known as Public Record Office (hereafter PRO), Kew, U.K.; *Dagongbao*, January 12, 1958.
10. Richard A. Johnson, *The Administration of United States Foreign Policy* (Austin: University of Texas Press, 1971), p. 211.
11. For a study of the American "Old China Hands," see Paul Gordon Lauren, ed., *The China Hands' Legacy: Ethics and Diplomacy* (Boulder: Westview Press, 1987).
12. This chapter draws heavily on the oral history interviews conducted by the Association for Diplomatic Studies, Foreign Affairs Oral History Program (hereafter FAOHP), which are housed in the Lauinger Library of Georgetown University, Washington, D.C. Extracts of the most important interviews can be found in Nancy Bernkopf Tucker, comp., *China Confidential: American Diplomats and Sino-American Relations, 1945–1996* (New York: Columbia University Press, 2001).
13. For example, Consul General Karl Rankin found Hong Kong a "most pleasant and interesting post." Jerome K. Holloway, an economic officer in the consulate, recollected that Hong Kong was "my best post . . . [E]veryone seemed to me to have a real interest in China and what was going on in China. And it was a very professional group." Rankin to Butrick, 2 November 1949, Karl L. Rankin Papers 1916–1973, Correspondence (April 1948–May 1950), Box 4, Folder 5, Manuscripts Division, Department of Rare Books and Special Collections, Princeton University Library (hereafter PUL), Princeton, New Jersey; Jerome K. Holloway Oral History Interview, June 16, 1989, FAOHP, p. 32.
14. Rankin to McFall, June 10, 1950, Karl L. Rankin Papers 1916–1973, Correspondence (June 1950–April 1953), Box 5, Folder 1, PUL.
15. Ralph N. Clough Oral History Interview, April 16, 1990, FAOHP, pp. 62–63.
16. Memorandum for Saltzman by Hanes, Jr., August 18, 1954, Papers of John Foster Dulles, Personnel Series, Chiefs of Mission Subseries, Box 1, Dwight D. Eisenhower Library, Abilene, Kansas.
17. Ralph N. Clough Oral History Interview, April 16, 1990, FAOHP, p. 57.
18. John H. Holdridge Oral History, July 20, 1955, FAOHP, p. 39.
19. Ibid., p. 55.
20. Lindsey Grant Oral History Interview, January 31, 1990, FAOHP, pp. 5 and 14.
21. For example, Lindsey Grant later served as Assistant to Marshall Green (Principal Deputy Assistant Secretary of State) in a China policy review in mid-1963. Both were key participants in the drafting of a speech by Roger Hilsman (Assistant Secretary of State for Asia) delivered in December 1963 (the famous Hilsman's China speech),

which called for a relaxation of U.S. policy toward China, one of the first of many long steps that culminated in the U.S. opening to China in 1972. Indeed, Green himself had also been U.S. consul general in Hong Kong in the early 1960s. See James C. Thomson, Jr., "On the Making of U.S. China Policy, 1961–9: A Study in Bureaucratic Politics," *China Quarterly*, no. 50 (April/June 1972), pp. 220–43.

22. Declassified material on the British Secret Service in Hong Kong is very thin. For some brief accounts, see Luo, Ya (Lo Ah), *Zhengzhibu huiyilu* (Memories of the Special Branch) (Hong Kong: Xianggang zhongwen daxue yatai yanjiusuo haiwai huaren yanjiushe, 1996), pp. 51–52; Stephen Dorril, *M16: Fifty Years of Special Operations* (London: Fourth Estate, 2000), p. 711.
23. Carroll to Heck, December 9, 1952, Record Group (hereafter RG) 59, Records of the Division of Acquisition and Distribution, Office of Libraries and Intelligence, Special Assistant for Intelligence (hereafter DAD) 1947–1955, Box 8; Zwolanek to Carroll, January 21, 1954, ibid., National Archives and Records Administration (hereafter NA), College Park, Maryland; Paul Kreisberg Oral History Interview, April 8, 1989, FAOHP, pp. 10–12.
24. John H. Holdridge Oral History Interview, July 20, 1995, FAOHP, p. 35.
25. A long-time CIA covert specialist revealed that his responsibilities included supporting "a refugee interrogation unit in Hong Kong operated jointly with the British" in the 1950s. Ralph W. McGehee, *Deadly Deceits: My 25 Years in the CIA* (New York: Sheridan Square Publications, 1983), p. 21. Also see Richard J. Aldrich, " 'The Value of Residual Empire': Anglo-American Intelligence Co-operation in Asia after 1945," in Richard J. Aldrich and Michael F. Hopkins, eds., *Intelligence, Defence and Diplomacy: British Policy in the Post-War World* (Ilford, Essex: Frank Cass, 1994), pp. 226–58.
26. The Hong Kong branch of the Regional Information Office was created in 1949 to produce propaganda materials, both anti-Communist and positive, for Asian consumption. It furthered the aims both of its headquarters in Singapore and of the Information Research Department in London, each of which was responsible for secret psychological operations at home and abroad. W. Scott Lucas and C. J. Morris, "A Very British Crusade: The Information Research Department and the Beginning of the Cold War" in Richard J. Aldrich, ed., *British Intelligence, Strategy and the Cold War, 1945–51* (London: Routledge, 1992), p. 21.
27. Zwolanek to Pope, January 14, 1954, RG 59, DAD 1947–1955, Box 8; Harris to Cook, August 26, 1952, RG 59, Records of the Office of Chinese Affairs (hereafter CA) 1945–1955, Reel 29, NA.
28. Hong Kong to State Department, February 15, 1951, 746G.00/2-1551, RG 59, Decimal Files (hereafter DF) 1950–1954, Box 3597; Strong to Clubb, March 1, 1951, 746G.00/3-151, ibid., NA.

29. For example, *Wenhuibao*, August 21, 1957; *Dagongbao*, October 7, 1958.
30. See e. g., Hong Kong to Colonial Office, February 20, 1950, FO 371/83557, FC1908/1; Singapore to Foreign Office, March 4, 1950, FO 371/83557, FC1908/2; Shattock to Graves, March 22, 1950, ibid., PRO.
31. Quoted in Frank Welsh, *A History of Hong Kong*, rev. edn. (London: HarperCollins Publishers, 1997), p. 447.
32. Alexander Grantham, *Via Ports: From Hong Kong to Hong Kong* (Hong Kong: Hong Kong University Press, 1965), pp. 169–70.
33. Ibid., p. 169.
34. Karl Lott Rankin, *China Assignment* (Seattle: University of Washington Press, 1964), p. 27.
35. Drumright to McConaughy, June 19, 1956, RG 59, CA 1954–1956, Miscellaneous File—1956, Box 15, NA; Rankin, *China Assignment*, p. 27.
36. Graves to Shattock, April 1, 1950, FO 371/83557, FC1908/4, PRO; FEIT D-9/8, "Hong Kong Government Concern over Size of U.S. Consular Establishment," September 22, 1955, RG 59, Executive Secretariat Conference Files 1949–1963, Box 83, NA.
37. In his memoirs, Peer de Silva, the CIA chief in Hong Kong in the early 1960s, talked about how, during his first day in the station, the U.S. consul general and principal British officials cautioned him about "the rules of the game in intelligence work in Hong Kong." Peer de Silva, *Sub Rosa: The CIA and the Uses of Intelligence* (New York: Time Books, 1978), pp. 192–93.
38. Paul Kreisberg Oral History Interview, April 8, 1989, FAOHP, p. 22. In the course of the 1950s, there was no evidence that U.S. secret agents used Hong Kong for covert operations against China. Even the most dramatic attempt on Premier Zhou Enlai's life—the *Kashmir Princess* incident of April 11, 1955—was attributed to the work of Guomindang secret agents, not the "hidden-hands" of the Americans. For a detailed account, see Steve Tsang, "Target Zhou Enlai: The 'Kashmir Princess' Incident of 1955," *China Quarterly*, no. 139 (September 1994), pp. 766–82.
39. Memorandum on Hong Kong, March 1953, RG 59, CA 1945–1955, Reel 18, NA.
40. Richard E. Johnson Oral History Interview, January 30, 1991, FAOHP, pp. 6–8.
41. Some economic historians have argued that the impact of the Korean War embargo on Hong Kong's economy should not be exaggerated: it merely reduced the level of trade to that which prevailed in the late 1940s before the Korean War boom. See Catherine R. Schenk, *Hong Kong as an International Financial Centre: Emergence and Development 1945–65* (London: Routledge, 2001), pp. 39–42.

42. State Department to Hong Kong, December 3, 1950, RG 84, Hong Kong Consulate General Security-Segregated General Records (hereafter HKCGR) 1943–1955, Box 14, NA.
43. In 1950, the United States came second (behind China) as the principal source of Hong Kong's imports, totaling about HK$655 million. Census and Statistics Department, *Hong Kong Statistics, 1947–67* (Hong Kong: Government Printer, 1969), p. 97. On the Hong Kong Governor's concern about the possible impact of the U.S. embargo on the colony, see Hong Kong to Colonial Office, December 16, 1950, FO 371/83371, FC1121/183, PRO.
44. Hong Kong to State Department, December 4, 1950, RG 84, HKCGR 1943–1955, Box 14, NA.
45. Hong Kong to State Department, December 19, 1950, RG 84, HKCGR 1943–1955, Box 14; Hong Kong to State Department, December 21, 1950, ibid., NA.
46. U.S. Congress, Senate, Committee on Armed Services and Committee on Foreign Relations, *Military Situation in the Far East*, 82nd Congress, 1st Session, 1951 (Washington, D.C.: Government Printing Office, 1951), Part I, pp. 51–52 and 121–22.
47. Hong Kong to Colonial Office, May 6, 1951, FO 371/92278, FC1121/164, PRO.
48. For the report, see Hong Kong to State Department, March 29, 1951, RG 84, Hong Kong Consulate General, Records Re Hong Kong Trade with Communist Controlled Areas, 1950–1954, Box 1, NA. As a matter of fact, the report quoted by MacArthur at the hearings was an enclosure to a confidential dispatch from the U.S. consulate in Hong Kong to the State Department (entitled Strategic Materials Bulletin). The enclosure contained information furnished at fortnightly intervals by the colonial authorities to the consulate for the purpose of scrutinizing the flow of goods to China. It listed a wide range of "strategic materials" which were believed to be of interest to the United States, but might not necessarily be of strategic importance in the strictest sense.
49. *South China Morning Post*, May 8, 1951; Memorandum of Conversation, May 7, 1951, RG 59, CA 1945–1955, Reel 24, NA.
50. Hong Kong to Colonial Office, March 31, 1951, FO 371/92277, FC1121/144, PRO; Hong Kong to State Department, December 10, 1951, RG 84, HKCGR 1943–1955, Box 14, NA.
51. Foreign Office Minute by Franklin, January 15, 1951, FO 371/92274, FC1121/37; Tokyo to Treasury, January 15, 1951, FO 371/92274, FC1121/46, PRO.
52. Hong Kong to State Department, May 26, 1951, Papers of Harry S. Truman, Department of State Selected Records Relating to the Korean War, Topical File, Box 11; State Department to London, July 17, 1951, ibid., Harry S. Truman Library, Independence, Missouri.

53. Hong Kong to Colonial Office, April 23, 1951, FO 371/92385, FC1905/6, PRO.
54. Hong Kong to State Department, December 7, 1951, RG 84, HKCGR 1943–1955, Box 15, NA.
55. USIS Hong Kong to USIA, March 16, 1953, RG 84, Hong Kong Consulate General, Classified General Records of the United States Information Service, Hong Kong (hereafter GRUSIS) 1951–1955, Box 3, NA.
56. Inspection Report to State Department by Olson, June 9, 1953, RG 84, GRUSIS 1951–1955, Box 1, NA.
57. Memorandum of Conversation, February 2, 1951, RG 59, CA 1945–1955, Reel 24, NA.
58. Frillman to Steiner, December 19, 1950, RG 84, GRUSIS 1951–1955, Box 4, NA.
59. Hong Kong to State Department, March 26, 1953, RG 84, GRUSIS 1951–1955, Box 3; USIS Hong Kong to USIA, August 19, 1953, ibid., NA.
60. Murray to Frillman, January 23, 1951, FO 953/1079, PB1066/14; Smith to Rayner, January 25, 1951, ibid., PRO.
61. Hong Kong to Colonial Office, February 6, 1951, FO 953/1079, PB1066/14, PRO.
62. Washington to Foreign Office, February 1, 1951, FO 953/1079, PB1066/14; Rayner to Murray, March 3, 1951, FO 953/1079, PB1066/11, PRO.
63. Hong Kong to State Department, March 26, 1953, RG 84, GRUSIS 1951–1955, Box 3, NA.
64. USIS Hong Kong to USIA, April 30, 1956, RG 263, The Murphy Collection on International Communism, 1917–1958, China, Box 34, NA.
65. USIS Hong Kong to USIA, August 19, 1953, RG 84 GRUSIS 1951–1955, Box 3; USIS Hong Kong to USIA, April 30, 1956, RG 263, The Murphy Collection on International Communism, 1917–1958, China, Box 34; USIS Hong Kong to USIA, March 14, 1955, RG 84, GRUSIS 1951–1955, Box 4, NA.
66. Wang, ed., *Xianggangshi xinbian*, vol. II, p. 477.
67. Hong Kong to State Department, December 7, 1955, RG 84, GRUSIS 1951–1955, Box 5; Hong Kong to State Department, August 24, 1955, 746G.00/8-2455, RG 59, DF 1955–1959, Box 3267, NA.
68. Inspection Report by Olson to State Department, June 9, 1953, RG 84, GRUSIS 1951–1955, Box 1, NA.
69. Arthur William Hummel, Jr. Oral History Interview, April 13, and June 16, 1994, FAOHP.
70. USIS Hong Kong to USIA, August 10, 1954, RG 84, GRUSIS 1951–1955, Box 4, NA.
71. Inspection Report by Olson to State Department, June 9, 1953, RG 84, GRUSIS 1951–1955, Box 1, NA.

72. USIS Hong Kong to USIA, August 10, 1954, RG 84, GRUSIS 1951–1955, Box 4; USIS Hong Kong to USIA, March 14, 1955, ibid., NA.
73. USIS Hong Kong to USIA, August 10, 1954, RG 84, GRUSIS 1951–1955, Box 4.
74. See Michael H. Hunt, "Conclusions: the Decolonization Puzzle in US Policy—Promise versus Performance," in David Ryan and Victor Pungong, eds., *The United States and Decolonization: Power and Freedom* (Basingstoke, Hampshire: Macmillan, 2000), pp. 207–29.
75. Thomson, "On the Making of U.S. China Policy, 1961–9," p. 226.
76. See Coe, *Eagles & Dragons.*

Suggestions for Further Reading

Adam Schall Catholic Community, the Chinese University of Hong Kong, 1972–2002. Hong Kong: Adam Schall Catholic Community, 2002.

Aldrich, Richard J., Gary D. Rawnsley, and Ming-Yeh T. Rawnsley, eds. *The Clandestine Cold War in Asia, 1945–65: Western Intelligence, Propaganda and Special Operations.* London: Frank Cass, 2000.

Archer, Bernice and Kent Fedorowich. "The Women of Stanley: Internment in Hong Kong, 1942–45." *Women's History Review*, vol. 5, no. 3 (1996): 373–99.

Baird, Kenneth G. *Letters to Harvelyn: From Japanese POW Camps: A Canadian Soldier's Letters to His Young Daughter during World War II.* Edited by Harvelyn Baird McInnis. Toronto: HarperCollins, 2002.

Bickley, Verner Courtenay. *Searching for Frederick and Adventures along the Way.* Hong Kong: Asia 2000, 2001.

Blake, Robert. *Jardine Matheson: Traders of the Far East.* London: Weidenfeld & Nicolson, 1999.

Blyth, Sally and Ian Wotherspoon, eds. *Hong Kong Remembers.* Hong Kong: Oxford University Press, 1996.

Bowie, Donald C. "Captive Surgeon in Hong Kong: The Story of the British Military Hospital, Hong Kong 1942–1945." *Journal of the Hong Kong Branch of the Royal Asiatic Society*, vol. 15 (1975): 150–290.

Brown, Deborah A. "The Roman Catholic Church in Hong Kong: Freedom's Advocate Struggles with the SAR Government in Electoral Politics and Education." *American Asian Review*, vol. 19, no. 4 (Winter 2001): 19–61.

Burton, Antoinette, ed. *After the Imperial Turn: Thinking with and through the Nation.* Durham: Duke University Press, 2003.

Cambon, Kenneth. *Guest of Hirohito.* Vancouver: PW Press, 1990.

Chan Cham Yi. *Ribenren yu Xianggang: shijiu shiji jianwenlu* (The Japanese and Hong Kong: Records of the Nineteenth Century). Hong Kong: Hong Kong Educational Publishing Co., 1995.

Chan, Ming K. *Luori Xiangjiang hong: Wei Yixin zhengquan de lishi tiaozhan* (The British Sunset in Hong Kong: Historical Challenges in the Wilsonian Era of Transition). Hong Kong: Hong Kong Economic Journal, 1989.

———, ed. *Precarious Balance: Hong Kong between China and Britain, 1842–1992.* With the collaboration of John D. Young. Armonk, NY: M.E. Sharpe, 1994.

Chen Ningsheng and Zhang Xueren, trans. and eds. *Xianggang yu Yihe yanghang: lishi de huigu ji youguan Yihe yanghang yiwen liangzhong* (Jardine, Matheson & Co., and Hong Kong). Wuchang: Wuhan daxue chubanshe, 1986.

Choa, G. H. "The Lowson Diary: A Record of the Early Phase of the Hong Kong Bubonic Plague 1894." *Journal of the Hong Kong Branch of the Royal Asiatic Society*, vol. 33 (1993): 129–45.

Chu, Cindy Yik-yi. *The Maryknoll Sisters in Hong Kong, 1921–1969: In Love with the Chinese.* New York: Palgrave Macmillan, 2004.

——. "From the Pursuit of Converts to the Relief of Refugees: The Maryknoll Sisters in Twentieth-Century Hong Kong." *The Historian*, vol. 65, no. 2 (Winter 2002): 353–76.

Coe, Andrew. *Eagles & Dragons: A History of Americans in China & the Origins of the American Club Hong Kong.* With a preface by Burton Levin. Hong Kong: American Club, 1997.

Connell, Carol Matheson. "Jardine Matheson & Company: The Role of External Organization in a Nineteenth-Century Trading Firm." *Enterprise & Society*, vol. 4, no. 1 (March 2003): 99–138.

——. *A Business in Risk: Jardine Matheson and the Hong Kong Trading Industry.* Westport, Conn.: Praeger, 2004.

Constable, Nicole. *Christian Souls and Chinese Spirits: A Hakka Community in Hong Kong.* Berkeley: University of California Press, 1994.

Crisswell, Colin N. *The Taipans: Hong Kong's Merchant Princes.* New York: Oxford University Press, 1981.

Crowell, Todd. *Farewell, My Colony: Last Days in the Life of British Hong Kong.* Hong Kong: Asia 2000, 1998.

Des Voeux, George William, Sir. *My Colonial Service in British Guiana, St. Lucia, Trinidad, Fiji, Australia, New Foundland, and Hong Kong, with Interludes.* London: John Murray, 1903.

Dew, Gwen. *Prisoner of the Japs.* New York: Alfred A. Knopf, 1943.

Dimbleby, Jonathan. *The Last Governor: Chris Patten & the Handover of Hong Kong.* London: Little, Brown & Co., 1997.

Drage, Charles. *Taikoo.* London: Constable, 1970.

England, Joe. *Industrial Relations and Law in Hong Kong*, second edn. Hong Kong: Oxford University Press, 1989.

England, Joe and John Rear. *Chinese Labour under British Rule: A Critical Study of Labour Relations and Law in Hong Kong.* Hong Kong: Oxford University Press, 1975.

Feng Bangyan. *Xianggang Yingzi caituan: yiba siyi nian zhi yijiu jiuliu nian* (British Corporations in Hong Kong: 1841–1996). Hong Kong: Joint Publishing (H.K.) Co., 1996.

Fu Wenling, ed. *Riben Hengbin zhengjin yinhang zai Hua huodong shiliao* (Historical Material on Activities of Yokohama Shokin Ginko in China). Beijing: Zhongguo jinrong chubanshe, 1992.

Fukuda, Kazuo John. *The Total Concern for People: An Empty Slogan of Japanese Management in Hong Kong?* Hong Kong: Department of Business & Management, City Polytechnic of Hong Kong, 1989.

Germany in Hong Kong: 50 Years Consulate General of the Federal Republic of Germany, 40 Years Goethe-Institut Hong Kong, 20 Years German Chamber of Commerce. Hong Kong: German Chamber of Commerce, Goethe-Institut, Consulate General of the Federal Republic of Germany, 2003.

Gittins, Jean (Hotung). *I Was at Stanley.* Hong Kong: n.p., 1946.

——. *Stanley: Behind Barbed Wire.* Hong Kong: Hong Kong University Press, 1982.

Grantham, Alexander William George Herder, Sir. *Via Ports: From Hong Kong to Hong Kong.* Hong Kong: Hong Kong University Press, 1965.

Ha, Louis. "The Foundation of the Catholic Mission in Hong Kong, 1841–1894." Ph. D. diss., University of Hong Kong, 1998.

Hammond, Robert Bruce. *Bondservants of the Japanese: Missionaries' Experiences during the Siege of Hong Kong.* Pasadena, Calif.: R. B. Hammond Voice of China & Asia, 1957, ca. 1943.

Higgins, Mary Tyng. *With a War On!: China, Haiphong, Hong Kong.* Sewanee, Tenn.: M.T. Higgins, 1984.

Ho Wai-Yip. "Historical Analysis of Islamic Community Development in Hong Kong: Struggle for Recognition in the Post-Colonial Era." *Journal of Muslim Minority Affairs*, vol. 21, no. 1 (April 2001): 63–77.

Hoe, Susanna. *The Private Life of Old Hong Kong: Western Women in the British Colony, 1841–1941.* Hong Kong: Oxford University Press, 1991.

Hoe, Susanna and Derek Roebuck. *The Taking of Hong Kong: Charles and Clara Elliot in China Waters.* Richmond: Curzon, 1999.

Holdsworth, May. *Foreign Devils: Expatriates in Hong Kong.* With additional text by Caroline Courtauld. Hong Kong: Oxford University Press, 2002.

Hong Kong: The Formative Years, 1842–1912. Hong Kong: Shell Co. of Hong Kong, 1963.

Jardines in Business in Southeast Asia. Hong Kong: Jardines, 2003.

Jardines Today. Hong Kong: Jardine, Matheson & Co., 1978.

Jeter, Jeremiah Bell. *A Memoir of Mrs. Henrietta Shuck: The First American Female Missionary to China.* Boston: Gould, Kendall & Lincoln, 1846.

Keswick, Maggie, ed. *The Thistle and the Jade: A Celebration of 150 Years of Jardine, Matheson & Co.* London: Octopus Books, 1982.

King, Frank H. H. *Survey Our Empire!: Robert Montgomery Martin (1801?–1868), Late Treasurer to the Queen at Hong-Kong, and Member of Her Majesty's Legislative Council in China: A Bio-Bibliography.* Hong Kong: Centre of Asian Studies, University of Hong Kong, 1979.

——. *The Hongkong Bank in the Period of Development and Nationalism, 1941–1984: From Regional Bank to Multinational Group.* Cambridge: Cambridge University Press, 1991.

King, Frank H. H., Catherine E. King, and David J. S. King. *The Hongkong Bank in Late Imperial China, 1864–1902: On an Even Keel.* Cambridge: Cambridge University Press, 1987.

——. *The Hongkong Bank in the Period of Imperialism and War, 1895–1918: Wayfoong, the Focus of Wealth.* Cambridge: Cambridge University Press, 1988.

King, Frank H. H., Catherine E. King, and David J. S. King. *The Hongkong Bank between the Wars and the Bank Interned, 1919–1945: Return from Grandeur*. Cambridge: Cambridge University Press, 1988.

Ko Tinming. *The Sacred Citizens and the Secular City: Political Participation of Protestant Ministers in Hong Kong during a Time of Change*. Aldershot: Ashgate, 2000.

Kwok Siu-tong and Kirti Narain. *Co-Prosperity in Cross-Culturalism: Indians in Hong Kong*. Hong Kong: Commercial Press, 2003.

Lau Sum-yin. "Escape, Exploration and Pursuit: Japanese Women Working in Hong Kong." M. Phil. diss., University of Hong Kong, 1998.

Le Fevour, Edward. *Western Enterprise in Late Ch'ing China: A Selective Survey of Jardine, Matheson and Company's Operations, 1842–1895*. Cambridge, Mass.: East Asian Research Center, Harvard University, 1968.

Leiper, Gerald Andrew. *A Yen for My Thoughts*. Hong Kong: South China Morning Post, 1982.

Lethbridge, Henry J. *Hong Kong, Stability and Change: A Collection of Essays*. Hong Kong: Oxford University Press, 1978.

Lockwood, Stephen Chapman. *Augustine Heard and Company, 1858–1862: American Merchants in China*. Cambridge, Mass.: East Asian Research Center, Harvard University, 1971.

MacDonell, George S. *One Soldier's Story 1939–1945: From the Fall of Hong Kong to the Defeat of Japan*. Toronto: Dundurn Press, 2002.

Marsman, Jan Henrik. *I Escaped from Hong Kong*. New York: Reynal & Hitchcock, 1942.

Mathers, Jean. *Twisting the Tail of the Dragon*. Sussex: Book Guild, 1994.

McLean, David Alexander. "British Banking and Government in China: The Foreign Office and the Hongkong and Shanghai Bank, 1895–1914." Ph.D. diss., University of Cambridge, 1976.

Meier, Richard L. *Life alongside a Revolution: A Hong Kong Diary, June 1989*. Berkeley, Calif.: Institute of Urban & Regional Development, University of California at Berkeley, 1989.

Munn, Christopher. *Anglo-China: Chinese People and British Rule in Hong Kong, 1841–1880*. Richmond: Curzon, 2001.

Nakano Yumiko. "The Experience of Japanese Expatriate Wives in Hong Kong: The Reproduction of Conservative Social Patterns." M. Phil. diss., University of Hong Kong, 1995.

Patten, Chris. *East and West: The Last Governor of Hong Kong on Power, Freedom and the Future*. London & Basingstoke: Macmillan, 1998.

Plüss, Caroline. "Hong Kong's Muslim Organisations: Creating and Expressing Collective Identities." *China Perspectives*, no. 29 (May–June 2000): 19–23.

Rewarding Success: The First Hundred Years of Jebsen & Company, 1895–1995. Hong Kong: Jebsen & Co., 1995.

Richardson, Sam S. *The Royal Marines and Hong Kong, 1840–1997*. Portsmouth: Royal Marines Historical Society, 1997.

Rogers, Glenn. *British Champions in Hong Kong*. Hong Kong: Mediazone, 2002.

Roland, Charles G. "Massacre and Rape in Hong Kong: Two Case Studies Involving Medical Personnel and Patients." *Journal of Contemporary History*, vol. 32, no. 1 (January 1997): 43–61.

——. *Long Night's Journey into Day: Prisoners of War in Hong Kong and Japan, 1941–1945*. Waterloo, Ontario: Wilfrid Laurier University Press, 2001.

Ryan, Thomas F. *The Story of a Hundred Years: The Pontifical Institute of Foreign Missions, (P.I.M.E.), in Hong Kong, 1858–1958*. Hong Kong: Catholic Truth Society, 1959.

Shell and Hong Kong: A 50th Anniversary Souvenir. Hong Kong: Shell Co. of Hong Kong, 1963.

Smith, Carl T. "The Gillespie Brothers: Early Links between Hong Kong and California." *Chung Chi Bulletin*, no. 47 (December 1969): 23–28.

——. "The Adaption of the Protestant Church to a Chinese and Colonial Situation." Working Paper, Centre of Asian Studies, University of Hong Kong, 1983.

——. *Chinese Christians: Elites, Middlemen, and the Church in Hong Kong*. With a foreword by James Hayes. Hong Kong: Oxford University Press, 1985.

——. "The German Speaking Community in Hong Kong 1846–1918." *Journal of the Hong Kong Branch of the Royal Asiatic Society*, vol. 34 (1994): 1–55.

Smith, George. *A Narrative of an Exploratory Visit to each of the Consular Cities of China, and to the Islands of Hong Kong and Chusan in behalf of the Church Missionary Society, in the Years 1844, 1845, 1846*. London: Seeley, Burnside, 1847.

Snow, Philip. *The Fall of Hong Kong: Britain, China and the Japanese Occupation*. New Haven: Yale University Press, 2003.

Stewart, Peter and Fernando Pereira, eds. *American Fortnight, October 15–28, 1973*. Hong Kong: Hongkong Standard Newspapers, 1973.

Tam Yue-him, ed. *Hong Kong and Japan: Growing Cultural and Economic Interactions, 1845–1987: A Special Volume in Commemoration of the 25th Anniversary of the Japan Society of Hong Kong*. Hong Kong: Japan Society of Hong Kong, 1988.

The Germans and Their Activities in South China and Hong Kong. Canton: National Publishers, 1934.

Ticozzi, Sergio. *The Catholic Church and the Early Village Life in Hong Kong*. Hong Kong: Centre of Asian Studies, Hong Kong University, 1983.

Tsai Jung-fang. *Hong Kong in Chinese History: Community and Social Unrest in the British Colony, 1842–1913*. New York: Columbia University Press, 1993.

Uhalley, Stephen, Jr. and Xiaoxin Wu, eds. *China and Christianity: Burdened Past, Hopeful Future*. Armonk, NY: M.E. Sharpe, 2001.

Vaid, Kanwal Narain. *The Overseas Indian Community in Hong Kong*. Hong Kong: Centre of Asian Studies, University of Hong Kong, 1972.

von Hansemann, D. *Jebsen & Co. Ltd., Hongkong*. Hong Kong: Jebsen & Co., 1988.

Wang Gungwu and Wong Siu-lun, eds. *Dynamic Hong Kong: Business & Culture*. Hong Kong: Centre of Asian Studies, University of Hong Kong, 1997.

Weiss, Anita M. "South Asian Muslims in Hong Kong: Creation of a 'Local Boy' Identity." *Modern Asian Studies*, vol. 25, no. 3 (July 1991): 417–53.

White, Barbara-Sue. *Turbans and Traders: Hong Kong's Indian Communities*. Hong Kong: Oxford University Press, 1994.

Whitfield, Andrew J. *Hong Kong, Empire and the Anglo-American Alliance at War, 1941–45*. Hong Kong: Hong Kong University Press, 2001.

Wong Heung-wah. *Japanese Bosses, Chinese Workers: Power and Control in a Hong Kong Megastore*. Richmond: Curzon, 1999.

Wright-Nooth, George (with Mark Adkin). *Prisoner of the Turnip Heads: Horror, Hunger and Humour in Hong Kong, 1941–1945*. London: Leo Cooper, 1994.

——. *Prisoner of the Turnip Heads: The Fall of Hong Kong and Imprisonment by the Japanese*. London: Cassell, 1999.

Xie Yongguang. *Xianggang lunxian: Rijun gong Gang shibari zhanzheng jishi* (Fall of Hong Kong: Historical Account of the Japanese Occupation). Hong Kong: Commercial Press, 1995.

Xu Xin. "Xianggang Youtai shetuan lishi yanjiu" (A Study of the Jewish Community in Hong Kong). *Jiangsu shehui kexue* (Social Sciences in Jiangsu), no. 4 (2000): 102–08.

Index